BONKERS BIRDING

JOHN LEE

Brambleby Books

Bonkers Birding
Copyright © John Lee 2017

The author has asserted his right
under the Copyright, Designs and Patents Act 1988
to be identified as the Author of this Work.

All Rights Reserved

*No part of this book may be reproduced in any form
by photocopying or by any electronic or mechanical
means, including information, storage or retrieval
systems, without permission in writing from both
the copyright owner and the publisher of this book.*

A CIP catalogue record for this book is available
from the British Library

ISBN 978 1908241 542

Cover design by Tanya Warren – Creatix
Cover images by the author

Typeset by JM InfoTech INDIA

First published 2017, reprinted 2019 by Brambleby Books
www.bramblebybooks.co.uk

Printed and bound in Great Britain by
Clays Ltd., Elcograf S.p.A.

To mum and dad
for their love, the memories and the 'gift' of birding.

To my brother, Tom,
for the rivalry and the companionship.

To my wife, Victoria, and my son, Jack,
for putting up with me.

ABOUT THE AUTHOR

Born in Derbyshire on the day that England won the world cup in 1966, John Lee was educated in Sheffield before studying English at Aberdeen University. After years working as an Inspector in the Royal Hong Kong Police Force, John returned to the UK to complete an MBA at Lancaster University in order to change his career to work in Financial Services. Presently he is Head of International Security at the European Investment Bank in Luxembourg. He is married to Victoria, with a 13-year-old son, Jack, and a 20-year-old step daughter, Molly. His passion is bird-watching or 'birding', as well as football, particularly supporting Sheffield United. Rugby, travel and nature are also up there.

CONTENT

Foreword	6
Introduction	11
How it all started: 1976–1977	27
Minsmere, Suffolk: 1978, 1979 & 1981	37
North East Scotland: 1984–1988	69
The Scillies: 1998–2005	101
Pelagics: 1998–2003	155
Hong Kong: 1988–1995	173
Cuba: April 2004	209
Canaries and Spain: 2006–2009	231
Hitting 400: 2013–2014	267
Index	299

FOREWORD

Jack's view on his dad's birding

A 'birder' is someone who likes looking at birds – and my dad likes to do that *a lot*. Whenever he has *any* spare time he wants to spend it birding. I saw him most excited about birds when we were on holiday in South Africa and he was seeing rare birds. When he gets excited he gets dead giddy and starts telling bad jokes. He'll never get fed up with looking at birds – no chance! His ambition is to see as many birds as possible – all the birds in the world if he can. He sets himself targets and he loves it.

I'm not a birder but I'm alright with my dad being one. My mum isn't alright with it and gets annoyed with him on holiday when he stays up really late doing his birding notes – these are the notes that show which birds he's seen that day. "He's been up all night again!" she says. "I didn't get a wink of sleep!"

We only go on holiday where there are new birds for Dad to see. The good side is that Dad's birding probably gets me on more holidays. I can understand his passion because I'm passionate about football – I'm a Sheffield United fan like my dad. I sometimes get excited about birds too – we are going on holiday to Panama and I'm looking forward to seeing the Blue Grosbeak, not because it's rare but because it's blue.

The most exciting time I've had bird-watching was at Minsmere when Dad took me to a viewing platform and said: "Look out for a Bittern." I had an idea what to look for because I watch a lot of nature programmes. Then he went on the phone to my Uncle Tom, who loves birding almost as much as my dad does, and they started talking about birds. I saw something that looked like a brown heron and I said: "A Bittern!" We all started laughing because I'd seen it first. In South Africa Dad also wanted to see a Knob-billed Duck. I was the first to spot that too – and I thought he'd made that one up!

Birding is not really good for me and Mum though because Dad goes into his own world – birding mode, we call it – when we are on holiday. He gets grumpy if you make a noise and frighten the birds. He says, "Jack, be quiet!" and uses the kind of voice from when he was still in the police and was arresting someone. I know that because he tells us stories about arresting people and he sounds the same as when I annoy him when he's birding.

On holiday, he gets up dead early – four or five o' clock every morning – and he goes out until nine o'clock. Mum says he's selfish and he does what he wants and I agree with her. By midday he's grumpy and starving because he's been up since four and missed breakfast at the hotel. If I could change anything about Dad it would be his grumpiness. When he sees a new bird he jumps up and down and is in a really good mood – that lasts about an hour until he gets grumpy again because he's been up for ages.

Dad's really good at bird-watching – he knows all the bird sounds and understands their environments. In South Africa there were some tiny birds that he wasn't sure about because they had such small differences, but on the whole he can tell.

I have never heard Dad say he can't be bothered with birding. We were in Costa Rica for three weeks and he got up at four every morning and stayed up late every night doing his notes and he never got fed up with it. When he comes back from his early morning trips he tells us all about what he's seen and exactly how it happened.  "I heard a little whistle... I looked up into a bush... there were leaves everywhere... I could hardly see a thing..." We get all the details. When we were driving into the bush in South Africa, he was gripping the steering wheel and sticking his tongue out – acting daft, showing it was a great treat and he could hardly contain himself. Then my mum had to do all the driving so Dad could bird.

He tricked my mum into going for a picnic once. "Do you fancy a picnic?" he said, and then he took her to Minsmere before disappearing off to the bird hides. He was quite pleased with himself about that one.

I don't regret Dad being a birder though – no one else has a dad like mine.

Jack Lee

BONKERS BIRDING

SONKER'S BIRDING

INTRODUCTION

Birding – it is my passion, my hobby and my crutch. In many ways, it has defined my life. For all this, I don't like talking about it much, certainly to anyone who is not a good friend, close family or who is not a birder. Admitting to liking birds has never sat well with me. I feel uncomfortable, embarrassed and self-conscious about it, especially with strangers. Why do I go birding? It is a question that has no easy answer – certainly not for me. I don't like to be asked about birding as I know that I have to open myself up a little and expose a bit of my soft underbelly. People are generally too nice to laugh in my face about it, but I know exactly what they are thinking. I have a paranoia about those conversations behind my back which I just *know* go on. People really don't get it and therefore they don't quite get me. They understand why I might have a casual interest, but going off spending a week on Shetland in October?! Come on! To them that is hard core. That metaphorical eyebrow is raised as soon as people find out. Still, I am what I am. Don't get me wrong – a handful of people do genuinely understand me, but most people, especially the ones that only know me a little, will inwardly think that it is a bit incongruous with the person they see. There is nearly always a smirk of derision, often latent, but always there. The sad thing is that if I did not have birding then I would most definitely be a signed-up member of the mickey-taking brigade too. I know what I would be thinking if I met me: *'He seems alright – he likes his football, but bird-watching? For God's sake – I didn't expect that!'*

When I ornithologically 'come out' I feel that people never quite feel the same about me. It is as if I have made a minor social faux pas that they did not expect.

'You go bird-watching? Oh…'

People pretend that it is okay, but I know there is a little doubt. It pops my head above the parapet just sufficiently so as to raise a question mark about my character and credentials. I guess it's just not cool to go bird-watching. Yes, I know Chris Packham and Bill Oddie have done their bit through *Springwatch* and other programmes to make it socially acceptable but, basically, they are both TV personalities, aren't they? They make great programmes but it is not quite my reality, unfortunately. Warming my hands over a blaze while sitting next to Michaela Strachan before going off to check out the badgers on livecam ('Oh, they are not there, but last night…') is not quite where I am at. I am sure there are many people who have been inspired to pick up a pair of binoculars and sign up to becoming a birder because of *Springwatch*. I do see more and more 'normal' people birding nowadays, including a few women. Birding for many years felt like it was being run by golf clubs; you never saw a woman – it was like they were banned. Today they are there, not in any great abundance and usually under sufferance by the looks of things.

Most people can take it or leave it though, whereas I am an extremist by comparison. For many it is the odd weekend out at an RSPB reserve or the thrill of seeing a Goldfinch feeding on the sunflower seeds that they have purchased from the shop at Titchwell. It sort of has a middle-class acceptability now. Roy Keane would describe it as 'the prawn-sandwich-eating brigade'. That is being cruel, but there is a sense of having all the clobber and a 4x4 to put it all in before heading off to Norfolk for a cup of that 'exquisite mulligatawny soup' and a naturally cured, locally sourced bacon roll from the servery at 'Titch'. Now this makes me sound like some kind of working-class, birding evangelist, which I am not. I am as middle class as anyone out there and love the finer things in life, too. My Dad was a doctor, so I can hardly play the working-class, council-house card. All I am saying is that I am there purely for the birds and the rest are just spin-offs which I quite happily and perhaps hypocritically indulge in, too. I love feeding the birds in my garden as much as anyone and the Titchwell soup is very good! It is a big help that birding has recently gained some middle-class kudos and acceptability, which it did not have before *Springwatch* came around. It definitely makes it slightly easier being a birder, but the fact remains that there are many people out there who still do not understand me and why I bird.

I also need to be honest with myself here. Being a birder does not quite fit the image I like to portray. I like to be seen as a 'lad'. I like football and rugby; I like a pint; and I like to think that I am a good laugh and good company. I am well educated, gregarious, I have had interesting jobs and I dress okay. I do all the things regular blokes do. Alright, maybe the dressing okay is stretching it a bit, but I don't have a beard, wear hush puppies and look like I work in IT (which a lot of birders do). So the birding thing presents most people with a curious dilemma. I tick the boxes but then there is the small print 'birder'. I don't quite add up. How can I be shouting and swearing at a Sheffield United match one day and then be 'dipping' an Eastern Crowned Warbler in South Shields the next? One day I am one of the lads and the next I am one of the geeks. Yes, admitting to being a birder means I have to come clean and announce to the outside world that I am not quite the real deal when it comes to the 'laddish' exterior that I like to present.

My other problem is that I'm a bit of a smart-arse too and like taking the Mickey out of people, sometimes mercilessly. Alcohol is usually involved and occasionally I go too far. My wife has a phrase which she trots out from time to time.

'John, you do let yourself down.'

It is said with a certain tone that I cannot really replicate in print, but you get the idea. The emphasis is on the 'John'. I know that I have been told. This usually follows a moment of crudeness or inappropriate behaviour on my part. I tend to be close to the line when it comes to my humour. Birding is an Achilles heel for someone such as me. It gives people the chance to hit back. I have my tactics to deal with it, but it is always there for a put down. It is a chink in my armour and another reason to keep quiet about my passion. I know that the issue is as much in my head as anyone else's. Of that I have no doubt. I just cannot help feeling that birding is some kind of social cross that I have to bear, like a kind of binocular-laden leper. Whatever, I like to keep the festering birding sores well and truly hidden if I can.

The people that ask me the birding question generally do not know me that well. They tend to be work colleagues or friends of friends. I am an ex-policeman and work in security now. People may stereo-type me a bit and I don't give off any other signals that would make them think otherwise. I think most people ask me because they cannot square the circle. I am a paradox. When I worked in Hong Kong, one of my mates summed me up quite nicely:

'You know what I like about you, John, is that one day you're getting drunk and shouting at a football match and the next you're reading poetry or going bird-watching. I don't know anybody else who is like that.'

He is right – nobody would have me down as a birder if I didn't admit it. Nice people nod politely, give approving smiles and make indulgent comments, but deep down they are thinking '*I never expected that of him*' and are making mental notes not to leave me alone with their kids. If I admit to people at work that I have been birding, then they give me a sort of look. It is a look of doubt and scepticism. That look tells me everything. They had me down as this sort of security monkey who used to give prisoners a good hiding in the cells, and suddenly that illusion has been shattered. They are no longer quite sure what I am and who I am. I think it makes them mildly curious and they have to ask. The conversation inevitably goes something like this:

'So, I hear you're a bit of a tweeter then…?'

'Yes. No. Well, I think you mean a twitcher. It's not a tweeter, it's really called a twitcher actually.'

'Oh right. Sorry. Twitcher is it? Ok. So how did you get into that then?'

'Well, a twitcher is just someone who travels a long way to see a rare bird. I'm really a birder. A birder is someone who likes birding but does not necessarily travel too far. I have done a bit of twitching, but since I have had kids I just bird now really.'

'Right. Okay. So what was it that made you become a tweet…a birder?'

'Well, it's hard to say. I just sort of got into it. I always liked animals as a kid. I guess it started when my Mum and Dad took us on holiday to Scotland where we saw some Ospreys and then I started looking at birds of prey and after that I moved onto all types of birds.'

'Oh right, that's really interesting. Anyway, I'm just nipping to the photocopier…'

'My Dad then bought us some bird lists and my brother and I started ticking off new birds. He used to take us out and show us different birds. As the years went by, both my brother and I got more and more into it. Then we started twitching.'

'Right. Okay, well I'll just…'

'I did loads at university and I love birding abroad. I don't twitch much now that I'm married and have kids but love birding even if it's just in the garden…'

'I must go – my meeting is about to start. Thanks anyway, yeah cheers.'

There is quite a lot going through their minds at this point. *Why the hell did I mention that? His bloody brother does it too? How can he be our Head of Security? I feel very sorry for his wife. She probably doesn't exist and he's made her up. Should I inform social services – he mentioned kids, didn't he?*

Meanwhile, I am left pondering on how I might have managed the conversation better. I feel like I must justify my birding somehow. I want them to approve. I want them to get it. But they never will. Even people who know me really well do not get it. Only other birders get it. I tell a lie actually, as the only non-birder I know who managed to empathise with me was a plane-spotter. Exactly, need I say more? The reason why he got it was because he suffered from exactly the same stigma, embarrassment and paranoia that I do. Perhaps worse – hopefully. Plane-spotting, I ask you! That work-place conversation is bad though on several levels. Firstly, I cannot help correcting them and lurching into a lot of unnecessary detail that describes the differences between birding and twitching. The sadness of it all is that they don't really care but, unfortunately for them, I do. Secondly, they have asked a question which is conversational and off the cuff. The answer that they get is anything but. The answer matters to me as I am justifying me and what I am about. I take that answer a bit too seriously for their liking. They do not need a helpdesk response on twitching or birding, or even tweeting for that matter. I am desperate for approval and for someone to leave the conversation thinking *'Wow. What a cool guy. A birder. I wish I was like him – maybe I'll give it a go.'* I want to hear them say (and this will never happen), *'John – we need to talk more. In fact, that meeting can wait. Let's sit down, grab ourselves a coffee and talk this thing through, mano a mano, because I need to make this birding thing happen.'*

The guy already sounds like a bit of an imbecile and possibly American – but that is purely coincidental. Let's face it; all I want is birding to be acceptable alongside boozing and football. My teenage stepdaughter, Molly, has derided me on a number of occasions, especially when I have had the telescope and tripod set up. It has hacked me off and I have hotly denied that there is anything wrong or 'funny' about birding. I have pointed out that she likes horse riding and it is each to their own in this world. They are both just hobbies. Yet we both know that horse riding is a far more acceptable thing to do for teenage girls than birding will ever be for anyone. Clearly, she has got a point as deep down I have always known that being a birder is just not cool. It is right down there with train-spotting. That dreaded tweeter question makes me confront my geekiness in public. It is dark territory that I do not want in the spotlight. People ask me about birding precisely because they find it odd. Nobody asks a bloke why he plays five-a-side every Tuesday, do they? For some it is an opportunity to take the Mickey. That is why I did not really admit to liking birds or being a birdwatcher when I was at school. Being a schoolboy birder in a Sheffield comprehensive was tantamount to wearing a T-shirt with 'Please Bully Me' written on the front. Birding was something you needed to keep quiet if you did not want to be picked on. That feeling has never really left me.

Birding is also undoubtedly not a cool thing to do when it comes to women either. It is no coincidence that you never saw any female birders in the past. It is definitely not a weapon to have in the 'bird-pulling' armoury at all (please excuse the sad pun). Admitting to being a birder is simply not part of my 'chat-up' repertoire. I have never once used it and remain quite certain that I am correct in that matter. White wine, trying to be witty and being a good cook are the main backbone of my approach, whereas conversation about birding is right out. It can all be going great guns. The pasta is perfect, the wine is flowing, she is laughing at the jokes and even pretending to be a bit interested in football. She's a bit tipsy and the trap is set. I have even cleaned the loo properly. It is all down to the detail. Things could not be going any better. Then disaster strikes. I have turned my back, possibly to crack open another bottle or to play that final trump card, posh chocolate. Then suddenly I hear those inevitable words: 'You've got a lot of bird books, haven't you?'

The bloody cat is out of the bag at that point. I curse that bookcase which is like a magnet to any vaguely attractive woman. I put the chocolates back in the drawer and take a huge gulp of wine while uttering the word 'bastard' silently to myself. I know exactly what she is thinking: '*OH MY GOD, get me out of here. This guy's a weirdo. I bet he's got a cellar too and is bound to be terrible in bed.*' She is right, I am fond of cellars. The other matters are of course true as well. It is at this point that I order her a taxi.

The other major passion killer is that object lurking in the boot of my car. I have offered to give her a lift and, to all intents and appearances, I am acting the part of the chivalrous gent. My motives, like with all men, are entirely ulterior though. Why else would I chime up?

'Oh, it's not a problem, I'll give you a lift. It's not out of my way at all. Twelve miles is nothing – honestly. Let me carry your bag for you.'

If it was a bloke needing a lift then it would be very different.

'Sorry mate – I'm a bit stuck tonight and I need to get back home. Oh, and I need to get some milk too before the shop closes. I'll drop you at the bus stop if that'll help.'

I then pop open the boot and there it is glowing like a beacon; this is the moment when she inadvertently spots the large, black Manfrotto tripod which I have left in there after the previous weekend's twitch. I curse myself for the lazy, stupid fool that I am. I should have moved it but just couldn't be bothered, could I? Well, that unmoved tripod is now very firmly biting me on the backside.

'What's this? Oh, are you into photography?' (Potentially this might be a positive for her at this point. Modelling, cat walks, etc.)

'No. Um – I'm a birdwatcher actually.'

'Oh – but it's for a camera, right?'

'Er, no, it's for my scope.'

The silent car journey that follows is naturally devoid of any flirtatious chat, indeed any conversation whatsoever. That tripod has seen to that. The car door slams firmly shut bringing closure on my pathetic designs. I am left with the scent of perfume and a clanking tripod rolling about in the boot on the journey home. You can imagine the conversation later when she sees her friends:

'God, you know John Lee, he kept this one quiet, but he goes bird watching. He's got all the gear and everything. It was all in his car.'

'You quite liked him, didn't you?'

'Well just as a friend – nothing else.'

Yes, if you want to lead a life of celibacy and being shunned by women, then birding is most definitely the hobby to have. It has always worked for me.

There is also another reason to dread a conversation about birding with a non-birder. As with all other birders, I am plagued with bad jokes from people who should frankly know better. If my birding comes up in any kind of social gathering then I can pretty much guarantee what will happen. Bill Oddie in his *Little Black Bird Book* sums it all up nicely on just how dull it is to hear umpteen repetitions of the same 'wink, wink, nudge, nudge, know what I mean Squire' routine. Like Bill and every other birder, I have had to endure endless variations of the following unoriginal catch phrases.

'I like birds myself – but the two-legged variety.' (This is undoubtedly the most common one and, when you think about it for a second, the most stupid. How many four-legged birds are there knocking around exactly?)

'I'm a bit of a birdwatcher too, but not the feathered variety; know what I mean?'

'I'm into my birds too, but not the ones that you are.'

'I like a Great Tit or two myself, actually.'

This is universally followed up by a bit of an elbow to the ribs and knowing looks to the assembled throng. Meanwhile, I wanly smile back and want to run. Boobies and Cocks are rather predictably both good for the 'phnaar phnaar' treatment, too. For those few moments, he (the Comedian) – is on the stage at the Comedy Club, emulating Peter Kay live on tour. The subtle difference, which he does not appreciate, is that Peter Kay is actually funny and that his material is new. The problem is that the 'joke' teller thinks that he is being original and that he is breaking new ground in the frontiers of birding humour. He is of the belief that I am being educated and entertained at the same time. He, and it is invariably a 'he', is blissfully unaware that this stuff has been said too many times before by idiots just like him. Even the very first time I ever heard these jokes they were not that good. I remember a Sheffield school mate of mine telling me that during the birth of his first child he had cracked 'funnies' right the way through the labour and birth. In his mind, he had been hilarious and in his own words had been on 'right good form'. That night, as he was leaving, the mid-wife took him aside.

'You think that you're really funny, don't you? Well not one of those jokes was remotely original. I've heard everyone a hundred times before.'

He was totally crushed. I often feel speaking up like that nurse too. Instead, I usually interject explaining that there is only one good birding joke to my mind, subtly insinuating at the same time that any others by natural implication are not so good after all. This particular joke I heard was recounted by an Isles of Scilly boat man, which he purportedly told a female passenger onboard of his boat. The joke involves two birds, a Cormorant and a Shag, which to the uninitiated are quite similar-looking birds. They are both black, have long necks and dive under water to catch fish. Both are resident on the Scillies, so it is quite a common question for a novice birder to ask.

'What's the difference between a Cormorant and a Shag?' she asked.

'Well, after ten pints I never fancy a Cormorant!' came the apocryphal reply.

Admittedly, it is the pick of a poor bunch but it is the only one that has ever made me vaguely smile. So please, no more bad jokes folks. You know who you are.

Going back to that photocopier conversation though and the tweeter/twitcher exchange, I do realise that there is a whole explanation of why I continue to be a birder. Yes, it does beg a question and there is not a simple answer. It is born out of many formative moments and experiences. As with any hobby, there are times in life when it takes a back seat or even gets ditched for good. Birding has had a few back seats for me, but I have always gone back to it. It has been a fantastic crutch during some bad times and has provided me with moments of wonderful escapism. I have been to unusual places, met some great people and it has kept me close to my brother (who is also a 'tweeter'). I have fantastic memories, many with my family. I can bird anywhere and can read about it when I am not birding. I love planning birding trips abroad and researching them exhaustively. I love seeing new birds. I love seeing birds abroad that I cannot identify and leafing through the field guide for the answer. I love finding rare birds. I love keeping lists and adding birds to those lists. It is all part of me and I genuinely love it.

Birding does have its bad side, or rather I have my bad side which comes out through birding. Sometimes it gets out of hand when it is all I can think about, particularly when I am abroad and the lure of new birds is there. Vicky, my wife, and my son Jack refer to it as 'Dad's birding mode'. This is when I become obsessive. I am like a man possessed. It eats me and haunts me; it is all I want to do and it makes me selfish and devious. To put it in perspective, it is similar to being a teenage lad thinking about sex. It is never out of my mind. I get like that.

Do I really want to get up at first light when I am on holiday with all my friends in Italy after a night of fantastic company, copious amounts of red wine and gorgeous Italian food? Of course, I don't! Why would I want to get up that early with a stonking hangover and venture into the Italian summer heat feeling rough and dehydrated. Unfortunately, I have to get up. Why could I not just have a lie-in like everyone else? I could be in bed having a kiss and cuddle with the wife. Oh no – not me. Instead, I am sneaking out the door at first light, trying not to wake her up. Why is everyone else relaxing around the pool while I am standing in a field trying to see a calling Quail that is annoyingly close by but still invisible? Why do I spend hours leafing through books revising birds before I go on a family holiday to somewhere exotic? Why? Put simply, I love it and it drives me. It motivates me and captivates me. If I did not do all these things then I would be annoyed and frustrated with myself. I wouldn't be me. All those formative experiences have made me what I am, and that is what this book is all about.

My worst moments are when I am abroad as all I really want to do is go out and see new birds. It just hits the spot at every level for me. New birds, identification challenges, exotic places, lots of research and reading, new lists, not knowing what I will see and, above all, the escapism. This is what I do. It is so much part of me and it makes me happy. That is why, when I was in Borneo a couple of years ago – on a family holiday – that I was desperate to see as many new species and Borneo endemics as possible. I will probably never go to Borneo again, so going birding while I was there became an all-consuming passion. It started to eat at me. The more birds I saw, the more birds I wanted to see. That is how it starts to spiral and I get the bug. The birds that I haven't seen become more important than those that I have, and there is always a bag full of birds that I have yet to see. That is 'birding mode'. I am still gutted that I have not seen the Bornean Bristlehead and only managed one of the four Malkoha species as well as missing countless other birds when we were there. It dawns on me now as I type this script that everyone else is in bed and what am I doing? Yes, here I am downstairs writing about birding.

There is one more thing. Nearly all birders are male. Why is it predominantly a man thing? It is only men who seem to get embroiled in a hobby or sport to such a degree that it starts to take over their lives. It might be going to the football, playing golf, or even train spotting, but men seem to be able to take their hobbies to ridiculous extremes. I guess women tend to like fads, whereas blokes stick to their guns for life. Men are in it for the long run, whereas women seem to do stuff obsessively for a bit and then mysteriously they will just stop. They can be drinking gallons of vegetable juice for weeks, yet one day that juicing machine is unplugged and is at the back of the cupboard, and a whole load of vegetables is left to rot in the fridge. Why? What prompted that? Blokes don't do that with their hobbies. We just plod on obsessively.

I have never had an eating disorder, but it feels a bit like that – once I get going I cannot stop – I just want to gorge on birds. By and large my birding is under control, but even at home I am consumed by my house list. I love adding new birds to it and trying to beat my year lists from previous years. It is a law of diminishing returns as every new bird is harder than the last one to get. My tactics get more and more silly. I regularly find myself on the top floor peering through a tiny window and scanning distant fields trying to pick up a Lapwing just to get it on the list. I have had the telescope up at that little window so I could get Canada Goose and Mute Swan on the list – little dots about three miles away at Rudyard Lake. It is ridiculous. A grown man, yes, a grown man squatting on his top floor landing for an ultimately meaningless list with only me being remotely interested in. Mind you, Lapwing would be my 52nd species for the house and it would take me a step nearer to my all-time house record of 64. Even worse are the birds that should be on that list which are not. I know that I have seen a Goosander flying over but not well enough to tick it. I just glimpsed it on the way to the car one morning. No binoculars and just a fleeting half glimpse. Just enough for me to know it was a Goosander but not enough to hundred per cent tick it. A half second longer and I would have had it. My wife Vicky has seen a Jay in the garden which I have not. I have seen thousands of them … but not in the garden. They are in the park less than a mile away, but will they come out for me? NO. Deep breaths. The irritation that I feel about this is indescribable. Like Lapwing, they are target birds and I want them. I need them. I will have to stop typing in a minute, just to calm down. The problem is that my house list matters a lot. It should not matter, but it does, and I cannot help it. I will get Goosander, Jay and Lapwing one day and I will be so chuffed. Ironically, the frustrations make the successes even more enjoyable when they come. I would not have it any other way.

All this explains my asinine fears and social incompetence, but it does not explain how or why. It is a tough question for me and takes a bit of answering. In what follows, I attempt to explain how I became a tweeter and why I will always be one.

HOW IT ALL STARTED
1976-1977

Being male and on the back-foot in life, I immediately need to look for someone to blame about my birding. I need an easy victim. Someone I can lay this on without any payback. That person is my Dad, or rather was my Dad as he is no longer alive. I used the same explanation when he was alive, so I am not being disrespectful in any way. He's just never been there to defend himself when I've been asked the question. The other reason that I cite my Dad is that it is true; it was because of him that both my brother and I got into birding. But before I lay everything at Dad's door, I need to be upfront about one thing, which is that I have always loved animals and therefore liking birds was a fairly natural progression.

As a toddler when asked what I wanted for Christmas it was always 'a baga ranimals'. I loved playing with my farm and my zoo. My favourite day out was a visit to Chester Zoo. Without trying too hard, I can still smell the Tropical House in my mind's nose now. Two of my favourite books, *The Ladybird Book of British Wild Animals* and *African Mammals*, another Ladybird Book, which I got for my fourth birthday. I can still remember getting them and opening them in my Mum and

Dad's bedroom. I also got some magnetic fish and a rod, but I never took up angling. I got far more out of those Ladybird books than the magnetic fish. My friends, Cathy and Cello, have a load of old Ladybird books in one of their book shelves on their landing. Amongst them is a copy of *British Wild Animals*. If I get up early when I stay at their house, I like to have a leaf through that book and stir up happy childhood memories. The thought has even crossed my mind to nick it, but even I am not quite that shallow. I guess that I am shallow enough for the thought to cross my mind, which is disturbing. Thinking about stealing from your best friends – it isn't good. Anyway, I know that all this is not really about birds and that loads of kids like animals. But loads of kids do not, and did not, like animals quite as much as I did. This was not 'learned' behaviour or 'copied' from others. No, this was a totally natural interest and love of animals which I have never really lost. My son, Jack, is similar.

As a five or six-year-old, I remember going downstairs one Sunday morning and picking up the *Reader's Digest Book of Birds* which was lying on the coffee table in the living room. It was a beautiful book, with fantastic illustrations and a Tawny Owl on the front cover. I no longer have the book but wish that I still had it for the nostalgia and sentiment. For some reason, I decided to have a stab at trying to identify the birds feeding in the garden. At some point, Dad came downstairs with the tea tray. I showed him a picture of a Bearded Tit. As Dads do when their children are trying hard but getting it wrong, he gently told me that it probably was not one and that it was a Great Tit. To my young mind it still looked much more like the Bearded Tit picture than the Great Tit picture.

I did feel a bit crushed by this early identification defeat and decided that I would not bother with birds anymore. It all felt a bit too hard. So there you have it, my first birding memory.

I only have two other young childhood birding memories. The first is finding a young Swift on the garden path one summer. I did not know that it was a Swift at the time but Dad told me many years later. It was exhausted and did not want to fly, so we hid it amongst some bedding plants at the bottom of the garden. The next morning, I was desperately excited to go and see if the bird had survived the night and remember asking Mum and Dad if it was okay to get dressed and go down. They were still in bed having an early morning cup of tea as was the Lee household tradition on a Sunday. I raced down the garden and parted the plants. I can still remember the wet dew on the plants now on that beautiful summer morning. I gently touched its feathers as it looked round at me for a few seconds before launching into the air. The second memory was again on a hot summer afternoon, probably in late June. I had just got back from school and was about to go in the back door. Mum had been outside polishing brass ornaments which were left next to the steps leading to the back door. A young fledgling thrush sat motionless amongst the candlesticks and pots. It did not move an inch as I approached. It was so perfectly still that I thought it was stuffed! I considered picking it up but did not dare. When I found mum, I asked where she had bought the stuffed bird from and if I could have it in my bedroom. Naturally, she denied all knowledge. Somewhat perplexed I went back downstairs to find the thrush gone.

I was actually nearly ten when birding took hold of me for the first time. We went on a family holiday to Scotland, staying on the Dollerie estate near Crieff. It was April, and Dad took us to Loch of the Lowes, one of the few accessible breeding sites for Osprey back in 1976. I can remember the hide well which had several high-powered binoculars on tripods pointing at the nest. As young boys, the chance to look through massive pairs of binoculars made the whole event special for us. They were like the size of machine guns and, as far as I was concerned, were the main attraction. The warden in the hide also told us a lot about the Ospreys. We had a fantastic time. Dad had won. He had managed to mix fun with birding. No doubt he had really wanted to see the Ospreys and was indulging himself a bit, I suppose. For once though, birding had won the day in the shape of big 'bins' and the nesting Ospreys, which even to a ten-year old were quite spectacular. Dad's two sons had started their birding odyssey. I guess Dad was a sort of a birder himself; he certainly had an interest in nature and liked seeing Grouse on the moors. He had studied Biology 'A' level and had a great all-round knowledge of wildlife and the natural world around him. Dad, for example, was one of the few people that could identify a Dead Nettle from a Stinging Nettle. One day when we were visiting my Grandma in Nottingham he burst in the living room where I was watching TV. He was brandishing a nettle and started to poke my bare legs with it. I shrieked at him in absolute panic until he told me that it had no sting. He had been weeding in the garden and just found it. They must be rare as I don't ever remember touching a nettle and not being stung other than that time at my Grandma's house.

Birds, I suspect, were an extension of this wider knowledge of the natural world, but in time as our interest grew in birds, so did Dad's. We saw a few other birds on that holiday, but

How it all started – 1976-1977 | 31

Tom (my brother) and I only really liked birds of prey at that time. I can still remember seeing a Buzzard and several hovering Kestrels, but it was hard to get us to look at anything else. My passion was very much mammals. I would get up really early in the morning and go looking for deer, even at the age of ten. It is strange to think that my parents would let me get up and go out on my own like that. I cannot even contemplate the thought of Jack doing that these days at roughly the same age. Times were very different back then. We had not quite got the birding bug but at least we had started looking at birds. My best memory of that holiday was seeing my first-ever Red Squirrel from the car window. Mammals were still ahead of birds by a long chalk. At that point Dad had never seen a Red Squirrel, so it felt great.

The following October, we went back to Crieff for another week's holiday. This time there were no Ospreys as their breeding season was at an end and they had already migrated south to Africa. Dad somehow managed to pull off another birding coup by taking us to the RSPB reserve at Loch Leven. This was a wildfowl wintering haunt of many species of ducks and geese. The real master stroke from Dad was buying Tom and me an RSPB bird field list each, as well as two YOC (Young Ornithologist Club) pencils. The pencils were white with various common birds running down the side. Dad soon had us ticking off various species of duck or goose and filling up our lists. Again, we loved it. I remember sitting in the car afterwards with Tom quizzing Dad about the birds that we had seen and he keenly checked off each bird. Being the younger brother by some three years, I copied him and soon we both had about a dozen sightings ticked off. For the rest of the holiday we were both devoted to adding more birds to our list. We had officially started bird listing. There was now no going back.

In the following year we returned to Scotland, this time on the Rahoy estate in Morvern, Argyll, a truly idyllic location in the middle of nowhere. It was sixteen miles from the nearest shop, a fact I loved at the time. The weather was fantastic on the way up, particularly the last stretch where we reached the coast after Fort William. I remember seeing Eider and Common Scoter which Dad identified before showing me their pictures in the field guide. This was probably the first time that I really connected birds with the illustrations. It was a penny-dropping moment for me as afterwards I started looking at the field guide quite a lot so that I knew bird names and more importantly what the birds themselves looked like. It rained a lot during that holiday, so there probably was not that much else to do when we were stuck inside our cottage. During the journey, I spotted a small bird with a bright red breast sitting on a rock at the side of the road and shouted out Redstart. Dad agreed – I had done it! I had identified a bird without Dad's help. My elation was short-lived as Dad later told me that it was actually a Stonechat. I was quite disappointed but still it was me who had spotted it and it was a new bird. Again, I was able to connect illustration with the bird that I had seen, reinforcing how important the field guide was. It was a Stonechat and I could see that from the plate in the guide.

We had a great holiday, seeing birds such as Red-throated Diver and Golden Eagle. One of the seminal moments for me took place one evening when I had gone out alone looking for Wild Cats. The love of mammals was still dominant at this point. I saw a new wading bird feeding in the brackish pools

Tom fishing and I am birding from the boat, Argyll.

near the road. I had a good look at it before running back to the cottage to look it up. Greenshank. I told Dad but did not really have the confidence to be sure about it. I also could not remember whether it had green legs or not. As Dad pointed out, this was a fairly key feature not to have noted. Why else would it be called a Greenshank? A couple of days later we all saw it again in exactly the same spot as my original sighting. This time Dad could confirm its identity. It was a Greenshank. I was chuffed and getting better but totally lacking in confidence when it came to making identifications independently. This was something that bedevilled Tom and me for many years to come. The Argyll holiday was a birding success. We

My parents and Tom during our holidays in Scotland, Argyll. Dad and Tom with binoculars.

saw some great birds but, basically, I had to rely on Dad to identify virtually everything but at eleven years old that did not really matter. I was just enjoying seeing new birds. Animals were still important to me. I would love to have seen a Wild Cat or a Pine Marten, but these were hard to see and, in the case of wildcat, nigh on impossible. By contrast, birds were everywhere and were much easier to observe. They filled the long dull gaps that inevitably occur when you are looking for mammals. We saw new birds every day during our holiday.

So that is basically how I started my birding life, but try telling that to someone in a photocopier conversation. I try to give a potted version when I get the tweeter question, yet somehow it is not really the answer they want to hear. It is long winded and, as the truth often is, a bit boring. The question that they really should ask is why do I go birding now, and that is what this book is about. These are my birding moments, my stories, my highs and lows as a birder. This narrative should help to explain why a few years ago, when we took a family holiday to South Africa with my best friend Cello and his wonderful family, I spent most of it on my own birding. I guess Cape Sugarbird beats talking to a Scottish Italian about Celtic and Italy's World Cup victories any day! There is a great photograph of everyone looking at zebras and giraffes while I am looking in the opposite direction with my binoculars raised. It epitomises that holiday.

MINSMERE, SUFFOLK
1978, 1979 & 1981

Nearly all birders of my generation will remember their first-ever trip to Minsmere. There is nothing quite like it. It was, and still is, a truly fantastic experience, particularly when you are young, as everything is so much better, bigger, rarer and more exciting. As a youngster, I dreamed for years of going to Minsmere and was absolutely enthralled when we finally decided to go to Suffolk on a family holiday. The tension, excitement and huge anticipation during the build-up was unbelievable. And Minsmere could really live up to all that expectation like nowhere else. A couple of years ago I was birding in Trinidad where I visited the excellent Asa Wright Centre and later the Caroni swamp. Three of us had gone on a guided day trip from Tobago and got over a 100 species during the day. We had a great time and quite literally did not know where to look at times as there were so many birds around the feeders, in the sky and woodlands. One of my fellow birders on the trip compared the experience to a first-ever visit to Minsmere. We all knew exactly what he meant. Yes, the Asa Wright Centre is that good, but that's another story.

Back in the 1970s, Minsmere was the flagship RSPB reserve in the country. These days, Titchwell seems to be vying strongly as the jewel in the RSPB's crown, but back then it was definitely Minsmere. Most people had not even heard of Titchwell. We certainly had not. Minsmere had the lot and a huge reputation as being a premier reserve. Avocets, Bitterns, Bearded Tits and Marsh Harriers were the prize birds to see. Seeing a Marsh Harrier was the height of my birding horizons in those days. It was to me the rarest bird in England. If we saw a Marsh Harrier then we had made it. Tom and I could not wait to get there.

One of Tom's Christmas presents in 1976 was a board game called *Conservation*, bought from the RSPB gift catalogue. It came in quite a thin box and had a picture of an Osprey on the front, sitting on a tree at Loch Garten. The game was essentially about collecting cards with rare breeding birds at various bird reserves on a map of Britain. The birds had values of either two or three points. To get the birds, you basically had to get a male card, a female card and a fledgling card. If you got all three of them for one species then you had a breeding pair and got the points. Certain birds, such as Marsh Harrier and Osprey, were worth three points, while the rest were only worth two. Each bird had a specific bird reserve where they could be found. Marsh Harrier was at Minsmere, Bittern at Leighton Moss, Osprey at Loch Garten, Avocet at Havergate Island and Dartford Warbler at Arne. The person with the most points won the game. Tom and I played that game countless times, often with Dad. I wish we still had it as I quite fancy a game now that I have sat and thought about it so much. I can even remember the pictures of the birds on the cards. Anyway, Marsh Harrier

The rules of the *Conservation* game that so inspired Tom and me.

being one of the three-points birds made it a really rare species in our minds. So when Dad told us that he had booked us into a hotel in Suffolk for a week and that we were off to Minsmere, we could hardly believe it. We had played *Conservation* so many times and always wanted to see those birds but it had always felt so out of reach. Now we had a chance of getting both three-points birds on our lists, Marsh Harrier and Osprey. Not only that, we had a fair chance of picking up Avocet and Bittern to boot.

Even Dad must have been excited as he had made a list of the birds we might see at Minsmere under the headings Abundant, Common, Fairly Common, Rare and Extremely Rare. This was taken from the book *Minsmere – A portrait of a Bird Reserve*. In order to jog my memory, I decided to check Dad's old field lists to make sure that I had got the chronology of the holiday correct. There, nestled in the back of the green RSPB field list binder in the plastic sleeve, was Dad's hand-written list (see right).

It makes me feel both sad and happy. It's a fantastic memento of a lovely and happy time. It is sad because it makes me miss him. I have a tear in my eye and I want him back. On the other hand, it's so nostalgic looking at the list and remembering that night when he showed it to me in the sitting room in front of the fire. When I think back it almost seems out of character for him to have bothered to write the list. He must have had the birding bug too. I can also remember the night when he showed us the permits for Minsmere and Havergate Island which arrived a few weeks before we were due to go. It was a Thursday evening and we were just back from school when Tom told me that Dad had got the permits. I immediately collared Dad and asked to see them. It felt so exciting holding them in my hand. It was a step nearer to the reality of going there and seeing all the great birds that the reserve was famous for. Yes, we were off to the Mecca of British birding.

> **MINSMERE**
> **July**
>
> **ABUNDANT**
> MALLARD
> TEAL
> GADWALL
> SHOVELER
> SHELDUCK
> PHEASANT
> MOORHEN
> COOT
> LAPWING
> BLACK HEADED GULL
> WOODPIGEON
> SWALLOW
> SAND MARTIN
> BLUE TIT
> WREN
> BLACKBIRD
> ROBIN
> DUNNOCK
> STARLING
> YELLOWHAMMER
>
> **EXTREMELY RARE**
> WHITE STORK
> AMERICAN WIGEON
> SCAUP
> BUZZARD
> MERLIN
> REDFOOTED FALCON
> SPOTTED CRAKE
> STILT SANDPIPER
> PECTORAL SANDPIPER
> BROADBILLED SANDPIPER
> RED NECKED PHALAROPE
> GREAT SKUA
> MEDITERRANEAN GULL
> CASPIAN TERN
> RAZORBILL
> GUILLEMOT
> ALPINE SWIFT
> GREAT REED WARBLER
> FIRECREST
> GREY WAGTAIL
> SISKIN

It was an exciting moment pulling up at the coastguards' cottages on Dunwich cliffs. I'm sure Mum insisted on having a cup of tea on arrival there. What torture. We could actually see Minsmere. It was within touching distance with all its birds and here we were having a cup of tea and wasting time. Typical of Mum. The weather was warm and balmy. We still had about half a mile to trudge down the beach as well. Still it was worth the wait. What a fantastic moment when we finally entered the Public Hide adjacent to the beach and overlooking the East Scrape. A whole array of waders and terns greeted us. The spectacle was amazing and so was the noise. We got ticks galore, including Black-tailed Godwit, Avocet and Spotted Redshank. Just as impressive was the clamour of gulls and terns nesting on the shingle islands. There were birds everywhere. It was a great start. I couldn't believe it. It was all too easy. Avocet straight away. It was like a zoo for wild birds. I remember Dad pointing out the East Scrape Hide in front of us where only the permit holders could go.

'Just look how close we will be on Monday', he said.

I looked enviously at the hide right on the edge of the scrape and a good thirty yards in front of the public hide where the second-class, 'permit-less' citizens had to make do. Back in those days you could not simply turn up at Minsmere and go round the reserve for the day. It was very much RSPB members only, with little or no access to the general public. Dad had to apply in writing for a permit several months in advance. On arrival, you had to go to the warden's hut to have the permit checked and signed. There was usually a queue and quite a wait. Then, and only then, were you granted the privilege of walking round Britain's number one bird reserve. It was a completely different culture to the one we know today when you can literally front up with the entire family, join as a member or get a day pass, hire binoculars, buy a bacon sandwich and go home with a car packed full of goodies from the shop. You even get a printed list with all the recent bird sightings on it with a map of the reserve on the reverse. I think that you could only buy RSPB badges and field lists in the old days. How times have changed!

The most important feature of the wardens' hut to us back then was the sightings board. This was a blackboard which held the key to the success of the day. If a new bird was on that board then Tom and I would want to go and see it straight away. It also had a bit of a negative effect because as far as I was concerned if it was not written up on that board then it was not on the reserve. I thought that the wardens and the information on that board were infallible. I trusted it implicitly and expected the wardens to know about every single species on the reserve. If we saw something slightly unusual and not listed on the board, I would be wracked with self-doubt about the identity of the bird and the validity of my latest tick. What a way to be, but that was exactly how I was. Basically, it was down to a lack of confidence in my birding ability. This was well founded as I was pretty crap in those days! Equally frustrating were bird updates on the board. Inevitably, at some point in the day we would end up back in the main car park hut and the urge to recheck the board was always irresistible. There were only three outcomes: no change which was a mixture of disappointment and slight relief in that we had not missed anything; there was a new tick available and we had yet to go to that part of the reserve; or there was a new tick which we had missed, a terrible eventuality which would lead to much consternation for Tom and myself.

Not only did you have the permit obstacle to overcome, the reserve was only open on certain days of the week, namely

Mondays, Wednesdays and at the weekend. So it was Monday before we could visit properly. Dad had arranged quite a nice itinerary with Havergate Island on the Sunday and Thursday, Minsmere on Monday and Wednesday. We had spent the previous day at Havergate Island, the poor sister of Minsmere. Havergate was quite a good day out as you needed to get a boat across to the island. This was definitely the best bit. We got one tick in the form of a Bar-tailed Godwit and saw plenty of Avocets, but to be honest it was a bit of a non-event. Minsmere was the real deal for us. Tom and I couldn't wait. We had a taste in the Public Hide and were at fever pitch to get to the main reserve.

Having got the permits and returned to the car where we were waiting excitedly, Dad went and did one of those things that only dads can do. He decided to give us a pep talk to calm us down.

'Now listen you two, just calm down. I very much doubt whether you are going to see very much more today than you did on Saturday, so just calm down a bit and try and enjoy the day.'

Come on Dad, we'd been looking forward to this for months and playing *Conservation* all year. There was no way we were going to be calm. This was Minsmere. We were desperate to go to one of the hides, so Dad decided to placate us a bit and take us to the North Hide which was practically next to the car park. I think Mum was still having a cup of tea by the car or had gone to the loo or both, but she did not come with us. There was one other person in the hide, a young lad aged about seventeen with glasses. He looked a bit 'brainy' in a nice kind of way. I can sort of picture him now. I guess he looked a bit like Harry Potter. Almost immediately a large brown bird flew right in front of the hide. It was a Bittern, literally the first bird of the day. I was so excited that I did not have a clue what it was. All I could think of was Marsh Harrier.

'I think that I've just seen a Marsh Harrier.'

'I've seen a Bittern,' my dad just replied,

Of course, that was it; it was a Bittern. What a start. I was so obsessed with seeing a Marsh Harrier that Bittern had not even entered my head. Minsmere was kicking in and doing what it has done to thousands of novice birdwatchers on their first visit in turning dream birds into reality. Bittern at last – two points on the *Conservation* game. I had vaguely noticed a white bird sitting on one of the islands which I had summarily dismissed as a swan and therefore had not even bothered looking at it properly. What a mistake. Suddenly the young lad spoke up.

'Have you seen the Spoonbill out there?'

SPOONBILL! SPOONBILL!!!??? I cannot describe how I felt as I heard those words. This was unbelievable. I was all over the place as I looked at the white bird properly, which quite clearly was not a swan. There it was, a white heron preening itself with its amazing spoon-shaped grey bill with a yellow tip on the end. This was a real rarity to me at the time. This was rarer than Marsh Harrier even.

On Dad's hand-written list we had just scored with a bird in the 'rare' category. I had never even contemplated that we might see a Spoonbill. What a start. Tom and I were absolutely ecstatic. Two ticks in the first minute in the first hide. We simply couldn't believe our luck. We had seen a Bittern and then a Spoonbill, easily the rarest birds that we had ever seen. It was all so unexpected. We simply had no idea that we would have such luck. The Spoonbill is a dramatic bird anyway, but there's nothing better than having a surprise sighting. We knew that Marsh Harriers, Avocets and Bitterns bred at Minsmere, but Spoonbills? No, we had not thought in our wildest dreams that we would see one. If 'get in' had been a popular saying at the time, I'm sure Tom and I would have said it, with accompanying high fives which were also not in vogue back then. Even better, we made Dad eat some humble pie on the walk back to the car park, considering his pep talk about not getting new birds and staying calm. In fact, Tom and I have subsequently given Dad serious stick on this matter over the years and have enjoyed many a good laugh about the irony of it all. It was so typical of our Dad, and dads in general, to try and restrain us and pour a bit of cold water over a kid's exuberance. Never mind, we had got Spoonbill, Bittern and one over on Dad, all in about ten minutes. Boys 3: Dad 0. It's funny looking back on it, how exciting seeing our first Spoonbill was. I have seen many since; in fact, we saw a total of five together at Minsmere by the end of the week. It is a good bird but really not that rare. Mind you, most birders I know still enjoy seeing a Spoonbill no matter how big their lists are.

Somehow as a youngster your perspective is different from that of an adult. Your horizons are much smaller and this makes everything so much more dramatic and exciting. It was simply a brilliant birding moment which I cherish and not just for the two birds but also for the memory of my Dad. The middle part of that day is quite a blur. I know we headed off down to the scrape and had repeat views of Avocet, Spotted

Redshank, Black-tailed Godwit and all the terns. This time we did not have to go into the public hide but were able to get into the East Scrape Hide and so get that much closer to everything. I can vaguely remember that it was all pretty good. We then completed the loop walk round through the sluice gate before stopping at the South and West hides. Finally, we made it back to the car park for lunch. I suffered a complete disaster there as I managed to slop coffee on my Heron 8 x 42 binoculars. Being cheap binoculars, they immediately leaked and for the rest of the holiday I could only see through one half of them. They were just about useable, but most of the birds that I saw that holiday were through a haze of coffee! The one bird that we had not seen was Marsh Harrier and this was beginning to play on our minds. Well it was beginning to play on the minds of Tom and me. We were obviously banging on about it as Dad decided to give us our second pep talk of the day.

'Look boys, we've had a really good day and I wouldn't be surprised if we don't see the Marsh Harriers at all. I'm sure that they'll be very difficult and not easy to see, so just relax a bit and enjoy the rest of the day. You both just need to settle down.'

You would have thought that he might have learnt his lesson. Dads always think they know best. Mum who had very sharp eyes in those days was always good at spotting distant birds. We used to call her 'Hawkeye Higgins' (Higgins was her maiden name). She was never the best at identifying birds and more often than not her sightings turned out to be crows but every now and then she would turn up a cracker. She also had the funny habit of claiming to have just seen a bird circling in the air, just as we were looking for birds of prey or talking about them. Even stranger was the fact that she never mentioned it at the time. This would always be accompanied later by vague pointing saying in her Irish brogue 'it was somewhere up that way'. The mention of Marsh Harriers naturally spurred her into one of her spurious claims. For once, Dad was able to explain that Marsh Harriers were more likely to be seen low down over the marshes and not circling high up in the air. Tom and I each breathed a sigh of relief – we hadn't dipped. You just never knew with Mum's claimed sightings.

With Dad's second pep talk ringing in our ears, we set off for the Tree Hide. To young boys this was quite simply the best hide that you could ever wish to go to. It no longer exists. It was basically a hide on stilts; to get in you had to go up a long straight ladder. It was like no other hide in Britain and was quite simply brilliant if you were twelve years old. This was before the days of 'health & safety' and the need for disabled access, so it was either climb up or – tough luck – you did not get in. I always feel a tinge of sadness when I go to the new re-named Bittern Hide. Obviously, it is nice and only right that everyone can get in but somehow the fun has gone. It is a sterile replacement for what was such a great place to go to as a child. There was something exciting and fun about that old hide. It was more like a tree house than a hide and could have easily been a set in one of the Tarzan films starring Johnny Weissmuller. As a youngster, I was not only out birding but also playing Tarzan or pretending to be a soldier or simply enjoying the exhilaration of the climb. Today it is safe and accessible, but it is also boring. No self-respecting WWII

Japanese soldier would be found in today's Bittern Hide – now that I do know!

The Tree Hide was packed when we got in, but fortunately a number of people made way for us and we were soon sitting down looking out onto the vast reed bed in front of us. I am not quite sure how long we had been in the hide but an elderly gentleman with quite a strident, posh voice suddenly called out.

'Marsh Harrier sitting on the bush to the right of K!'

What? Where? K? What was he on about and where was the Harrier? The voice rang out again.

'Female Marsh Harrier perched on the bush to the right of K.'

I had not noticed but there were lettered posts all over the reed bed, but could I find K? No. My coffee stained binoculars were not helping either. It was like looking through cataracts. To make matters worse, Tom shouted out that he'd got it. Hang on, here was the rarest bird in the *Conservation* game and I was going to miss it! Dipping was unbearable, particularly with the added pressure that Tom had now got on to it. Sibling rivalry was very much at play when it came to spotting new birds. Sadly, it still is to this day. Dad had also fortunately got it and he very quickly made sure that I was looking in the right direction. Suddenly I saw post K. Then I saw a bush just to the right of it and there was a brown lump sitting in the top of it. Not a coffee smear but a Marsh Harrier! What a relief and what a moment! What a day! Bittern, Spoonbill and Marsh Harrier were all in the bag. Fantastic. What's more, Dad's second pep talk of the day had been proved wrong too. Tom and I were on cloud nine. We had just had the best day's birding of our lives.

That was Minsmere. It was simply magical. I know so many people who have had similar experiences. That is why years later, when I was totting up the day's total of birds at Trinidad airport after a particularly successful day and one of the birders I was with compared it to his first-ever visit to Minsmere, I knew exactly what he meant. It is the language of my birding generation. It means bird after bird and tick after tick. They are all new and they are all crackers. You do not know where to look next and you cannot keep count of the lifers. It is back to being a kid again with the same emotions and excitement. It is a rollercoaster and it is pure one hundred per cent birding. It is fun, and you are like a novice again as half the birds you cannot identify and you are having to ask the guide what such and such is. Just as I had to ask Dad back in 1978. The male Tufted Coquette hovering in front of you at Asa Wright Nature Centre in Trinidad is like the Bittern at Minsmere and the Scarlet Ibis at Caroni Swamp, Trinidad, is the Spoonbill. When the guide points out a trogon high in the tree and I cannot see it straight away, I am overcome with that same sense of panic about missing it. I am then no longer an adult but that twelve-year-old boy again desperately trying to see a Marsh Harrier on the bush to the right of 'K'. Nothing else matters apart from seeing the bird, trogon or harrier. The emotion is the same in spite of the years. And suddenly, I finally see the trogon in all its glorious resplendent colours and the relief sets in. I become a man again as my emotions normalise. The twelve-year-old boy is gone, but those latent memories of trying to desperately find post 'K' have been revived and relived. In my subconscious the old man's voice is ringing out in the hide.

'Marsh Harrier sitting on the bush to the right of K.'

I am sure that lots of people visiting Minsmere in the 70s will remember him. He was a very kindly old fellow who loved helping young birders and showing people the harriers. He was always in either the Tree Hide or the Island Mere Hide and must have shown hundreds of people their first Marsh Harrier. He certainly made my day back in 1978. He has, no doubt, died long since, but his memory lives on with me. I like to think that he himself would be happy about this.

Obviously, with all the highs in birding there are also the lows. Later that week, Minsmere delivered me a terrible blow, a crippling thump which very nearly reduced all the previous sightings to nothing. It was a sickening moment. The incident happened later that week at the East Scrape Hide. Everything had been reasonably sedate when suddenly a mutter went round the hide that there was a Curlew Sandpiper out there. Curlew Sandpiper? This was a bird that I had barely heard of. It sounded rare, and I was desperate to see it. It was in the Spoonbill category – exotic, rare and having a great name. The 'official' cry went up 'Curlew Sand' and some directions were shouted, too. The problem was that I had no idea what a Curlew Sandpiper even looked like. Also, I had rubbish bins that were covered in coffee. If I remember rightly the light was not that great either, so the odds were stacked against me. It transpired that the bird was on one of the islands out on the scrape. Tom, for the second time in two days, was on to it almost immediately. Dad saw it, but I could not find it. I remember Dad painstakingly describing where to look but by the time that I focussed on to the right island it had disappeared. I had dipped out. Not only had I dipped but I had been gripped off by Tom. I was inconsolable and he was elated. His enjoyment of seeing a cracking new bird was clearly augmented by the fact that I had missed it! Conversely, I was even more aggrieved by the fact that Tom had got it and, boy, did he go on about it. My misery compounded his joy and *vice versa*. I now had to live with this. Life was going to be truly unbearable. I was going to have my nose well and truly rubbed in the mud by a jubilant and merciless elder brother. I did what I do best at such moments. I sulked. I looked on morosely while Tom and Dad poured over the field guide studying the Curlew Sandpiper illustration.

'Yes, that's it. It's that red one, isn't it Dad? This really is a rare bird, isn't it? That's definitely the rarest bird that we've ever seen.'

It went on seemingly all afternoon and all evening. I was disconsolate and Tom was at his merciless best. I did not know it then, but Curlew Sandpiper is not rare at all, but in our limited birding experience at the time it was an absolute mega tick. I also deserved a bit of stick as the previous day I had seen my first Kingfisher during a walk at Walberswick Marshes and Tom had missed out. I was hardly sympathetic. In fact, I too had gloated horribly. The whole experience of seeing my first-ever Kingfisher had been improved immeasurably due to the fact that I had scored one over on Tom. I had seen a Kingfisher – a tick for me – and Tom had not. A flash of vivid blue and I had hit a double whammy. The Curlew Sandpiper dip was payback time and I was absolutely gutted. What goes round comes round I guess. Dad was very conciliatory, but there really was not much anyone could do.

The story does have a happy ending as the next day, the Thursday, we went to Havergate Island. Tom had gone on ahead and was sitting in the hide with another birder. I had lagged behind with Mum and Dad, no doubt still stewing on the previous day's dip. However, when we got to the hide I was greeted by Tom and a middle-aged man. Grudgingly he told me that there was a Curlew Sandpiper out there. I did not believe him. This was just the sort of sick sense of humour that Tom was capable of. He persisted and showed me the bird. Out there in pristine summer plumage sat a beautiful Curlew Sandpiper. The relief and elation that I felt was unbelievable. Tom was pleased in that he had been involved in the finding and correct identification of the bird but I could not help detecting a hint of disappointment in his voice. He knew that I had got one back big style and he was going to miss out on a good deal of pleasurable gloating. Fate was to deal Tom a decent card later that day when we stopped at a small marshy pool. It was very fortuitous as I think we only stopped due to the call of nature. We left Mum in the car. Dad spotted a fantastic Kingfisher perched in the reeds. We had excellent views in the warm afternoon sunshine. List parity had been restored. I think Dad was the most relieved person of all of us, not just because he had just emptied his bladder but also he no longer had two moaning boys on his hands. I remember feeling a wave of disappointment about seeing that second Kingfisher as it was very nice having a bird on my list that Tom did not. Anyway, all's well that ends well.

Minsmere had most certainly met all of our expectations. We saw a bag full of birds during that first week in Suffolk and had a fantastic time. I learned a huge amount about birding as well and really improved my identification skills. Above all it provided great memories of my youth and of my Mum,

Dad and brother. Going back home knowing that I had that *Conservation* 3 pointer, Marsh Harrier, as well as the 2 pointers, Bittern and Avocet, firmly on my list was simply the icing on the cake. Tom and I could not wait to go again, and that is exactly what we did the following year.

We returned to Minsmere in the summer of 1979. We saw some good birds, including my first-ever Little Gull and a male Garganey together in the same scope view. We also saw Bearded Tit, a Minsmere speciality, which we had managed to miss the previous year. We did not know the calls on our first visit which drastically reduced our chances of seeing the species.

I have not quite got the same vivid memories that I had of my first visit, but one mystery bird stands out distinctly. Tom and I still occasionally talk about it even now. I remember one very warm afternoon towards the end of the week birding near the old car-park. A pale, thrush-sized bird sat up on a bush for about thirty seconds. It was quite washed out and had an obvious down-curved bill which looked like an extension of its chin, giving it an exaggerated, almost curlew-like appearance. I knew that it was something I had never seen before. Dad couldn't even identify it. We rummaged through the *Collins Field Guide* and still could not put a name to the bird. As luck would have it, we bumped into one of the wardens and asked him what we might have seen. Having heard our description, he immediately said it was a juvenile Cuckoo. But it was definitely not; we had seen several during the week and had great views of both adults and juveniles. This bird was no Cuckoo. While we were looking, the warden caught a fleeting glimpse of a Nightingale. Tom saw it, although I didn't.

You can imagine the scene! There were also quite a few juvenile Starlings around which the warden thought might be our mystery bird. No, clearly not again. We were adamant, and he clearly couldn't help us. We left not knowing what it was that we had briefly seen.

Some months later the autumn edition of the (at the time) RSPB magazine, *Birds*, arrived through the post. I was idly thumbing through it while having my tea in the kitchen after school when I stopped dead in my tracks. There was a picture of our mystery bird with its elongated neck and curved bill. Golden Oriole, a female. My God, that was it. I read on and there, hidden away in the text, it confirmed that a female Golden Oriole had been seen over the summer at Minsmere. They kept that one off the sightings board. I saw Dad later when he came in from work.

'Dad, Dad, do you remember that bird we saw at Minsmere that we couldn't identify…?'

'Yes, I've seen it in *Birds* already. Golden Oriole. That was surely it, wasn't it?'

Golden Oriole went straight on my list that night and it's still on today as my first-ever sighting. To this day, I have no doubts that it was a female Golden Oriole that we saw. I have seen many since but none so well and so close as that particular one. A great bird, but it was certainly quite a strange way to first see it. Minsmere had delivered the unexpected again. The other bird which causes me a bit of consternation during that holiday was Savi's Warbler. They had been seen regularly near the Island Mere Hide and both Tom and I were very keen to see one. I can remember seeing a many Reed and Sedge Warblers but not really having the skills to pin down a Savi's.

During the mid-part of the week we were all in the Island Mere Hide when Tom suddenly shouted 'Savi's!' Literally everyone in the hide wanted to know where it was. I remember Dad pooh-poohing Tom's snap identification.

'Really Tom, you mustn't go shouting things out like that when you're not sure.'

I think Dad was a bit embarrassed by the reaction in the hide after Tom had shouted out. I remember Tom being indignant as he had clearly seen the fanned tail as the bird flew. According to Tom, the night before he had asked Dad how to best identify a Savi's Warbler. Dad had apparently tapped the picture of the Savi's in the *Collins* guide with his forefinger saying, 'fan tail'. Dad did not seem to have much recollection of this but Tom remembers it clearly. I am not sure what Tom really saw that day but I guess it was a Reed Warbler. On our final day at Minsmere we left the Island Mere Hide and, instead of heading back in the direction of the Tree Hide, headed along the loop trail in the other direction. Just on the right of the path lies an opening in the reeds where we could hear a faint reeling noise. A bird briefly sat up on a dead tree. It looked bigger than a Reed Warbler and that is about all I can now remember. Tom, Dad and I all agreed it was a Savi's Warbler. It went on the list and there was another great Minsmere moment in the making. Years later I 'un-ticked' that bird. Everybody has had stringy birds on their list at one time or another. The problem is that I was not good enough at that time to categorically identify a Savi's. We had been trying to see it all week and miraculously finally saw it. Or was it that we made it happen through our desperation? I like to think that we genuinely saw one but unfortunately the bird was 'stringy'.

The simple answer is that I am not sure. It probably was a Savi's, but I have my doubts and cannot now truly remember all its discriminating features. So Savi's was the bird that never was and has only recently crept onto my list. I had previously heard one in Kent but was more intent on trying to see a Baillon's Crake at the time and did not get the chance to look for it. I've even missed them while birding in Spain. It has been a tough bird to reclaim. Birding sometimes works like that. Ironically, I managed to identify the Golden Oriole weeks after seeing it, and yet the bird we did identify at the time is no longer on my list.

We gave Minsmere a miss in 1980 but were back again in the summer of 1981. I was now fifteen and had turned into quite a decent birder. The year 1980 had proved to be a disaster as far as getting lifers was concerned, but I had done a fair amount of birding, largely at Blacktoft Sands, with Dad. We had seen some good birds and I had really got to terms with identifying the more regular waders, particularly Godwits, Sandpipers and Stints. I had also become a lot more confident in my own abilities. The other improvement to all of our birding had come with the introduction of a new piece of equipment, as Dad had acquired an Optolyth 30x telescope. It was a cracking scope, one of the old draw-tube kind with green rubber around it. I still had my rubbish Heron bins but at least they didn't have coffee on them anymore. I tended to hog the scope quite a bit as my bins were so bad. The other area where my birding had improved was in my note taking and record keeping. The previous year, I had been on two YOC birding holidays to Gibraltar Point, near Skegness in Lincolnshire. I had spent nearly two weeks of intensive birding on these holidays and picked up some good habits as well as really improving my identification skills. My notebooks for 1980 really reflect this all-round improvement in my technique. In fact, I did not really keep records until then, so it was quite a dramatic change for the better.

Anyway, we arrived at Dunwich Coastguards Station on the Saturday afternoon and after our obligatory cup of tea set off to the Public Hide overlooking the East Scrape. As often in July at Minsmere, it was a lovely warm and balmy afternoon. We did not know it at the time but this was about to herald the start of a phenomenal week of birding. We had decided to drop Havergate Island from our schedule this time. Instead, Dad had agreed to take us into the Norfolk brecklands. I had a list of sites from a birding friend called Jonathan Ross (JR as we referred to him), whom I had met on the Gibraltar Point YOC holidays. He used to write to me regularly about his birding exploits from Stowe School where he was a boarder. In these letters Jonathan had sent me a load of information about where to go and what to see. The only problem was that I had forgotten to bring the letters with me! Fortunately, I had read them so many times that I knew most of the contents off by heart. To be honest, the trip into central Norfolk was going to be our best source of lifers. We had already seen all the Minsmere specialities, so there were not too many ticks on the cards, or so we thought.

From the Public Hide we saw and heard the typical cacophony of screeching terns and gulls with a good array of mid-summer waders. There was only one other birder present, a bearded twitcher type, who did not speak at all. No doubt he had us down as a group of Minsmere novices not worthy of his acknowledgement. I had the telescope and was checking through the Sandwich Tern colony on one of the shingle islands when I came across a very large tern with a red bill. I remember saying, 'God, there's a massive tern out there.' It was clearly something different. I knew all my commoner terns quite well, including Arctic, Common, Little and Sandwich, but I couldn't place this one. It was a big tern and had an obvious orange/red dagger-shaped bill with a faint darkish spot towards the tip. Otherwise, it was the standard tern, grey and white but with a shaggy crest at the back of its head. At one point, it flew across the scrape and looked more like a gull in flight than a tern. We had left the field guide behind in the car. I was thinking it might be a Caspian Tern but couldn't quite remember the full details. The silent, sulky twitcher packed up his stuff and left without enlightening us. He must have overheard our conversation about the tern and had clearly seen the bird but had decided not to speak, for whatever reason. It would not have taken much to tell us what it was. Anyway, I didn't need his help. We had seen everything we needed to know about that bird. We had all had great views of it through the telescope. Back at the car, Dad, Tom and I immediately laid our hands on the *Collins Field Guide*. It only had an illustration of the head of the Caspian Tern but that was it. No doubt. Caspian Tern was my first proper rarity and a self-found bird to boot. I had come a long way since my first visit when I couldn't even identify a Bittern. Now I was nailing Caspian Tern without any help or need for confirmation. It was such a good moment and a personal milestone. I must admit though that I still felt it necessary the next day to ask one of the wardens if I might have seen a Caspian Tern.

'Oh, is it still around?' he asked. 'It was up in Norfolk the last I heard of it. It seems to be commuting up and down the coast.'

There it was – game, set and match. It had been confirmed by a warden. I was chuffed when I saw that it had been recorded on the board later on. That was my bird and it was a rare one at that. A lot of people were asking about it and we were about the only people who had seen it. I saw only my second British bird very recently at Rudyard Lake in Staffordshire. I did see one in the Algarve a couple of years ago. I enjoyed that Algarve bird so much more for the memories it evoked. Caspian Tern put me on the birding map, certainly in my own head. It was a seminal moment in so many ways. I had tasted the sweet enjoyment of finding a true rarity and experiencing all the tension and excitement that goes with it. In birding, there is no better feeling than finding your own find – so to speak. Granted, the bird was known to be around but we certainly were not in the know, so it was a true find in every sense of the word as far as I was concerned. It was also a true rarity in terms of the British List, i.e. it would appear in *British Birds Magazine* in the annual *Rare Birds* review. It was a good bird and a great find and I wanted more of it. I was now a birder, fledging my wings with my first decent find. It is the same feeling that I still crave for now when I am out and about. It might be a Waxwing in the garden or a White-browed Shortwing on Mount Kinabalu, Malaysia; it does not really matter. As long it is a find or I need to piece together some key features to clinch identification, then I get a tremendous buzz. 'Caspian Tern moments' are all-absorbing. All you are thinking about is the bird. What is it? What are the features? Your senses are heightened as you try to absorb every minute detail of the bird, not just what it looks like but also how it behaves and what it reminds you of. There is nothing else on your mind. It is pure concentration. There is no thought of work or your troubles or anything else. It is all about the bird as you try to suck every ounce of it into your head, so the identity can be secured and the tick nailed down. It matters so much. It is pure unadulterated escapism. I love birding for these moments. Minsmere had taught me that through such iconic birds as the Bittern, Spoonbill, Marsh Harrier and, most importantly of all, Caspian Tern.

Tom and I went out for a quick stroll on Dunwich Heath that evening and got chatting with an older birder. He mentioned that there had been an Oriental Pratincole around and it might just still be about. Unfortunately it was not, otherwise we would have been in for the most fantastic week. As it turned out there was another British rarity on the way.

In the meantime, we had our trip to the Brecklands to satiate our appetite for new birds. The day was an instant success as we saw a male Crossbill in the middle of Santon Downham village, perched high in a pine tree. This was part of JR's letter that I could remember. Next it was off for the major bird of the day at Weeting Heath – Stone Curlew. In between the Crossbill and getting to Weeting, we stopped for a pub lunch or a 'bit of a bar-snack' as Mum and Dad used to call it. For a few years they became obsessed with bar-snacks. I guess it was a hangover from pubs being strictly 'no-go' areas for kids.

The highlight for Tom and I was an old fellow saying, 'thank you, boy', in a rich Norfolk accent to Dad when he held the door open for him. Tom and I had the giggles for most of the meal and made a point of referring to Dad as 'boy' for the rest of the day. Naturally we assumed our best Norfolk accents. It must have been quite annoying for the 'boy'.

By the time we got to Weeting, the weather had become very hazy and warm. Weeting Heath is basically rolling, rabbit-cropped grassland that can be viewed from hides located in a shady pine belt. The land falls away and is deceptively cratered and uneven, meaning that birds can hide quite easily. Conditions were far from ideal and there were not many signs of life, as seen from the first hide that we visited. I was beginning to feel a dip coming on and was losing concentration in the summer warmth. There were not too many birds about full stop, so it was dull to say the least. Eventually, Dad produced the goods when he spotted a movement on the far edge of the heath. Despondency turned to joy as I got the scope onto an unmistakeable Stone Curlew. The 'boy' done good as they say in football. This was a bird that I really wanted to see as it is very much a Norfolk speciality and a classic Brecklands bird.

While I was ogling the Stone Curlew, Dad produced another lifer when he got onto a Green Woodpecker. When Tom saw the bird, he let out that he had already seen it but thought that it could not be a woodpecker as it was feeding on the ground. I was inwardly a bit disappointed at Tom as I felt that he should have known better. It might come as a surprise to some that Green Woodpecker was a tick, but I was at that funny stage when I still had some glaring omissions on my list. Anyway, we had two out of two lifers under our belts as well as Green Woodpecker as a complete bonus bird. Weeting Heath had produced the goods. I knew that there were Red-backed Shrikes breeding near Santon Downham at a picnic site, but unfortunately without my precious instructions we could not quite find the site. These birds proved to be the last breeding pair in Britain as sadly the species has contracted its range and is now only a passage migrant to our shores. To cap the day, we stopped at Westleton Heath where we had heard Nightjars calling a couple of evenings previously. It had been a bizarre experience, as for some reason Mum and Dad had dropped us off on the heath and told us to follow a path to the other side where they would pick us up an hour or so later. For reasons beyond our comprehension they must have fancied a break from us!

Anyway, as we walked on, the path became increasingly overgrown until it petered out into complete wilderness. There was absolutely no way through. I remember Tom getting a bit agitated, particularly when the light started fading. It was at this point that we heard the distant 'chirring' of Nightjars. I was not that bothered about being stuck out on the heath in the dark and suggested that we simply retrace our footsteps back to the car park. Tom was anxious and had convinced himself that we would not find our parents. I had never seen him stressed out before, whereas I just felt totally calm about our situation. There was nothing else for it but to go back. It was a decent walk back and it was pitch black by the time we got to the car park. Dad's car was waiting for us as I had hoped. I quite enjoyed this little adventure but, more importantly, it had also given us vital information as to where we might pick up the Nightjars. That is how we ended up on Westleton Heath two nights later just before dusk where we were greeted to the unique chirring of these strange nocturnal birds. Hearing Nightjars is easy but seeing them can be tricky. We could hear them alright but not see them. Just as the light was really fading, a couple of birds finally showed for us. It was magic when it became truly dark. Tick number four of the day. We were delighted. It had been a cracking day, one that we would all think fondly of for many years to come. It was our first real twitch and would be the first of many for Tom and me.

The following morning, we were back at Minsmere. The day started well when we found our first-ever Little Owl on the road close to the reserve. Our lists had a few bad gaps in them with glaring omissions such as my bogey bird at the time, Nuthatch. The Little Owl was a typically grumpy individual swooping in front of the car and proceeding to glare at us menacingly down from its perch. Minsmere was and still is a great place for novice and developing birders and is ideal for seeing a wide variety of species while throwing in the odd rarity. It is a great list filler. In those early years, I got a lot of birds such as Reed and Sedge Warblers, Wood and Green Sandpipers, Little Owl and many more species which helped fill a lot of gaps in my list. I seem to remember that the rest of the morning was fairly steady, nothing too exciting, just decent birds. We were somewhere near to the car park when news broke that there was a Marsh Sandpiper showing from the South Hide. We headed off on my very first forced route march for a bird. I have done a few since, particularly on the Scilly Isles, but this was the first occasion when I really had to step on the 'gas' to get to a rarity. It was a tense fifteen-minute walk, knowing that the second official British rarity of the week was awaiting. We got to the hide quickly and managed to find a seat. It rapidly filled up as news spread around the reserve. The Sandpiper showed itself readily in the end. My emotions were a mixture of relief and cool excitement. It felt like we were hitting the big time by being in on the act. It was a beautifully delicate bird, reminiscent of a Greenshank but only superficially. Greenshank is a bit of a monster by comparison. I think I appreciated the Marsh Sandpiper for its rarity more than its aesthetic appeal to be perfectly honest, but what a great tick to add to the Caspian Tern and our bag full of goodies from the Brecklands.

The following day, a Thursday, saw the arrival of a few hundred twitchers to see the bird. The reserve had been partially opened to allow them access to the South Hide. We enjoyed watching the unfolding spectacle, particularly as we had the bird safely in the bag. Our parents had left Tom and me to our own devices, so we headed off down the beach and had a fairly idle day. We did get some splendid views of a Grasshopper Warbler, but the highlight of the day strangely did not involve a bird at all. It was probably one of the most amazing wildlife cameos that I have ever witnessed. It was quite a violent and savage encounter which in some ways was out of keeping with the calm Suffolk countryside on a warm July afternoon. We were enjoying a bit of a teenage lounge around in the dunes near the sluice gate, taking in the sun and idling the afternoon away. Suddenly we saw a stoat break cover and run into one of the bushes and grab a baby rabbit by the throat. The rabbit let out a huge squeal. The next instant a larger rabbit, which I presume was the baby's mother, appeared and gave the stoat what I can only describe as a 'boot' in the stomach. She took one sniff of her dead baby and ran off into the bushes. The stoat looked completely stunned for a few seconds before it recovered sufficiently to drag the baby rabbit through the Marram Grass towards us. The whole episode lasted only a matter of seconds. It was like *Wildlife on One*. Some sixth sense must have stirred in the stoat as it stopped and dropped the rabbit. It sat stock-still looking directly at Tom and me. We did not move a muscle as we were literally only a few feet away. After what seemed like ages, the stoat started dragging the baby rabbit through the grass once more before disappearing out of sight. Again, that is the beauty of birding; it is not just the birds, it is also the other wildlife and the places that you visit. I cherish that memory of the stoat and rabbit. It was an amazing experience and for a few moments we were very privileged to share an incredible scene – less so for the rabbit – from wild Britain.

I think it is fair to say that Minsmere is not quite as good as it was back in the glory days of the 1960s and 70s. The scrape clearly is not what it was. I understand that it has lost some of its nutrients over the years and consequently does not hold the same attraction to feeding birds as previously. The other memorable features now lost are the breeding terns. The shingle islands are gone and so too are the Sandwich Terns which used to nest on them. The raucous noise and clamour of the terns met you like a greeting mat at the front door. Also, some of those near mythical species such as Marsh Harrier are far more widespread than in former years. Even Spoonbill is now breeding in Norfolk. There is no way that if a game called *Conservation* was invented today that Marsh Harrier or Osprey would be worth three points. Sadly, we would be collecting breeding pairs of Yellowhammer, Grey Partridge and Cuckoo, such is the plight of so many of our once common birds. As I have already mentioned, Titchwell seems to have eclipsed Minsmere as the number one RSPB reserve. I hope that Minsmere still has the same impact for young birders today, but times have changed a lot and so have the birds. For me it is still a cracking place to go birding. I still get a thrill from seeing Bitterns, Bearded Tits and the sheer variety of birds on offer. I took my son Jack there recently and he had a great time. He too spotted a Bittern, which proved to be a poignant moment for us both. I guess I love Minsmere more for the memories and nostalgia. It is good thinking about Mum and Dad on those holidays but also remembering that Caspian Tern when I earned my birding spurs. They were fantastic days and brilliant holidays.

NORTH EAST SCOTLAND
1984-1988

Many people have asked me how a lad from Derbyshire could end up studying English at Aberdeen University. I get it almost as much as the dreaded 'tweeter' question! The other one that I face regularly is 'how on earth did you end up in the Royal Hong Kong Police Force?'

I can understand the curiosity about the Hong Kong police as it is hardly a regular career choice, but not so much studying in Aberdeen. Granted, it was a long way from home but, as I saw it, the distance did not matter. I was leaving home and moving on. Perhaps it is the irony of studying English in Scotland. Again, it is not a straight forward answer as to how I ended up there, and like many things in life it just sort of happened. If I am totally honest it is probably because Scottish universities were a bit easier to get into in those days, particularly on the arts side. Aberdeen was my fourth choice on my UCCA form and, in many ways, it was an insurance policy if I did not get my grades. At some point, I had looked at average acceptance grades for studying English and noted that the grades were not quite as demanding as in England. I quite fancied doing something a bit different as well, so why not Scotland? I was not stupid and did not put down St Andrews or Edinburgh where I would have no chance of getting in. I was not sufficiently well-heeled, did not have a double-barrelled surname nor came from the 'right' school. I ended up putting Aberdeen and Dundee as two of my five choices. The other good thing about Scottish universities was that it secured you entry into the faculty, the Faculty of Arts in my case. This allowed a huge degree of flexibility and the ability to change subjects in your first year. A friend of mine, Simon Monaghan, also applied to both Aberdeen and Dundee. We both ended up north of the border. He was in Dundee reading History, while I was further up the east coast studying English. Bizarrely, we both joined the Royal Hong Kong Police Force after graduating and were in the same batch of recruits at the Police Training School.

As things transpired, Aberdeen was the only university that I managed to get into anyway. My first choice, Manchester, did not even make me an offer. Neither did Leicester, my fifth choice. That left me with Aberdeen, Dundee and Liverpool. Aberdeen required three G.C.E. Cs or a B and a C. I ultimately got a 'B' in English and a 'C' in French, as well as a 'B' in General Studies. My third 'A' level was Economics which I hated and completely flunked. Why I ever decided to take Economics in the first place is really down to a very odd piece of advice by my school. I should have taken History instead. Unfortunately, I had not done History at 'O' Level and was told that it would be very risky for me to consider it at 'A' level. As only schools can, they demonstrated a complete absence of consistency and logic by offering Economics as an 'A' level subject when no one had studied it at 'O' Level, as it was not even on the curriculum.

Like a fool, I fell for the hard-sell rhetoric of this new social science and went for it. As the terms went by, I completely lost interest and quite often went to the pub on a Tuesday afternoon instead of going to double Economics. It was pretty boring though. The sum of my learning was that Milton Keynes and Sigmund Freud were both famous economists! As my A levels approached, I realised that I had no chance of passing Economics. I was in for an 'E' at best, so I put all my efforts into English and French as well as drinking bitter, playing rugby, watching Sheffield United and going out on the town. So, as a result of a mixture of trying to be a bit different following on from some research, an exam results 'insurance policy', a bad 'A' level choice and the B-C offer from Aberdeen, I found myself 380 miles from home in north-east Scotland, studying English. Yes, I know what you're thinking. How could someone who writes this badly have studied English?

Birding had never really featured in my thought processes but, as the summer slipped by, I began to realise that there might be some good ticking prospects ahead. Mum and Dad were both delighted that I had managed to get through my 'A' levels and secure a place at Aberdeen. My older brother Tom would readily admit that he had disappointed them by his lack of academic achievement. It just was not for him. He was clever but not really cut out for the world of academic study, although to his credit he did go on to get a degree as a mature student. I know this meant a lot to him and it is sad that my Dad did not live to see him succeed. I was prepared to study and naturally had a bit of a flair for English, so I was always in with a chance of getting reasonable grades. I could have worked harder and achieved better grades, but the main thing was getting into university. I was one of those kids who had a bit of a balance to life in that I was not bone idle but also knew how to have a good time. Academically, I have always underachieved but have always lived life to the full. My mates were all the same and all have gone on to have successful careers, so we cannot have been that bad. Outside of our group there were two types of student; the brainy studious and boring kids or the 'nutters' who just had a laugh and never studied. We were somewhere in between.

I loved sport and was captain of the school rugby team as well as playing for De La Salle Rugby Club. I used to play for the school every Saturday morning and then again for my club in the afternoon. Sundays were spent doing homework, lying on the floor battered and bruised from the matches. I played hooker and, even at 17, could feel like an old man the day after playing two games in a day. The job market was also hideous at the time. This was 1984, the height of the Thatcher years and the miners' strike. We were brought up with demonstrations, riots and anti-Thatcher sentiment with Sheffield at the heart of it. Arthur Scargill would be leading rallies in the city centre, the police would be everywhere in town and hatred was in the air. As there were precious few jobs, I never really felt that there was any other option than to go to university. This was also all my parents wanted for me but were never obsessive about it.

As a parting gift before I went up to Scotland, Dad bought me a pair of 10x40 Swarovski 'Habicht Diana' binoculars. He had a pair himself and it was like looking at a different world through them. This was his way of saying, 'Well done'. It was a complete surprise when he gave them to me. What a great present. Even better, I could at last ditch those terrible Heron binoculars. The coffee stains had gone but they were totally substandard. I still have the Swarovskis to this day and they are still going strong. They were – and are – simply fantastic with a beautiful, bright image coated in golden light. When Dad died, I treated myself to a pair of Leica Ultravids with some of my inheritance money. The Swarovskis stand up well but the Leicas do have the edge. Leica served me well for many years but I have recently reverted to Swarovski.

My first outing with the new Swarovskis produced a great tick at Spurn Point with my first-ever Red-breasted Flycatcher.

My prized Swarovski Habicht Diana. Present from Dad for getting into University in 1984.

I am not superstitious but it is always nice to christen new optics with a new bird. Ironically it took me ages to get my Leicas off the mark. It was as if they were cursed. It took nearly a year to get a tick with them, with a Sora Rail on the Scillies, eventually breaking my run of hitherto bad luck. The wait was worth it as the Sora had been an absolute bogey bird for me. I had already dipped two of them and had also gone to see one on Tresco in the Scilly Isles, which ultimately proved to be a more common bird, the Spotted Crake. Without doubt, my best new optical christening was with the AT 80 HD Swarovski telescope that I bought in 1996. The day I got it, a Woodchat Shrike turned up in Kearsley, about ten miles away from my house in Manchester. The following day, I successfully twitched three lifers in the form of Great Reed Warbler, Marsh Warbler and Honey Buzzard with Black Tern, Osprey and Pied-billed Grebe amongst the supporting cast. The Marsh Warbler was literally crawling around my feet in the reeds, so I never got the scope on to it, but as a lucky omen and a positive start it doesn't get much better. Anyway, back in 1984 I was rather chuffed with my new bins and what better present to have for my four years at Aberdeen.

Fresher's Week saw me at the Students Union building going round the various clubs and societies touting for membership. There was a large variety, including all the political parties, sports clubs as well as a few real oddities like the Clangers Society. I joined the Bird Club and the Rugby Club. The Bird Club could not have been more stereotypically geeky and epitomised most people's concept of the bearded anorak-touting introvert. The two men sat behind the desk were certainly classic stereotypes, both sporting beards and were clearly completely ill at ease with the situation of having to speak to strangers. Christ knows what they thought of me with my wedge hair-cut, Yorkshire accent and stupid, 'trendy' clobber that I was no doubt decked out in on the day. I probably looked more like a football hooligan than a birder. They muttered something about the first meeting being at the Zoology Department the following week. I somehow doubt whether either of them managed successful careers in sales. In fact, I know they did not as they were both postgraduate Zoologists. I got to know them in years to come, but at the time they did not come across too well and I was not overly inspired to go along. To my mind, they appeared as if half a pint of mild and a sausage roll was the height of a good time. Unsurprisingly, I missed that first meeting and it was some while before I went along to the bird club. In fact, it was not until my second year that I finally became an active member. It took me some time to do any birding at all. Fortunately, a lad called Colin who had a room along the corridor from me in my Hall of Residence told me that one of his best friends, Owen Hayward, was a very keen birder. Eventually, Owen and I were introduced.

Owen was a very cool guy who I instantly liked. You could not help but like him. He had spent the summer in the USA doing sports coaching and had managed to develop a pseudo-middle-class Edinburgh / American accent. Owen was quite a distinctive figure as he was nearly always dressed in a red and white bomber jacket, faded jeans and baseball boots. Basically, he dressed like an American college kid. I know he does not sound very cool from this description but Owen somehow carried it off. He was not like a birder at all. He was charismatic, funny and, dare I say, quite good-looking. I think the nice thing about him was that he did not take himself too seriously and took the Mickey out of himself quite a lot. He knew that he had a fake accent and looked like a yank but he could also laugh at himself. We got on well straight away. I guess I did not quite fit the birding mould either. He was the sort of person who would lose a daft bet and have to eat a handful of rabbit droppings as the forfeit. Owen was not only a birder but was massively into rock climbing. I went with him a couple of times, although was not that keen due to my fear of heights. There were other factors, too. The last time I went with him was memorable for one thing. Owen was helping me get my harness on and checking my gear before I abseiled down a sea cliff. I was wearing MTV's (Meat and Two Vegs), the tight lycra pants that all rock climbers wore back then. Instead of clipping the carabiner onto my harness he deliberately fastened it onto my privates. I have the scar to this day. Still, it is a memento of our friendship and that little cameo pretty much depicts Owen as he then was and shows you why I never took up rock climbing.

Owen mentioned that there was a good walk close by to Hillhead Halls of Residence, down the River Don leading to the estuary. He was amazed to hear that Long-tailed Duck was a lifer for me. This was a bit of a trash bird to him but, as I explained at the time, sea ducks were uncommon in Sheffield. We agreed to have a wander down that weekend, not too early as we were students after all. The following Sunday, Owen turned up about two hours late, nursing a monster hangover touting his bins and scope. As promised, Owen found me my first Long-tailed Ducks as well as a few other decent birds, including Red-throated Diver and Eider. This was my first taste of birding in Aberdeen and it was obvious that the selection of birds up there was rather different to what I was used to. Also, the walk from the Bridge of Don down to the estuary was not a bad little local patch. A Caspian Plover had even turned up there in the early 80s. More recently, a very rare Harlequin Duck spent several weeks in the area. I did very little birding that first term which was a real shame but everything was new including total freedom, so birding (along with studying) took a back seat to drinking and hangovers, unfortunately.

After returning from my Christmas holidays back home with Mum, Dad and Tom, I had a cracking start to the new term. Owen had shoved a message under my door telling me to get in touch if I fancied going twitching that weekend. Before I could get to him, he appeared at my door very excited.

'Johnnie, you fat northern git, where have you been? I've been trying to find you for ages. Anyway, how do you fancy coming on a twitch at the weekend for Desert Wheatear, Ross's Gull, King Eider and there's Grey Phalarope as well. Rory's given me all the gen. If you're up for it there's a space for you in the car.'

Owen always called me Johnnie and always liked to be a bit derogatory about my northern English origins as well as my figure. I did not take much persuading with the birds on offer. Every bird was a lifer. All the birds were right in the north-east corner of mainland Scotland, literally a few miles away from John o' Groats. The twitch was on. All was set for an early start on Saturday morning. Well, all was set apart from my alarm clock which meant that I awoke to Owen banging on my door.

'Johnnie, you lazy northern sod – get up. We've all been waiting in the car. Come on.'

Not my most auspicious moment. I could not believe it. As a rule, I have always been good at getting up when I have to, so this was rather out of character for me. Fortunately, my clothes and kit was all out and ready. As an afterthought, I decided to put a pair of tracksuit bottoms on under my trousers. Aberdeen was a cold spot in January and we were going way up north. Little did I know just how glad I would be of that extra layer. It did not take me too long to get to Owen's Datsun.

Besides Owen himself, awaiting me were two other birders who I had not met before, James Stephen and Dave Steele. Both were later to become stalwart birding companions as well as good friends. James hailed from Somerset, while Dave was from Northern Ireland. Owen was behind the wheel and we were soon off on our way. There must have been some birding small talk en route but the first real memory of that journey was a 'gentlemen's stop' at a lay-by in the middle of nowhere. Mid-flow the first half decent birds of the day flew over; a small party of Siskins which Dave picked up on call. This was the first of many birds that Dave would latch onto before me. I did not know it at the time but he was a red-hot birder. He was the sort of bloke that you could easily underestimate as he was quite shy and had a slight stutter in unfamiliar situations. He was a lovely guy who had a good turn of dry humour. James was also a very solid birder, not quite in Dave's league but still very good. He was a quintessential Englishman, with a reasonably posh voice, quite straight-laced and had good strong middle-class values. By comparison, Owen and I were a pair of gobby and cocky hooligans. I also found out that day that James had seen the Cheddar Gorge Wallcreeper, an absolute megastar bird in the UK. I think we were all a bit envious of that one. I had a nice little gem on my list in the form of Marmora's Warbler, which also gave me some megatick credentials, but the Wallcreeper was – and still is – a major tick. I would not say that I was out of my depth, but Owen, Dave and James were all far better field birders than I was. They also had telescopes whereas I just had my binoculars. Thank God, Dad had bought me a decent pair and I was not relying on those old Herons.

Owen whacked on the music and we speeded on our way north to the sound of Dire Straits and Asia. If I ever hear *Sultans of Swing* or *Heat of the Moment* I am immediately transported back in time to the inside of Owen's Datsun and that twitch. At some point, Owen announced that he was knackered and needed a 'doss' as he used to call it. I am much happier as the driver than as a passenger, so I was more than pleased to take over behind the wheel. Owen turfed whoever was sitting in the passenger seat into the back and promptly fell asleep. I decided to put my foot down (if that was possible in a Datsun) and did some great overtaking along the way. James said afterwards that he was terrified by some of my manoeuvres. It was not the fastest car in the world and took a bit of winding up but it seemed safe enough to me. I think Owen's car was well known in the area because everybody kept flashing at us!

Our first proper stop was at Wick Harbour for the Grey Phalarope. It was a bit foggy when we got there and cold. There was even an iceberg floating around in the harbour, but no sign of our bird though, which was not a good start. Owen explained that this was the weakest bird on our target list and that his mate Rory reckoned it might have already departed.

Now you tell me, I thought. We were just about to jump back in the car.

'Let's go boys, there's nothing here apart from a couple of tysties,' Owen said quite casually.

Now if he had been a Brummie I might have had a clue what *'tysties'* were and would have probably asked him for a bite of one, especially if it was cheese and ham. As it happened, he was Scottish, so I asked him what the hell he was on about.

'Oh yeah, I keep forgetting you're not from up here you great English fat boy. They're Black Guillemots. They're just over there.'

There they were. Two winter plumage Black Guillemots floating serenely in the calm misty waters of the harbour. I was not too serene though as I had scored my first lifer of the day. They had literally just appeared out of the gloom and Owen had nearly not bothered pointing them out. He had seen loads of them but here was a bird that does not occur in central England. I let on to Owen that they were lifers and he immediately started celebrating and made me do an American style high five.

'Hey Johnnie boy, you stick with your old mate Owen and he'll get you the birds…'

Just as we were completing our slightly OTT celebrations, a birder appeared and asked if we had seen the Grey Phalarope. We got talking to him and explained that we were heading up north for the Desert Wheatear, Ross's Gull and King Eider. He asked if he could join us as he was hitchhiking. Apparently, he was a part-time warden at Loch Garten and had just been dropped off by a colleague in Wick. To this day, none of us were sure whether he had decided to join us on the spur of the moment or was planning to hitch up to Freswick

Bay under his own steam. Whatever, it was a massive stroke of luck for him to run into us as he would never have got to those birds in a hurry. It was just so remote. While we were talking, lifer number two of the day appeared in the form of a flock of Purple Sandpipers. This was getting good. Well it was for me at least as I was the only one getting any ticks. Purple Sandpiper was a bit of a duff bird in terms of its rarity but they tend to be locally common in England and I had never caught up with them. They are far more widespread in north-east Scotland and this was the first of many sightings for me. We did not hang around long and were soon back in the car listening to more Dire Straits. This time it was a lot more uncomfortable as there were now five of us, having acquired our birding hitchhiker. It dawned on us that the guy (I have long forgotten his name) might not cough up any petrol money which we thought was a bit rich as we were all penniless students. Technically he was hitchhiking and would not normally have to pay. In reality, we were all skint students. We had not thought about it properly at the time when he joined us at Wick but over the course of the journey all had clandestine conversations about it. We were over two hundred miles into our journey but still had a fair amount of travelling to go if we were to see our target birds.

The day had turned out to be an absolute cracker with clear, blue skies and hardly any wind. Dare I say it, but it even felt warm at times in the winter sunshine. Freswick Bay just south of John o' Groats was our next destination. It was an idyllic spot. What made it all the better was that the male Desert Wheatear showed immediately. It was an absolutely fantastic bird giving excellent views down to a few feet away. This bird alone was worth the journey. I was sitting pretty with three lifers now but to be honest the others were just padders (uncommon but not really rare birds). Don't get me wrong, every lifer is welcome, and it was nice to plug some bad gaps on my list, but Desert Wheatear was definitely a big one. You just do not expect to see a bird which has 'Desert' in its name in the far north of Scotland. It felt quite incongruous to be watching this delightful bird in mid-January. Just as incongruous was a wintering Chiffchaff that also put in an appearance. Chiffchaffs overwinter regularly but none of us had expected to see one this far north. A flock of thirty-seven Snow Bunting was a more fitting sighting for the locality, more especially since these had 'snow' in their name rather than 'desert'. It was lovely birding but all too soon we had to move on along the coast to Thurso where we hoped to connect with the Ross's Gull.

We decided to take the scenic route via John o' Groats. None of us had ever been there before, so it would have been criminal not to have a quick stop when we were so close. We had brilliant views of the Orkney Isles as we drove past against a bright blue sea and sky. There was a fair amount of discussion as to which islands they were and I confess to getting the atlas out in the end. It was all absolutely beautiful, with stunning scenery. We had a quick stop and a much-needed brew but soon had to get back on the road as there were birds to tick. The harbour at Thurso was full of gulls when we got there, but the Ross's was not showing. We spent about thirty to forty minutes scanning without any real success. I was struggling without a scope and my concentration was beginning to waver. We were all a bit hungry as well. As the afternoon progressed, it was getting distinctly colder. Owen and I volunteered to go into town and get some food for the boys. He was driving and we were having a bit of a laugh about something inane as we got out of the car. We went off in search of a pie shop but without much success. Everywhere seemed to be closed or sold out. We managed to buy the last two sausage rolls from a bakery which we scoffed immediately. Being lovely lads, we made a pact not to tell the others. A cover story was agreed; all the places we had visited were either sold out or closed. We decided to cut our losses and go back to the car. As we approached, Owen started checking his pockets.

'Johnnie, did I give you the keys?'

'No, I don't think so. You were driving.'

'Well, I've not got them. Are you sure? I gave them to you, didn't I?'

'No, definitely not. You had them.'

'You must have. Come on, hand them over you great English git.'

The banter went on until we reached the car. Clearly neither of us had the keys or one of us was playing a very childish joke. I knew that I did not have them. When we reached the car, it was locked and on looking through the window there they were in the ignition. We tried the doors, the boot, checked the windows, but we were locked out. The rest of the team were at the harbour, possibly watching one of the most beautiful and most sought-after gulls to grace these shores and we had no way of contacting them. Mobile phones were a thing of the future. We were stuffed. Not only was the journey home in jeopardy but so was the Ross's Gull. Time was now ticking on and we were stuck in downtown Thurso. We set off for the police station to see if they had any spare keys or advice on car break-in. Owen seemed confident that the police would be able to help us out.

The local sergeant soon crushed those elevated expectations by telling us that we would have to smash the window or call the AA. And, 'No', the sergeant did not know how to use a coat hanger to hook the lock. I suspect car theft and 'TWOC' were not quite the crimes in vogue in the metropolis of Thurso back in the 80s. Sheep rustling, drunkenness and incest were far more likely. On a good night, they might even get a single culprit committing all three crimes simultaneously. The red bulbous nose and six fingers of the Sergeant were a bit of a give-away on two fronts. I thought that I could hear a faint bleat from the cells but was perhaps wrong. Owen was not in the AA, nor was I. Back at the car, we used all our combined intellectual powers to gain entry to the vehicle. The English and the Zoology students from England and Scotland, respectively, pooled all our life experiences and intelligence to come up with the cunning solution. Seconds later a small pile of glass and a house brick were littering the Thurso pavement. There was a triangular hole where a triangular window had once been in the Datsun's near-side back door. Owen reached in and popped the lock. We were in but now had the prospect of a 250-mile journey in mid-January in Scotland with the backdoor window half smashed open. Thank God that I was one of the drivers on Owens's insurance.

We raced back to the harbour to the lads, giggling at the stupidity of it all. We reaffirmed our pact not to mention the sausage rolls and keep to the script that there was no food to be had in Thurso. This had to rank as one of the most unsuccessful pie stops of all time. Not only had we failed to get the boys any food but also one of the backseat passengers was going to get a stiff neck. We arrived back at the harbour to find the boys absolutely freezing and starving. We had been away well over an hour and a half and they had begun to wonder what was going on. Little did they know that Owen and I could be so incompetent as to lock the keys in the car. The temperature was really plummeting as the sun started to dip and had easily dropped to somewhere around the freezing mark. The good news was that they had got the Ross's Gull. Bingo. We were in! Dave painstakingly gave me directions to find the bird which was sitting on the sea. There was a mass of gulls out there, so it was very much a case of:

'Can you see the red buoy about half way out? Then count ten birds to the left. Then there's a white plastic bag in the water. Well, if you get the Herring Gull that is preening just behind it, at ten o'clock to that, there's the Ross's.'

'Right, I've got the red buoy…'

To be fair, Dave was among the best at giving directions and getting you onto a bird. It was a magical moment when I finally clocked that Ross's Gull. What a bird. Small, pinkish and petite – this classic arctic gull was like no other gull I had ever seen. This one was certainly not going to swoop in and steal your ice cream. I was not into gulls at all at this point but here was something very different. Scanning through flocks of gulls was anathema to me back then. I had hardly looked at them. They were boring, and the vast array of plumages and ages meant that gulls were a tough nut to crack in terms of identification. However, here was a reason to look at gulls more closely. Through my binoculars it was obviously small and delicate but that was about all I could make out. The boys were very good and all let me look through their scopes. The bird in question was transformed into something beautiful to behold which is not a ready description of any gull. The faint pinkish hue of its breast and the finer structural details of this arctic wanderer could just be made out in the fading afternoon light. It was a magnificent birding moment. Lifer number four of the day and an absolute cracker. It was and remains to this day a very rare bird. Ross's Gulls are very special birds.

In passing, Dave mentioned that he had also seen an Iceland Gull. True to the script, this was another lifer for me. I asked Dave where it was and to my dismay he said that he had lost it. He obviously recognised a note of anxiety in my voice and, realising it was a lifer, set about relocating it. As luck would have it, the adult Iceland Gull was about six birds to the left of the Ross's. There it was, my first-ever White-winged Gull. Tick number five of the day. This was fantastic. It was also freezing and now getting a bit dark. At about half past four, I decided to get the keys for the car off Owen so I could hear the football results. Realising that there was a fellow wimp in tow, Owen came with me. He was flabbergasted when I started retuning his radio to Radio 2 so that the time age music for Sports Report could blare out and momentarily replace Dire Straits. Naturally this was followed by the dulcet tones of James Alexander Gordon reading out the classified results. Sheffield United had managed a goal-less draw away at Notts County. It was not quite a perfect day, but an away draw would do. The main thing was that we were getting warm in the car and I had some great ticks under my belt. James quickly joined us demanding food and enquiring how Bristol City had got on. He was disappointed on both fronts as I had missed the score and we had not brought any food from town. He could not believe that we had been gone for nearly two hours and come back empty-handed. We did not dare confess about the sausage rolls. Owen and I glanced at each other in a knowing but guilty way. The code of Omerta prevailed. Years later when we were recounting the tale, our code of silence foundered when we accidentally mentioned the sausage rolls in front of James. His violent reaction said it all.

'You pair of bastards. We were f***ing freezing and starving while you locked us out of the car and ate the sausage rolls. If we'd known, we would never have shown you the Ross's Gull.'

Now James is a well-mannered and reserved kind of chap, so the reaction says it all. Those boys had gone through the ringer for us to get that Ross's Gull. Owen and I were a pair of lazy charlatans whereas they were dedicated, decent lads. In hindsight, being a charlatan was the way to go. I would rather take my chances with my belly full of sausage roll and 'pull the wool' over my freezing mates than go hungry. It is a philosophy that has stood me well throughout life and I've never looked back. Being overweight and possessing a lack of friends have always been issues though.

We had earlier decided to sack the King Eider as we had lost too much time. Our itinerary was packed anyway, but with locking ourselves out of the car and having spent quite a long time searching for the Ross's Gull, we had simply run out of daylight. At that time of year and so far up north, there is not a great deal of daylight time anyway. It was a shame, but we were all well satisfied with our haul of birds. We had scored on the two main rarities and had some neat padders as well. I was sitting prettiest of all on five lifers. Eventually, Dave joined us back at the car. He was an insatiable gull watcher and could never drag himself away from them. It had taken near-pitch darkness to get him to pack up his scope. He was also in danger of suffering from frost bite, hypothermia and any other cold-related condition. The weather was really becoming arctic like. All of us had been struggling during the final hour or so. Buoyed by our success, we decided to head into Thurso town centre for a chip supper and a few pints.

We had a celebration in the pub before setting off on the long journey back to Aberdeen. Owen said he would drive the first stint so long as I could take over. That meant that I was limited to two pints of '80 Shilling'. A crying shame as I was right in the mood to get on the ale. We had already spoken with Scotland's finest once in the day and I did not fancy a second meeting, so the beers had to be capped. We hit the road and headed off down the A9 to the coast. It was not long before we had to have the obligatory road side 'gentleman's stop'. The pints had worked their way through our systems. Owen and I swapped over as he needed another 'doss'. Well we did not quite swap over. He got in the passenger seat and kicked Dave into the back seat. I guess ownership has its privileges. It was now pitch-black outside and all I had was Dire Straits for company. The conversation had completely dried up as the boys were all getting their heads down. I was under instructions to look out for the turn-off to Dornoch as we would need to fill up with petrol. Owen woke up after about an hour and we successfully negotiated our way into Dornoch. To our dismay, the only petrol station in town was closed for the night. We were also all starving again. It was as if we had not had anything at all back in Thurso. Mind you, we had been on the road for some two hours since leaving the pub and our last 'feed' as Owen liked to call it. There is nothing like a day of birding in the cold to give you an appetite. We piled into the chip shop and ordered fish suppers all round. That was with the exception of our hitch hiker friend who was a vegan. He was going to order chips but wanted to know if the chips were cooked in vegetable oil or animal fat. The chippy man looked at him as if he were mad.

'I dinna ken to be honest. I guess it'll be animal fat in here pal.'

Anyway, he just sat there starving while we all stuffed ourselves with fish and chips. It sometimes pays not to have too many principles. Still, it was an impressive display of self-control as he must have been ravenous, but that was his choice. Coming from the Sheffield area, I had not met many vegetarians before, let alone vegans, so I was not too sympathetic to his cause. I live with two of them now! It is far more common these days. Back then, I was naively insular and classed veggies along with people who did not like football – someone to be avoided. I found it quite amusing to see him suffering in the back of the car listening to the sound of our happy 'feeding' and smelling the wonderful aroma of our fish suppers. I was not alone as the other boys were quite amused too as they all admitted afterwards. If it had been me in his shoes then I would have cracked and tucked in. We pushed on with me in the driver's seat, with hardly any petrol left, and were regretting not filling up in Thurso when we had the chance. The chippy man had told us that we might get petrol in Tain which today is only about ten miles away by road. In 1985, there was no Dornoch Firth Crossing, so you had to drive the long way round and cross the firth at Bonar Bridge. This added a good twenty miles to the journey. It quickly became clear that we had no chance of making it to Tain. We were running on fumes. As luck would have it, we found a small private petrol station at a tiny village called Spinningdale. It was closed and there was no sign of life in the house at the back. We knocked on the door but it was clear that no one was at home. There was nothing for it but to park up nearby and wait for the owners to return. We found a small farm lane nearby and pulled the car onto a grass verge next to a rusting car. It was a beautiful winter's evening with a full array of stars in the sky. It was also bitterly cold and already well below zero. By now it was about nine o'clock, so we did what only students can do in moments of adversity and headed to the local pub, the Old Mill Inn. Considering where we were, the pub was a disappointment. It was nondescript and modern inside when you would really expect an 'olde worlde' kind of place. We spent the next two hours playing pool and darts, as well as sinking a good few pints. We made sure that we dropped several massive hints to the landlord that we had run out of petrol and had nowhere to stay for the night. We all felt fairly confident that he would show pity on us and let us kip down on the floor for the night. At about eleven the bell went for last orders. We got another round of pints to make sure that we had given him a decent trade and to make that act of generosity easier for him. The minutes ticked by and soon we were swilling the dregs around the bottom of our glasses. There was not even a 'lock in' on the cards. The bell rang again.

'Night boys. It's time for drinking up now.'

What? He was turfing us out? We must have trebled his takings that night and yet there was not even a hint of compassion from the landlord. In some ways I cannot blame him. After all he did not owe us anything and who would want a group of students dossing down on their pub floor? On the other hand, it was well below zero out there and we were obviously decent lads. Mind you, two of us were English, one of us sounded like an American and if you shut your eyes Dave's voice was a dead ringer for Gerry Adams. We were all students to boot. Little wonder there was no room at the inn! We would have even paid him, but no – we were shown the door. Clearly, the parable of the Good Samaritan had not been read out at the local Kirk for some time. If it was cold when we arrived at the pub, it was absolutely freezing when we left as the temperature had fallen through the floor. We piled in the car and ran the engine for a few minutes to warm the interior. I was in the driver's seat and with a fair bit of beer inside was ready to fall asleep after a very long day. The last thing I remember was looking at the clock and seeing that it was about midnight. With that I promptly dropped off.

I woke up because I was shaking so much with cold. I looked at the clock in disbelief. I felt like I had been away for hours and that it must be about three in the morning. The clock was saying half past twelve. Surely something was wrong? It must have stopped but, oh no, I had only been asleep for about thirty minutes. I was now wide awake with the cold. In fact, we all were. It was just too cold to sleep. I spent the next hour or so grabbing fitful snatches of sleep until I had to get out again for a call of nature. Owen got out, too. It was even colder than before. I was shaking uncontrollably. This was not fun, and time was dragging interminably. We had a quick scout round and found a horse box loaded with hay bales but in the pitch dark we could not find a way in. We ended up getting inside an abandoned car and climbing into some empty fertiliser bags which theoretically would provide insulation. We both lay there chatting until we started giggling like a pair of teenage girls. It was basically a slightly more pleasant way of shivering. At some point, we must have fallen asleep only to awake absolutely perished by the cold. There was nothing for it but get up and get the circulation going with a walk round. Thank God that I had had the foresight to put on my track-suit bottoms under my jeans but to be honest they did not seem to be making much difference. We headed back to Owen's car where I clambered in the back next to the broken window which was stuffed with a piece of card board. I spent the next couple of hours dozing on and off. James told me afterwards that I had been snoring like a drain. Apparently, I was the only one not awake.

Eventually dawn broke and we headed off to the petrol station. What bliss to get the car heater on. Naturally, it being a Sunday morning, the petrol station was closed so we hammered on the door. A temperature gauge at the back door read minus 13°C. It must have been even colder in the dead of night. No wonder we had been suffering. It was like Siberia. Eventually a rather bleary-eyed owner appeared at the door. He had been out on a belated Hogmanay party at his neighbour's the night before. Hogmanay on January 12th! It was apparently a complete one-off, normally they would have been in on a Saturday or at the Old Mill Inn. It was just our luck. He was a really decent sort and turned on the pumps especially for us. We had fuel. The good news was that we were only about ten miles from Embo on Loch Fleet where the adult male King Eider was supposed to be, so we headed back up the coast.

At Embo, there is a long harbour wall overlooking the sea with the sea loch on the other side of the promontory. The winter sun was getting up but we were all still perished and hungry. All I can remember is seeing a mass of Common Eider and Long-tailed Ducks out on the sea. It was also scope work by and large, although some of the Long-tailed Ducks were fantastically close inshore. I think we were all getting a bit disheartened when Dave saved the day by finding the King Eider. What an exquisite bird. It was an absolute stunner with its bright orange knob above its bill and housewife-eye-shadow-blue-coloured head. Dave also picked out a Slavonian Grebe which was another tick for me. Within minutes I had racked up lifers six and seven of the trip. The night in the freezing cold all seemed worth it.

We probably spent about an hour or so at Loch Fleet but all of us were feeling the cold badly in the arctic conditions. It was well below zero, not to mention the wind chill factor and none of us had really got back our core heat from the previous night. We were all really famished, too. Owen out of the blue said that he had some bread, peanut butter and jam (jelly as he had taken to calling it!) in the boot. His mum had filled the car up with his American favourites before he had headed back up to Aberdeen from Edinburgh at the start of term. A week on he had still not emptied his boot! That was Owen all over though. The bread was still reasonably fresh as it had been nicely chilled over the week. Not that we were complaining as peanut butter and jam sarnies made with week-old bread seemed like manna from heaven at that point. He must have had about ten loaves in his boot, so there was plenty to go round. We tucked into it with gusto, standing round the boot of his car and stomping our feet trying to get our circulation going. Breakfast never tasted so good, particularly after the night we had spent and with a male King Eider on our lists! Why Owen never mentioned that his boot was stocked with supplies remains a mystery to this day. Knowing Owen and his casual approach to life, it is entirely possible that he had simply forgotten about it!

The journey back down to Aberdeen was all a bit of a blur. I think Owen drove most of it. We stopped in Inverness to drop off our hitch-hiker companion who must have been wondering what had hit him. He had got some good ticks though. He also coughed up a few quid for the petrol. It would have been seriously tight of him to have just walked away. We were not totally skint but also not exactly flush. The first thing that I did when I got back was pop the kettle on and go and run a hot bath. That bath and brew were absolute bliss. It was late afternoon and we had been away for thirty-six hours and I still had not properly defrosted. It was a fantastic twitch full of great laughs, fantastic birds and a bit of arctic drama to boot. We all forged a special bond on that trip. I am sure all the other guys remember it as fondly as I do. Owen, James and I went on to share a house for our final two years at Aberdeen. We had many cracking outings together with Dave but none to match this particular one.

Ironically, the following year history very nearly repeated itself. A male Surf Scoter had been seen at Findhorn Bay as well as a drake American Wigeon at Culbin Mudflats near Inverness. The scoter would have been a tick for all of us. I had seen

American Wigeon at Minsmere back in 1982 but I think it was a lifer for the others. For some reason, we made the trip twice in a matter of days, probably to get another shot at the scoter as on the first visit we dipped it but got the Wigeon. For the next outing, we were joined by Mark Hannay who had just acquired a new car. I cannot remember the model but it was a brand new red hatchback. Mark must have been keen to get a twitch under his belt in his new wheels. Whatever, for the second time in five days we all crammed in and headed off up to Inverness. It was the usual crew of me (obviously), Dave, Owen and James. Mark was also a student at Aberdeen and a stalwart of the University Bird Club. He was a pukka gent, very well spoken and privately educated. He had something of a Boris-Johnson look about him, being a bit baby faced, with a spanked back-side complexion, a mop of blonde hair and the aristocratic accent to match. In those days, Boris Johnson had not even been 'invented' so to speak – which was fortunate for Mark as he would no doubt have acquired the 'Boris' nickname and been ribbed mercilessly. Findhorn Bay was our first port of call. From the shingle bank on the beach, we were confronted by hundreds of scoters. I have never seen so many Common and Velvet Scoters as on those two days but, unfortunately, we could not find the Surf Scoter amongst them. There were so many birds to check that we could never quite finish going through them all. You always felt that you had missed some which you clearly had. After hours of checking and re-checking we decided to call it a day. It was a bad dip.

We headed up to Culbin mudflats and pulled into the Forestry Commission car park before heading down the access road through the plantation of spruce trees to the flats beyond. We got on to the American Wigeon again easily and actually had better views than on the first visit. The highlight though was seeing three otters feeding and frolicking in the pools. We watched them until the light was beginning to dwindle and then headed back to the car. We were just about to go when a couple of Tawny Owls started hooting down the track we had just come from. We decided to go and have a look, but to save time Mark drove the car down the forest track. We had a go at calling to the owls but did not manage to see them in spite of them coming close to us. As darkness fell, we headed back up the track and into the car park. Disaster had struck. While we had been looking for the owls, the ranger must have turned up and locked the car park gate. Obviously, he must have thought that the car park was empty. We were locked in and absolutely miles from anywhere! What we could not understand was why the Commission felt it necessary to pay a man to lock up that car park each evening. It was not exactly near anywhere. Alright it might have been a good spot for one of the local lads to park up with his girlfriend, but did that really justify employing someone to lock it up each night and then unlock it the following morning? Anyhow, that is what happened. This question, although important to our situation, was not the burning issue of the moment. How the hell were we going to get out? It was Spinningdale II. It was nearly dark and here we were trapped in the car park. It was not as cold as at Spinningdale but it was still going to be a sub-zero night. Mark had obviously heard about our earlier experiences but had clearly *not* realised that we were cursed. Which birding god we had offended I do not know.

The Forestry Commission make good robust car parks. The gate was solid, with a strong chain and padlock. That was definitely a no-go. We started to have a good look at the fence which consisted of barbed wire between wooden posts. It was in very good nick and looked quite new. We had a go at wobbling the posts and with some effort they became loose in the ground and could be lifted out. Eventually we did this with about six posts and were able to lay them flat on the ground. Fortunately, Mark had a sheet of tarpaulin in the boot of his car which we could lay over the barbed wire. It also needed the combined weight of a couple of us to keep the fence flat and stop it from twisting back upright. Mark nursed the car through the rough grass, over the tarpaulin and across the fence. We were out. In the darkness, we put the posts back in and gave them a bash with a stone. They were a bit of a mess to be honest, rather wobbly and leaning at all angles. God only knows what the ranger thought when he came back to unlock the car park the next day. I bet they have a twenty-four-hour guard on it now! The rural crime statistics for criminal damage must have soared that year. The main thing was that we were on our way home and did not have to spend the night in that bloody car in the middle of nowhere AGAIN!

Our final trauma as a twitching crew came the following May. Every year, we would do a sponsored bird watch with the aim of seeing as many bird species in one day as possible. We would start off locally and make our way up the coast, crossing over to Inverness and into Speyside before hitting the woods at Ballater and back through the mountains into the Don Valley. We all used to get great birds this way, including Scottish specialities such as Golden Eagle, Osprey, Crested Tit, Scottish

Crossbill, Slavonian Grebe, Capercaillie and Black Grouse. It was always a great laugh if not something of a birding marathon. In 1986, I had personally totalled nearly 120 species in twenty-four hours, which was impressive for Scotland. The idea was to raise funds for the bird club but it was also a great birding day out. Well that is, it was a great day until our minibus broke down in the middle of nowhere and we had to wait two hours for the RAC to turn up. This pretty much wrecked our outing in 1988 when we were out for a huge target with the possibility of setting the Scottish record for species in a day. We had more or less connected with everything, and all we needed was a bit of luck in the hills and we would have done it. It was not to be and we ended up losing the last couple of hours of daylight sitting on the minibus bemoaning our lack of success. I guess that this was nothing compared with our previous tribulations though.

On a final note, my exploits in Aberdeen would not be complete without mentioning the annual Capercaillie Count to which we were invited on one of the larger estates in the Don Valley. The reward for us was a day of birding in beautiful surroundings and a lunch of piping-hot venison stew, washed down with malt whisky. Clearly, student birders were the target market. In return, we would spread out in a long line and count any Capercaillies and Black Grouse that we flushed out along the way. The day consisted of a number of drops where we would be pointed in the right direction and effectively set off to beat and count the birds. We were ferried about in lorries and dumped at various parts of the estate. It was a cracking, bright and crisp winter's day. On our first drop, I was at the end of a diagonal line about 20 yards away from James. He disappeared over the brow of a hill and out of sight along with the others. It was akin to being in the outside lane of a running race, so in effect I was a long way behind the others to my right. By the time I reached the ridge line, everyone else had completely disappeared from sight. I walked a bit further and arrived at the track signifying the end of this particular beat. My dilemma was which way to go. Nobody had waited and I was on my own. Did I go left uphill or right and head down the track? A couple of footprints in the dirt seemed to suggest that people had gone left, so that was the direction I chose. Wrong. After ten minutes or so I realised that I had made a duff choice. I turned tail and retraced my footsteps. After about a mile, I arrived at a point where the lorries had obviously picked everybody up. Tyre tracks and footprints marked the spot. They had buggered off without me! The air turned blue. What's more, I did not have a clue where I was.

It seemed sensible to head downhill. All I could do was keep walking and walking until hopefully I could get my bearings. I walked about twenty miles that day, possible more, without seeing a soul. I had nothing on me, not even a chocolate bar. At about the half-way point, I finally managed to confirm my whereabouts and could see the University minibus parked miles away in the distance in the bottom of the valley next to the river. Thank goodness, I had my binoculars. This was quite a relief to me at the time as up to that point it was beginning to turn into something of a 'lost on the moors' ordeal. The words 'beware the moon' and 'stick to the road' were echoing in my head. I arrived back at the bus fully expecting it to be locked. Fortunately, someone had left the door open. I clambered into the bus and listened to the Scottish live commentary game on the radio. It was a pretty boring and hungry afternoon. I was the only member of our party to see a Dipper that day, which was an appropriate bird considering I had missed out on the venison stew, the whisky and a Golden Eagle, too! The lads seemed pleased to see that I had made it back okay, although I did not half get some stick for getting lost. Well-deserved really. Apparently, they had raised the alert to the lorry drivers that I was missing but had decided to leave me marooned commenting that I would either get back or the foxes would have me after I had died of exposure. Not my best-ever day out.

My years at Aberdeen were brilliant in terms of the birding. We spent a huge amount of time in the field and made some good finds over our four years there, including King Eider, Snow Goose, Tawny and Richard's Pipit. My personal highlight was finding a Snow Goose with another student birder called Roddy Maver. I put it on the telephone information service, Birdline, that night. While I was in the kitchen, the phone rang. James came through to get me saying that Richard Millington was on the phone asking for me. If anyone does not know, Richard is one of the UK's leading twitchers and a founder of the rarity hotline, Birdline, and leading bird magazine, *Birding World* (or *Twitching* as it was called back in those days). I thought James was joking but it really was Richard ringing me wanting exact details of where we had found the bird. I was on cloud nine, feeling like I had finally made it on the twitching scene. I left Aberdeen with a far bigger list and a much better birder than when I arrived in 1984. Hours in the field had brought me on no end and I was mad keen to continue my birding endeavours. Birdline, a car and a desire to expand my list were the key to that.

THE SCILLIES
1998-2005

Scilly has a unique place in most birder's hearts of my generation. Certainly for the twitchers. I have been on Scilly a number of times over the years and absolutely love the place, so much so that I want my ashes spreading at Giant's Castle on St. Mary's. It means that much to me. I have had great times there, seeing some belting birds and also having a couple of shocking dips, too. It is just a fantastic place to be. The scenery is breath-taking, the birding dramatic and the social scene was fantastic. It is a holiday of solid birding and nothing else. You eat, drink and sleep birds for the whole time that you are there. Most days I will be birding from dawn to dusk and in the evenings mixing with other birders at the daily bird log. During the downtime in between, Tom and I will be discussing birds that we have seen (or not seen as the case may be) and discussing tactics for the following day. It is hundred per cent birds. I am sad to say that October on Scilly now seems to be very much in decline. It has become ridiculously expensive to get and stay there. For the cost of a week's holiday on Scilly, you could easily go abroad for half the price. I think many birders are now opting for the Continent or the States instead. Even top twitcher and year lister Lee Evans has been giving it a miss. The birding is not what it was in the seventies and eighties by all accounts but also without the mass flood of birders onto the islands, less birds are being found.

I have not visited since 2005, partly due to family commitments but also because of the ridiculous prices. It all just feels like a rip off. I still get yearnings each October to go to the Scillies but I now think Shetland is the place to be. I first went to the Scilly Isles in August 1981 with a mate called Jonathan

At my favourite place on the Scillies.

Ross who I had met on one of my YOC holidays at Gibraltar Point. I was fifteen and Jonathan was seventeen. We camped in his tent up on the Garrison camp site for nearly two weeks. It was rather early for any really good birds, but we picked up a fair collection of lifers including Wryneck, Icterine Warbler, Dotterel, Roseate Tern, Nightingale and the resident female Black Duck. The holiday was somewhat marred by Tom getting Baird's Sandpiper, Common Rosefinch and Icterine Warbler in Yorkshire while I was away. He always seemed to pull the cat out of the bag when I was not around. My next trip was in 1985 when Tom and I decided to have a couple of weeks there in September before I returned to University for my second year. We did not do too badly, picking up Bee-eater, Short-toed Lark, Buff-breasted Sandpiper and quite a few decent 'padders'. A lot of them were actually lifers for us though, including Richard's Pipit, Ortolan Bunting and Lapland Bunting. We had a good time, but literally the day after we left, the islands were flooded with Yankee warblers. We missed an absolute bag full of megas. I could almost cry when I think how close we were to ticking some of those birds.

That is the quintessential problem with the Scillies in that you always miss birds when you fly off the islands. The last day is often like a knife being twisted in your guts. That was certainly the case in 2001 when a Swainson's Thrush was showing at Porthellick House on St. Mary's. Birders could see it while we were standing there, but because of the crowds and the restricted views we just could not get on to it. To twist the proverbial knife a bit further, we had to endure flying over the throng of birders some two hours later on our way back to the mainland. It was a horrible moment looking down on them no doubt enjoying fantastic views of the Swainson's as we headed home. What a bloody sickener. It was a bad dip and left a really sour taste in my mouth and cast a major cloud over the holiday.

My next visit came in 1994 while I was back on leave from Hong Kong. My years in the Royal Hong Kong Police Force meant that my British list had taken a bit of a pummelling in that I had missed stacks of major birds. As a result, I was somewhat off the whole twitching scene and somehow Tom and I had got it in our heads that we would be better off in Cornwall finding our own birds rather than just going from tick to tick on the Scillies. How we came up with that idea, I do not know. I guess it was some sort of purist and ethical birding stance we were taking at the time. Anyone who knows me half well will vouch that purity and ethics are not words that people generally associate with me.

'It's a bit unethical, but we can get really a result if we do this,' I said to a colleague at work recently.

'Since when have ethics ever bothered you?' came his sardonic reply.

So Cornwall it was. We stayed in a caravan at Kelynack near St. Just. It was a good trip, but the birding was hard going. There were very few migrants about. We spent lots of birdless hours going down the various Cornish valleys, particularly Kenidjack which we had taken a perverse shine to. We got Ruddy Shelduck and a superb adult Franklin's Gull at Hayle Estuary on our first and last days, respectively, but not that much in-between. The Franklin's Gull was literally squeezed in by the skin of our teeth, right at the end of the trip. We had decided to stop at Hayle Estuary for an hour's birding and have some lunch at the pub before heading back home. As we arrived, a very excited birder came running up to us.

'Did you know that you've just dipped out on an adult Franklin's Gull? It was showing superbly and it's just gone. It flew over your car as you pulled into the car park.'

He had a horrible gloating smugness about him but at the same time was pretending to be alright about it, as if he was our mate. Birders call it being 'gripped off'. I instantly disliked him, not for seeing a Franklin's Gull but for revelling in the fact he had seen something that we had not. He was cock-a-hoop. He was also a cock. I resisted the urge to issue summary violent justice. Nobody seemed to have a clue where it had gone. We stood around for a while and fairly soon there was a decent crew of birders milling around the car park, all chatting, but no one was really looking. It was as if everyone was just expecting someone else to find the bird. Now I was just back from Hong Kong where I had really got used to looking for my own birds rather than ticking somebody else's. Also, I had done my time on working gull flocks with the boys in Aberdeen, so I knew the score. I just set up my scope and started scanning. There were a hell of a lot of gulls out there and more were arriving by the minute. Suddenly, a dark grey mantle appeared in my scope and there it was, a pristine adult Franklin's Gull in winter plumage. A beauty.

'I've got it. Quick Tom, come and have a look.'

Everybody's ears pricked up around me as Tom peered through the scope.

'Are you sure John? All I can see are Herring Gulls.'

The people around all started giving me withering looks and rolling their eyes. I grabbed the scope off him and put it back on the bird. He peered through again and stood there silent and uncertain for a few seconds before slightly adjusting his stance.

'No. I can't see it, just Herring Gulls. Are you sure? Wait a moment. Oh God, it is it. I've got it. What a beauty.'

The withering looks stopped, and suddenly there was a clamour for me to tell them where it was. I got a few pats on the back for that one and a lot of 'well done mate' from the assembled throng. Everyone was elated. So was I as I had re-found the Franklin's and I was buzzing. After giving it a thorough grilling we headed into the pub where the gloating git from earlier stopped us with a pint in his hand. He clearly did not recognise us. He had obviously spoken to every birder possible in his grip-off frenzy and had completely lost track of who was new meat.

'Did you know that there was an adult Franklin's Gull here about an hour ago? I saw it before it went.'

'Yeah, I did mate because you told us already. I've just re-found it though and had belting views.'

His face dropped. The 'grip-off' had backfired. Scampi and chips washed down with a celebration ale never tasted so good after rubbing (metaphorically speaking) his smug face in it!

So the holiday ended on a really high note, but it had been hard work throughout. We had dipped out on an Arctic Warbler which cleared out of Kenidjack on the day we arrived. It had been around for a few days and there had even been an 'unconfirmed' sighting during the morning on the day of our arrival. Needless to say, we saw no sign of it. The next few days saw us getting very little. Finally, we both broke and decided to day-trip Scilly. We flew from St. Just airfield in a small turbo prop plane. The pilot was late arriving and when he finally did turn up he looked like he had been out on the ale all night.

The journey out was okay, but on the return, he nearly carted the plane into a hedge. As we came into land, he got the trajectory completely wrong. Cows were scattering in all directions as we approached the airfield only about ten feet from the ground. It was clear to both Tom and me that we were far too low and were going to smash into the hedge. Suddenly he jerked the plane upwards and we literally hopped over the hedge and hurtled onto the landing strip with a massive jolting bump of a landing. It was a close one for sure. My fists were clenched tight when it happened, but somehow he missed that hedge. It did make us laugh afterwards and certainly reinforced the 'on the piss' theory. We picked up Little Bunting, Yellow-browed Warbler, Red-breasted Flycatcher and Red-backed Shrike on our Scilly jaunt. Unfortunately, we dipped on a Radde's Warbler which was our main target bird. I had a fleeting view of a good candidate near Porthellick. It was re-found the next day at the pumping station round the corner, but unfortunately not seen on the day that we were there. I guess it was not the greatest day trip to the Scillies and I was not too keen on the large numbers of people at virtually every bird. Even the Red-breasted Flycatcher had quite a big crowd. One or two of the twitchers there were either poor birders or half asleep. The flycatcher gave its characteristic 'tik tik' call, like two coins being tapped together, before showing. Half of them did not even react. I was not that impressed. The Yellow-browed Warbler was a British first for me, but they were two-a-penny back in Hong Kong, so I was not overly enthused by the latest addition to my list. Tom added the Little Bunting to his life list, leaving Scilly at 1:1. At least we had not been killed in the plane. The Radde's Warbler might have been worth dying for, but definitely not the Yellow-browed or the Bunting.

In 1997, we were again on holiday in Cornwall but this time were accompanied by Tom's then wife Louise. I had now finished my time with the Royal Hong Kong Police Force and had joined the Greater Manchester Police Service, so I was back into British birding properly. I had decided to have a go at getting a half-decent year list as there were a lot of British birds that I had not seen for some time. Working shifts in Manchester meant that I had a fair amount of time off in the week. Birding was a great way of doing something constructive while most people were at work. Without birding, I would have had bugger all to do. I mean what is there to do on a damp Tuesday in February in Manchester? The year list also gave me that incentive to get out and about. For the first time since my university days I got well over 200 species for the year, not a great feat when compared with the serious year listers who score over 300 species, but I was pleased with it.

We had rented a cottage at Porthgwarra and spent a lot of time sea-watching, picking up some good birds, including several Sabine's Gulls. This was a self-found lifer for both Tom and me. We had put in a lot of hours sea-watching, knowing that the conditions were good. We got two or three Sab's, but that first one was fantastic. It is not often that you find your own lifers, so we were both elated. We had seen juvenile Kittiwake after Kittiwake, which is superficially quite similar to a Sabine's gull. Suddenly, a Sabine's appeared – there could be no mistaking that wing pattern. For someone who does not like gulls that much, I seem to get my kicks from them. Ross's, Franklins and Sab's all have their stories to tell. Again, the birding was hard work, so we decided to do a day trip to the Scillies. I think it was as much to show Louise the Scilly Isles as to pick up any lifers as there was nothing about on the islands when we arrived. I seem to remember that there may have been a Little Bunting near the airport but little else. I was trudging along behind Tom who had the pager when he quite literally turned round in his tracks saying:

'Mega. Yellowthroat. Lower Moors.'

Without another word, he did a U-turn and marched off. All I heard was the word 'Mega', so for the first thirty yards I was just following him not knowing what the bird even was. I could hear the news crackling through on the CBs (Citizen Band radios) around us, and eventually I ascertained it was a Yellowthroat, a very rare warbler from the States. This was a massive stroke of luck, a complete jam-in if we could see it. We managed to get a decent position in the general area where it had been seen. Anyway, I had a couple of fleeting glimpses of it before finally getting brief but cracking views of the bird in the brambles. Now this was proper Scilly. This was why people flocked to the islands each year. I had got the bug and was beginning to wonder what I was doing scratching around in Cornwall. It may have been the fact that I had scored a mega tick, but somehow the crowds seemed far more acceptable. Never let it be said that I am anything but fickle. You know what you can do with your ethics Johnnie Boy! Tick a Yellowthroat and all is well in the world. Scilly was very much back on my birding agenda.

The following October saw Tom and I with a full two weeks booked on Scilly. I was beginning to really hate my job in the police, especially on nights when I used to dread the thought of going into work each evening. The only upside for me was the time off. We used to work seven consecutive nights followed by six days off. I used to live for those six days off. It was a very unhappy time for me professionally. In many ways, I never really acclimatised to police life in the UK after being in Hong Kong. I also had problems at home as my personal life was beginning to fall apart, too. My relationship with my girlfriend at the time was beginning to show cracks. She had a new job and was completely wrapped up in it. She would spend the evenings tapping away on her laptop and I would watch sport in the other room. I felt that I had no one to turn to and had gradually become more and more of a recluse. We got on okay, but the relationship was certainly getting stale and tired. It was like being brother and sister without the incest. Birding was my crutch and my main distraction. Sheffield United was also a big interest at the time for me, so between birding and football, I kept myself as happy as I could. There cannot be too many happy couples where the bloke goes off on a two-week holiday without his girlfriend. It was a statement, I guess, that I was too cowardly to say openly. It was the elephant in the room which both of us ignored. I am the biggest moral coward in town and was incapable of dealing with it. Anyway, that was what I was doing and I could not wait to get away.

Birding was my main outlet for all this crap that I was going through. I did not realise how unhappy I had become. The only thing that gave me real pleasure was birding. I do not think that I was depressed but definitely would have been without birding and my beloved Blades. When I was not birding then I was reading up about Scilly and swotting up on rarities. I could not wait to get there. I would read everything and anything about Scilly or rare birds. I had fastidiously read about virtually every possible rarity that I might see. I had whetted my appetite by studying many previous year's sighting for the dates of our holiday. If the conditions were right we could pile on the new birds. It is always dangerous looking at old records from previous years as one thing is for sure – no two years are the same. If the weather conditions are poor then generally the birding is poor.

All I had to get through were my seven nights and then I would be off for nearly three weeks. On one of my last night shift, I saw a cracking Tawny Owl perched in the woods in Blackley. Even the other bobby that I was with was impressed; mind you, he did spot it. It was a year-tick to boot. Five days later I was on the road heading south, starting my holiday. The plan was to stay at Tom's place in Hampton before setting off for Cornwall and then getting the helicopter flight across to Scilly. As luck would have it, there was an immature White-tailed Eagle in Graveney in Kent, so I decided to go for it and get the holiday off to a flying start. As I was heading south on the M1, the pager informed me that the Eagle was still there, so it was game on. Great news. I was not far off the M25 when the pager flashed up a message that there was a Sociable Plover at Graveney, too. Sometimes your luck is in and mine was in big style. This was a excellent bird and another lifer. They were literally about a mile apart. My luck held and I scored with them both. The Eagle was dead easy, just sitting in a field surrounded by crows. The plover was also straight forward. Within a couple of hours both were in the bag. Tom was green with envy when I told him that night. He insisted that we get up and go for them the next morning even though we were supposed to be driving down to Cornwall. I really did not want to trog over to Kent and back from Hampton before driving off to Penzance. Tom was insistent and said that he would even go on his own. Eventually, I succumbed after hours of badgering from him. God knows what time we got up, but I know we were in Graveney well before first light. We had to park up in a lay-by where we promptly got checked out by the local cops.

As it turned out, the Eagle had gone. We headed over to the plover field. As we arrived, the Lapwing flock with which the Sociable Plover was mixing took flight. I got onto it straight away, but Tom struggled to pick it up in spite of my best commentary efforts to get him onto the bird. It was right at the back of the flock and I kept telling him exactly which bird it was. After a couple of turns the flock landed absolutely miles away in a field completely out of sight. We hung around for a bit but they were not showing, and time was not on our side. Tom had seen the bird, but not conclusively. It was an NTV, a Non-Tickable View. This is what every birder dreads. All that bloody way and back for nothing. It was just typical of Tom; he had dipped one and technically could not tick the other. I guess he was more fed up than I was as at least I had seen them both and they were both on my list from the previous day.

The only good news was that the Olivaceous Warbler was still on Scilly. It had been there for a few days and we were now in with a real chance of connecting with it. If it was there tomorrow we would be straight off to St. Agnes to get it. Because of our delayed start from the Graveney excursion, we arrived in Cornwall a lot later than we had originally planned. We managed a quick stop at the Hayle Estuary before going to our B&B for the night. How I wish we had spent an extra day on Scilly rather than meander our way down as by the time we flew there the next day, the Olivaceous Warbler had gone. We had missed it by a day. It turned out to be a funny holiday. The birding was okay and we had a first for Britain in the form of a Wilson's Snipe. Anyone who has seen Wilson's Snipe will know that it is pretty much identical to a Common Snipe. It was a good bird to get on the list, but it was hardly riveting stuff. We started off well seeing Common Rosefinch, Rustic Bunting and Corncrake in the first few days, but it never really got going. While we were watching the Corncrake, a mega alert came up on the pager:

'Yellow-rumped Warbler feeding in pines at Watermill.'

This was bloody miles away, right on the other side of the island. Virtually everyone set off on the trek up there as this was a good bird. It also turned out to be the perfect bird for a string. It was a complete hoax. News filtered through that Rare Bird Alert could not verify the informant's details and then we were all hit with the crushing disappointment that Yellow-rumped Warbler was not going to be on our lists. It was never even there. It was clearly somebody's idea of a joke. A couple of years later there was a similar hoax call made really late on in the day with the report of a Philadelphia Vireo on St. Martin's. The weather was absolutely appalling, too. A few birders went for it, but it also proved to be a hoax. Thank God, we had learnt a salutary lesson with that mythical (as it turned out) Yellow-rumped Warbler.

The best bird of the trip was not actually a lifer. We were on Tresco towards the end of the first week. It was a warm and balmy afternoon and we decided to have our lunch at the Rowesfield Crossroads near a clump of likely looking bushes. Tom had a doze in the warm afternoon sun, while I kept an eye out on the bushes. There were a few Goldcrests moving through but also another bird which was really staying deep in cover. I woke Tom up and told him that there was something odd lurking deep in the bushes. I had a sixth sense about it. We kept getting half glimpses of it. It was like making a jigsaw puzzle with a piece of wing here and a bit of head there. We watched for about fifteen to twenty minutes, getting frustrating glimpses as it flitted through the undergrowth. Occasionally it made an odd 'tik' noise, which sounded like a Flowerpecker call, almost as if two coins were being tapped together. Even Scilly was not going to produce a Flowerpecker, but I had been in Hong Kong for seven years so it was not surprising that Asian birds were springing to mind. We both knew that we were onto something different, but what? The coin tapping noise had me thinking Red-breasted Flycatcher, RBF. Neither of us had really seen anything diagnostic. Eventually, it started to move slightly to the front of the bushes and, finally, I saw that it had white outer tail feathers. Red-breasted Flycatcher. Not the greatest rarity but still a cracking little bird and, what is more, we had found it. As soon as we had clinched the ID, it decided to come out into the open and pose for us. It's funny how birds seem to play with you and then just go for it, giving tantalising glimpses before putting on a show. It was obviously a female! I guess it is the ornithological version of a striptease. After it disappeared out of sight we got up to spread the news and put some nearby birders onto it. A couple of Scilly 'faces' put it on the CB and quite soon a fair few birders appeared to look for it. The next thing, it flashed up on the pager:

'Red-breasted Flycatcher at Rowesfield Crossroads, Tresco.'

There it was, our find on the CB and on the pager. It was the only RBF on the islands, so a lot of people needed it for their holiday and year lists. It was a well-watched bird over the next few days. That night at the 'Porthcressa' bird log, it finally came round to Red-breasted Flycatcher being called out. Will Wagstaff was doing the log.

'Red-breasted Fly. There was a report of one from Tresco today?'

I had to shout up. I was nervous but also proud.

'Yes. That's right.'

'Was that at the Rowesfield Crossroads?'

'Well it was near the fruit cages in the bushes if that is Rowesfields.'

'Yes. Sounds like Rowesfields to me.'

That was it, our moment of glory. I remember Lee Evans, who is a real 'name' in twitching circles, looking me up and down. Now for the uninitiated, Lee is to birding or certainly twitching what José Mourinho is to the Premier League. He is talented, outspoken, controversial, even flawed and certainly not everyone's cup of tea. He is undoubtedly a character and very Marmite in birding circles. I like Marmite and I like Lee. Others differ in their opinions – I know that. Yes, he is rather controversial and divisive at times, but birding has been a lot richer and more interesting because of him. He is also a good organiser and gets things sorted when leadership is required. I've met him on quite a few occasions and given him directions to birds a couple of times. He has always been spot on whenever I have spoken to him. Tom and I were fairly new kids on the block as far as Scilly was concerned, and it felt like Lee was just taking a mental note of us. To be honest, he may just have been looking at us like everyone else and I thought more of it just because it was Lee. Maybe it was all in my head, but he did seem to give me the once over. I remember one time being on the Garrison with Tom doing a bit of sea-watching. I had just found a Great Northern Diver when Lee turned up. He let on to us and Tom mentioned the diver. As always, he was keen to see it. He wants to see every half-decent bird, so I had to relocate the diver and put him onto it. Now, it was clearly a Great Northern, but for those thirty seconds or so, while I was directing Lee to the bird, I was having a confidence crisis thinking, '*Please don't cock this one up Johnny boy. Anyone else, but not with Lee Evans.*' My reputation was at stake and I did not want to show my ignorance in front of the UK's most famous and notorious twitcher. I was racked with fear that the diver would suddenly swim a bit closer and morph into a Cormorant. I was so relieved when he saw it. He was genuinely appreciative and said well done. He was obviously totally oblivious to the stress and pressure that I was under. Thanks a lot Tom! After Lee had gone, I told Tom that I had been bricking it in case I had dropped a clanger. We had a good laugh, and I am glad that we could show Lee the bird. He has shown many other birders good birds over the years. Back in 1998, we were in a field near the airport looking at a flock of Meadow Pipits, which included a single Red-throated Pipit. Superficially, the two species are very similar in autumn plumage, so the main identification diagnostic is the call. We could hear the Red-throated Pipit calling occasionally, but it was hard to pick out the actual bird amongst the many Meadow Pipits. Lee was there, kneeling in front of us. I managed to locate a likely candidate for the Red-throated Pipit, a bird that was quite neatly marked and just that bit smarter than all the other pipits present. Suddenly, the pipits started to fly off in little clusters. Lee characteristically chimed up:

'They're going to go. The Red-throated will sit tight though. It will be one of the last to fly.'

Now I did not know this about Red-throated Pipits, and I am sure many others did not either. However, Lee did, and not only that but he was also prepared to pass on his knowledge. What is more, the Red-throated Pipit did sit tight and was among the last couple of birds to fly, giving its characteristic call as it went. It turned out that it was my smart-looking bird after all. This incident really impressed me on two fronts: Lee's knowledge but also his generosity with it. Tom and I both learned something that day and it was thanks to Lee. It is not the sort of thing that you will read in any field guide or bird book. It was a pure and practical birding tip and I am grateful to Lee for it. There are many birders who have it in for Lee just because of who he is and the fact that he stands up to be counted. A lot of it is done behind his back in a silly school boy kind of way. It makes them look good if they slag him off. He courts controversy and notoriety and is outspoken in the extreme at times. He is a one-off and a maverick but, love him or hate him, he has been good for both British birding and twitching. I am sure he has made mistakes like everyone else, but the twitching scene and October on Scilly are a lot better when he is there. For me, he is birding box office.

The rest of that 1998 holiday was a bit of an anticlimax. We did get Olive-backed Pipit, which is a good bird, but it was not a tick for either of us. I had also seen loads in Hong Kong. I left Scilly with just five lifers on my list. Alright, one, the Wilson's Snipe, was a first for Britain, but it did not really feel that exciting at the time. It did not actually have 'full' species status in that it was deemed to be a subspecies of the Common Snipe when we saw it. The world of bird speciation is very much a moving feast with the development of DNA testing and a more malleable approach to awarding full species status being used. As a result, Wilson's Snipe was in the likely to be 'split' category. It was a pencil tick waiting to be overwritten in ink, not quite 'the Full Monty' yet but certainly on the cards. I had the pleasure of an 'armchair tick' some months later when Wilson's was awarded full species status. A lot of the big names came across to get it as an insurance tick. This meant that if it was upgraded to a full species then they could add it to their lists. I think I spent more time ticking off famous birders than birds that day. I also saw the first for Britain that never was in the form of what became known as 'that starling', which had originally been identified as Britain's first-ever Spotless Starling. Many travelled over for it when it was first discovered, and to all intents and purposes it looked like the real deal. It was eventually re-identified as a Common Starling, so I imagine rubbers were out on many lists. I cannot imagine how excruciating it must have been to 'un-tick' that bird. I must say, having seen the bird in question sitting on the rooftops in Hugh Town, it looked nothing like a Common Starling. Rumour had it that it was an eastern form of starling but superficially at least it looked like a 'Spotless'.

The weather over the final few days was atrocious with a huge westerly front coming in from the Atlantic. If only it had come a few days earlier. Literally a day or so after our departure, American Robin, Pied-billed Grebe and Rose-breasted Grosbeak were all found on St Agnes. These were exactly the kind of birds that you go to the Scilly Isles for. I was absolutely gutted. Not only was I back at work doing my job in the police but I had dipped on two Yankee lifers by days having spent two weeks there. Leaving Scilly is always a wrench because of the dip factor. Once you are off you do not want anything else to be found. Before you go there you want anything already found to stay there until you arrive. While you are there, you just need to make sure you get everything. Scilly is great, but dips before, during and after the holiday are agonising. Bizarrely, that is what makes Scilly so good as you just never know what fate has in store.

The year 1999 was for many the best-ever year on Scilly and I could not go. In May, I had thrown my job in with the police, split up from my girlfriend, moved out of her house and left her with my cat. It was a tumultuous time on many fronts, but I was particularly attached to that cat. I had enrolled to do an MBA at Lancaster University after having the summer off. I was supposed to be going with Tom, but the term dates clashed with the holiday. My first week at Lancaster coincided with my week's holiday on Scilly. I was paying a lot of money for my MBA and it was a serious career move for me, so I decided to do the mature thing and be there for the first week. It was the first truly mature decision that I had ever made in my life. However, I cannot believe that I was so sensible looking back. Tom went on his own and what a week he had. All week I had to put up with text messages from him as he scored megabird after megabird. Short-toed Eagle, White's Thrush, Siberian Thrush, Radde's Warbler, Yellow-billed Cuckoo, Upland Sandpiper, Blue Rock Thrush and a possible Eleonora's Falcon were all available and he got the lot as well as loads of padders. I was distressed…to say the least. Meanwhile, Tom was elated and still is. I have yet to hear the last word about that holiday from him.

The following year, I was determined to make amends and get a decent October holiday on Scilly. The week before I was due to go I landed a new job at Britannia Building Society, having successfully completed my MBA. The job did not start until December, so there was nothing to get in the way this time. I was on the back of another badly failed relationship, but I now did not really care anymore. I needed to focus on me, my new job and my new life. At least I had not had to give up another cat! Birding was one of the few constants in my life and I really felt that I could not be involved with women any more. Bachelor birding was the way to go! I just had to hope that the birds performed. It was looking good as there were a number of quality birds on offer in Cornwall and on the Scillies. I did my usual trip to Hampton and picked up Tom. The following day, we headed off to Cornwall. News came through on the pager that the Red-eyed Vireo was still at Nanquidno. This would be my first Yankee passerine since the 1997 Yellowthroat…if I connected. They are cracking birds, and it was a tick that I was desperate to get. I was also catching one up on Tom who had already seen this species in the UK. Cornwall produced. We got the Vireo almost immediately and had good views of it feeding in the trees above us. It was not quite what I would call a 'hyperzonky megacrippler', as described by Richard Millington in his book *A Twitcher's Diary*, but it was still a damn good bird. This was the start of a strange phenomenon where I would do well in Cornwall in terms of seeing birds that Tom had on his list. The only downside was that Tom would do the same to me on Scilly. It did not always follow that pattern but I have generally had the better of it on the mainland. He has eclipsed me with loads of ticks on Scilly – which has always been galling from my perspective. We then headed up to Sennen where we picked up a fantastic Buff-breasted Sandpiper as well as a couple of Lapland Buntings. Both species showed beautifully in perfect light in a ploughed field by the roadside. It had been a cracking afternoon all round.

The other good news was that the Solitary Sandpiper was still at Porthellick on Scilly. One more day and we were in. I had that familiar feeling of nervous anticipation before flying over, but this time we were not disappointed. We had a great first day, easily picking up the sandpiper and then finding a Red-breasted Flycatcher in Holy Vale. Suddenly, news broke of an Arctic Warbler on the Garrison. We raced over and had very good views of it as it fed along the wall between the Upper and Lower Broom platforms. We saw the Arctic Warbler on each day of its stay, an absolute fantastic little bird and a lifer for us both. In a classic case of east meets west, we also got our second Red-eyed Vireo of the trip, with a well-marked bird in the tamarisks near Old Town churchyard. What a start. On the first day, we had just about eclipsed our whole two weeks of 1998. We had a few more days of easy birds with nothing too special knocking about until news broke of a pair of Blue-winged Teals on Tresco. True to form, this was a lifer for Tom but not for me. We got the bird. We were back on Tresco again the next day following up a spurious report of a Grey-cheeked Thrush, which proved to be a complete 'red herring'. Every year on Scilly there is at least one metaphorical 'wild goose chase'. It had been mentioned at the bird log the night before and the sighting seemed to have some substance to it. With few options on other birds, we decided to give it a go. We spent several fruitless hours seeing very little.

On our final day, we reconnected with the Red-eyed Vireo getting excellent views of it feeding in trees near the school. It had been a good week. I was quite eager to get off the islands for once as there was a Yellow-billed Cuckoo at St. Leven in Cornwall. Now this was a 'big' bird. American Cuckoos are often sick when they hit our shores and prone to dying, so it was touch and go. I drove like a madman from the heliport as we were tight on time having had an afternoon flight from Scilly. We rushed to a group of birders who were watching the cuckoo sitting on a fence post. I do not know whether it was nerves, excitement or what, but I could not see it. Tom had it in his scope and told me to have a look. As I peered through the scope, it almost instantly started to fly. I followed it with my binoculars as it darted into a small copse. I saw it well, but the brevity of the views did not do justice to such a fantastic rarity. Try as we might, we could not relocate the cuckoo. Where it had gone or what happened to it is anybody's guess. It had probably snuffed it like nearly every American cuckoo that hits these shores. It was never seen again. We were the last people to see it. Still, my Cornish luck was in but only just. I had got one of Tom's 1999 birds back. It had been my best Scilly trip yet.

2001 proved to be a poor year for us on Scilly as the weather was bad and our tactics were not much better. We also made some poor decisions, had some bad luck and missed out on a lot of 'padders' mainly through a bit of laziness on our part. I had picked up a lifer in Cornwall in the form of a Baird's Sandpiper at Dawlish Warren which had got things going. Tom could not believe that my Cornish hoodoo was working again. I was pleased with this tick as it was turning into a bogey bird. I had twitched one earlier in September when I had been doing a Leach's Petrel session at Leasowe in Merseyside. While I was there, a Baird's Sandpiper was reported near Southport on the pager. I shot off through the Mersey tunnel to go for it only to have it re-paged as a misidentified Little Stint. Lancashire has been bad for me on misidentified birds that have been paged prematurely. I have also twitched a Greater Yellowlegs at Martin Mere which proved to be a Greenshank and a Slender-billed Gull at Leighton Moss which turned out to be a Black-headed Gull. Both were totally annoying experiences for me as, on both occasions, I literally dropped everything and hit the road. I was pleased to get the Baird's as well as a nice Kentish Plover in what was a lovely morning's birding at Dawlish. It had laid one Lancashire ghost to rest, but there are still two more haunting me.

The holiday was blighted from the start as Tom had just moved to a new house with his girlfriend. Unfortunately, they had a leak in the kitchen which she just seemed incapable of dealing with. He spent hours on the phone to her and also to various plumbers trying to get them to come round, which apparently is not an easy thing to do in London. When one of them did finally arrive at the house to fix it, she turned him away because he looked scruffy! Tom was beside himself, but Maria was playing the 'damsel in distress' role very well and at the same time ruining his holiday. Being a cynic, I think that it was probably her intention from the start. God knows what his mobile bill was like at the end of the holiday. Anyway, we really struggled for birds early on, but eventually a Yellow-breasted Bunting turned up on St. Agnes. It proved a tough bird initially but eventually gave good views. We also saw a fantastic Hummingbird Hawkmoth and a huge Convolvulus Hawkmoth which pretty much took my moth list to two. Well, it was a start. It is now on three having added Death's Head Hawkmoth in 2003.

It was one of those holidays when we kept getting drawn back to Tresco. Now I have mentioned that Baird's was a bogey bird that I had managed to get rid of, but little did I know that I was developing another. During my MBA year, I decided to do a decent-sized day twitch down to Devon to get a Sora Rail and hopefully pick up a Booted Eagle that had been seen in Somerset. There was also a Siberian Chiffchaff available in Worcestershire if I was desperate. The Sora had been frequenting Stover Country Park for weeks and had been showing very well, so I was very confident of seeing it. I set off at some ungodly hour from Lancaster to make the long journey down to Devon and arrived there not long after first light. I took the path and found the right area where I was soon onto a Water Rail, but after a while the birding really went dead. It turned out that there was a team of people harvesting lilies and they were creating one hell of a disturbance in and around the reeds where the Sora Rail was supposed to be. I waited hours, but it did not show, so I eventually gave up. What unbelievably bad luck to travel all that way on the day they harvested the lilies. I had dipped big time. To compound matters, the eagle failed to put in an appearance at Chew Valley Lake, so I ended up cashing in my claim on my insurance tick, Siberian Chiffy. It was a massive trip to undertake on my own, only to come back with just a Siberian Chiffchaff.

So here lie the origins of making Sora Rail as my number one bogey bird. Back on Scilly in 2001, Tom and I were ambling along Penninis when the pager went.

'Mega. Adult Sora on Great Pool, Tresco.'

We headed straight for the harbour and caught the first boat across. We got to the right spot and even on the right bird. The problem was that it was not a Sora. It was a Spotted Crake which we had seen two days before. The final part of the Sora saga came on New Year's Day in 2005 when Tom and I decided to kick off our year lists with the long-staying Sora at Attenborough Pools in Nottinghamshire. True to form, it had gone. Another dip. The fact that this time it had been a genuine bird was little consolation. While we were on Tresco that day, we also picked up a Shore Lark and a Rough-legged Buzzard, both of which may have been the American forms, but no one really seemed to know. Anywhere else in the country they would have been ticked without any second thoughts. I had very good views of the lark while Tom was predictably on the phone to Maria. It was a cracking little bird, but it had some kind of tick on its head. It was the only tick that I saw that day at any rate.

Unfortunately, we fell for the old 'probable' sighting again, this time it was a Sardinian Warbler that had been 'reliably' heard calling from some brambles on Tresco. Like the fools we were, we headed off to Tresco again the next day to try and get the warbler. We saw nothing but Blackcaps. While we were on Tresco, a Rose-breasted Grosbeak was found on St. Martins. Now this was a biggy and a bird I desperately wanted. Being marooned on Tresco meant that we had a fair old wait before we could get over to St. Martins. While we were anxiously pacing up and down, news came in from St. Mary's that another lifer, a Paddyfield Warbler, had been found. Bloody hell, what were we doing on Tresco? Why on earth were we chasing yet another half-baked sighting? It was absolutely crazy and now we were stuck on Tresco potentially missing out on two major birds. By the time we arrived on St. Martins, the Grosser had flown. We had missed it by minutes. We waited and waited but it just did not return. To make matters worse, there was a Melodious Warbler on St. Martins too at the other end of the island. We just could not risk leaving the Grosser spot and ended up missing the Melodious Warbler completely. We caught the last boat back to St. Mary's and legged it to the Paddyfield Warbler. It performed beautifully, showing no signs of fear by hopping about just a few feet in front of us. To a non-birder it would just look like a little brown bird. To the assembled crowd it was magnificent. As one chap described it, 'it was a birder's bird'. And that is exactly what it was. It was certainly one of the best birds that I have ever seen.

We were due to fly out the next day, but there was still the Grosser to see. I was not under any time pressure as I had another week of holiday left, but Tom had strict instructions to get back to Maria. In an Oscar-winning performance, he played an absolute beauty by ringing her up and telling her that all flights from Scilly had been cancelled due to fog and that we would be delayed by a day. What a star. The power of birding had won. Lies and deceit were called for. We rehearsed our story time and time again to make sure that we could back up the lies when we got back to his house in Shepperton. The Grosser was back on. You just cannot beat a bit of subterfuge every now and then. This called for it. We booked into the Bell Rock Hotel for our impromptu extra night. Unfortunately, the Grosser let us down badly the next day. It was seen first thing by a handful of birders but could not be relocated. We spent all day looking for it and once again did not go for the Melodious Warbler, which was apparently a really exquisite bird. To make matters worse, another British lifer, a Dusky Warbler, was on Bryher. We left the Scillies dipping on three lifers. A truly atrocious state of affairs.

The only consolation came in the form of a first winter male Pied Wheatear on that final morning, not a tick, but a decent bird. Now I can imagine that many women reading this will be thinking that we got what we deserved for lying to Tom's girlfriend for the sake of a bird. It could be easily construed as callous and selfish, but we needed that Grosbeak. They would also be thinking that lying does not pay and that we had been justly served by the birding gods. Well, Tom must have been feeling some remorse about lying to Maria as he was very keen to get straight back home. I was having none of it as there was a rare American sparrow, a Bobolink, at Prawle Point in Devon. Having dipped on the Grosbeak and two species of warbler on Scilly, there was no way that I was going to drive straight past a 'big' lifer. What else were we down here for anyway? Besides,

Bobolink has to be one of the best names of any bird on the British List, and I wanted that name on my list too. Tom was clearly feeling uncharacteristically guilty about the extra day on Scilly, but I talked him through a very reasonable scenario of how he would ring Maria and tell her that we had set off and he would see her soon. He would then call again after about an hour or so to say that we were delayed in traffic but not to worry. He would then ring a third time to say that there had been a jack-knifed caravan and hence we were horribly delayed and how sorry he was and how much he loved her, etc. I am good at this sort of stuff and I coached him like a pro. After all, I was a police officer for several years, so I can lie with the best of them. A true professional. For the second time in as many days, Tom got on the blower and gave another Oscar-like performance in the art of lying to your girlfriend. To be honest, he did not have much choice as I was driving, and I was going for the Bobolink. So, did we see it and does lying pay? You bet we did. Bobolink was on my list and all thanks to subterfuge! Mind you, my conscience is clean, she was not my missus. Maria and Tom split up a year later. I cannot think why.

In 2003, Tom and I had enough of messing around with just having a week on Scilly, so we decided to go for another fortnight's holiday. He was single again, not surprisingly. Whether he had confessed about the 'Grosser' and the Bobolink in a moment of weakness, I don't know. Whatever, he was emotionally unencumbered this time around. For me it was a slightly different story, having reneged on my Bachelor birding vows. I was seeing Vicky who is now my wife and mother of my son, Jack.

With Vicky, my future wife, here in Costa Rica.

We were going steady at the time but I still had some personal freedom. We had not quite got to the joint holiday stage. Lads' birding holidays on Scilly was an avenue of pleasure that was still open to me. This time round I was driving direct to Cornwall as I was getting fed up of the diversion to London as it ate into my holiday allowance too much. Unlike previous years, Cornwall was rather on the dead side with no lifers for me to go for. Even so, I felt that I ought to try and land something, so I headed to Helston to see the resident Ring-billed Gull, a species that I had only seen once before back in 1991. As we had missed it the year before, I was keen to connect with it this time round. Helston Boating Lake is not an easy place to find. We struggled to find it in 2002, and 2003 was no different. Eventually, I got my bearings and pulled into the car park. I had to make a beeline for the loos as the large Americano coffee I had on the way down was pushing my bladder to the edge. As I was leaving, the pager beeped and remarkably the message read, 'Cornwall: Ring-billed Gull showing well at Helston Boating lake.' I glanced up to see two birders packing up a tripod and camera midway along the lake. The gull surely had to be somewhere nearby and instantly there it was sitting on the water. The onset of drizzle caused me to cut short my observations and so I went back to the car to send Tom a text 'RBG OMYL' which to the uninitiated translates as 'Ring-billed Gull on my year list'. Tom joined me later that night having come down on the train.

As ever, the flight to St. Mary's was an enjoyable experience. I saw several Gannets and roughly at the halfway point caught sight of a dark fin, which I thought was a whale, plunging into the water. The brevity of the sighting left me wondering whether I had really seen it or not. Later that day there was a report on the pager of a possible Great White Shark. It certainly made me think.

Soon we were on the airport bus heading into Hugh Town. We were staying in the Cornerhouse apartment in the centre of town, directly above the Chicken Shack fast food stall and, more importantly, opposite the Bishop & Wolf pub. It was very strategically located as far as we were concerned with beer and food on the doorstep. It took us only a few moments to find the flat. We were very pleased with our home for the next fortnight. It was a lot more spacious and far less dingy than the lodgings we had stayed in before and had the added benefit of some major luxuries in the form of two bathrooms and two televisions.

After unpacking we decided to nip to the nearby Co-op to stock up for the week and make the first sizeable dent to the kitty. Tom is always kitty holder for our holidays. I am not too sure how this developed because it is quite onerous, as he ends up buying everything from pasties to boat tickets. In return, I manage security in the form of the flat key which prevents us being exposed to two of Tom's foibles, namely checking and re-checking to see if the door has been locked and 'losing' the key in one of his pockets. I clearly get the better deal from this arrangement and it makes for an easier life all round.

Finally, it was time to get in the field and go birding. There was actually sod all about with virtually no target birds to go for. It is always nice to arrive on Scilly with a few birds in play that have been present for a few days, although it can make for a nerve-racking build-up to the holiday. It is great when birds stay but a killer when they leave hours before you land, like the Olivaceous Warbler back in 1998. There had been a clear-out a couple of days earlier with Hoopoe, Lesser Yellowleg and American Golden Plover, all departing. Fortunately, none of these were new ticks for us. It would have been nice to have something to go for though. The only available bird was a Richard's Pipit that had been visiting the fields near Sandy Lane. On the plus side, we had not just missed out on a hatful of rarities either. Our first port of call was – naturally – Sandy

Lane, but as we approached it started to drizzle. We sheltered with a few other birders under some trees and gathered that the Pipit had not been seen for quite some time.

News of a Yellow-browed Warbler on the Porthellick loop trail drew us away. We sat there for nearly an hour with only an occasional Chiffchaff, a few Goldcrests and a Blackcap to alleviate the boredom. We decided to head back to Hugh Town. En route we picked up a couple of Firecrests – well I did. Tom had one of those 'blind' moments that strike us all when you just cannot see the bird. It turned out to be a monster year for Firecrests; they were absolutely everywhere. You could easily see over ten different individuals in a day. On the way back, news came over the CB that the Richard's Pipit had returned to Sandy Lane and fortuitously we were close by. We quickly got to the field and very soon were treated to cracking views of it feeding amongst the tussocky grass, hopping in and out of view. I had not seen a Richard's Pipit for several years, so it was nice to catch up with this one. It was impossible not to be impressed by its large size, more like a wagtail than a pipit. It eventually hopped out of view for good after twenty minutes and we decided to head back home and get an early tea. The pipit and the Firecrests had at least provided some excitement, but nonetheless it had been a rather inauspicious start. In the last decent light of the evening, we approached the outskirts of Hugh Town where a birder shouted he had got a Yellow-browed Warbler. As we got alongside him, it disappeared from view. A bit of a poor end to the day as that was the second one that we had dipped. I like to get padders under my belt early in a holiday. We headed into town and went straight to the Scillonian Club, a regular haunt in previous years, for our evening scran. I had chilli, which was overpriced, tasteless and not spicy. What is the point of making bland chilli? For God's sake, it's called chilli for a good reason! Tom's curry looked a bit more appetising, but our overall opinion was that the food quality had deteriorated. We decided that we weren't going back.

The following day continued in a fairly low-key way. It was relaxed but unexciting, with just a couple of year ticks in the form of a Wryneck and a Snow Bunting. We were slightly concerned at the lack of any decent rarities and the limited numbers of 'padders'. All in all, it was too quiet and uninspiring. In fact, the main highlight for me had been two Merlins seen dashing together over the fields near Carn Vean. With few target birds available, we headed to Carn Vean tearoom for our first 'brew' of the day. Cafes and tearooms are an integral part of life for most birders on Scilly, but we only really discovered them in 2002. Neither of us is particularly keen on cakes and pastries, but the prospect of a pot of tea outside in the fresh air was just what the doctor ordered. While Tom was settling the bill, I heard the familiar 'double tap' of the pager (which I had set to beep twice for Scilly news), so I had an air of eager expectancy as I surveyed the news on the screen. 'Immature Red-rumped Swallow on St. Agnes. Perched on wires.' This was a bird that I had only seen once in Britain – at Cley in 1987, so I was keen to end a barren spell of nearly seventeen years. Tom still needed it as a British tick and was looking to end an equally long crusade for what had become his worst bogey bird. This was yet another opportunity for him to gain a tick over me on the Scillies – typical. I was pleased that there was at least a decent bird around but could not help feeling a bit gutted that it was not going to add to my list. I would have been much happier if it had been a lifer for us both, or even better, a lifer for just me. When Tom returned I silently passed the pager to him. His face was a picture as his expression instantly changed from 'I've just seen a few common padders' to 'impending lifer on the cards'. Hirundines are very wide-ranging birds, notorious for being short-stayers and difficult to pin down to a single locality, so this was potentially going to be a difficult bird. We decided to steadily make our way down from Carn Vean and head towards the quay in Hugh Town, a good four miles away. There was every chance that boats would specifically run to St. Agnes, but we were also wary that the swallow might disappear at any time. At last there was an air of excitement.

As we walked back to town, we were interrupted by a quick succession of pager beeps. There were so many that I could not tell whether they were 'double taps' or single beeps. The bloody thing had gone mad.

'Mega: Grey-cheeked Thrush on Tresco,' Tom announced.

We were no longer going to St. Agnes but to Tresco. Grey-cheeked Thrush is a mega bird to get in Britain, a lifer for both of us and 'a Yank' to boot. It is one of those birds that you always hope to see on Scilly and one of the prime reasons why so many birders make their annual October pilgrimage there. It was also a bird that we had dipped out on during previous Scilly visits, usually involving unconfirmed, spurious sightings. We had wasted hours on these duff birds, so we had a degree of scepticism about this one. There was absolutely no time to waste and we immediately embarked on the high-speed, 3-mile trek down to the quay. A first-day yomp was the last thing that I needed, but under the circumstances it was necessary. To compound matters, the weather had become warm and sultry such that it was not long before we were both getting hot and sweaty. I was also getting shin splint pains, but there was just no choice but to keep on going. The road to the quay from the outskirts of Hugh Town is hook-shaped, so it is possible to see the quay from quite some distance as it arcs in a long right-hand bend around the harbour. It's a real tonic when you first see the quay, but that last mile or so across is a killer. Psychologically you have arrived but physically it's still a right old trek. Like a mirage in a desert it never seems to get any closer either.

We arrived to find a big queue at the ticket office. You never think that there are many birders on Scilly until that first big bird appears and suddenly there are thousands of birders everywhere, or so it seems. We were pleased that we could get on board the second boat, quite a feat considering our starting point when the news broke. The boat trip between islands provided a welcome respite from the rigours of walking at top speed and also a moment to reflect on the chances of actually seeing the bird. I was not feeling confident that it would show but for once it seemed to be genuine with reports coming through that the bird had been showing well. Some fifteen minutes later the boat docked. We were straight back into endurance marching the two miles up to Borough Farm. A lot of birders were between the bird and us as we were amongst the last off the boat. I would think that we passed a good sixty or seventy birders on the way, and for the last half mile I tucked in behind the well-known twitcher Anthony Bridges, finally passing him in the last hundred yards. A great dash for the line to win a race in which Anthony was blissfully unaware he was competing.

There was already a decent number of birders at the scene and many of the best viewing positions were occupied. That's why it is vital to get on site rapidly to secure the best vantage point possible. Also, we were greeted by the very news that we did not want. The bird was not showing and nobody seemed to have seen it, certainly in the immediate vicinity of where I was standing. We were on a road looking across a series of mixed grazing and bulb fields separated by high hedges. We had managed to secure a reasonable position overlooking the field in which the bird had apparently been seen. Minutes passed and nothing happened. It was getting really tense. Suddenly, there was an audible mass murmur to our right and the shout went up that it was showing. Not from our position though, as nobody near me was on to it. Dick Filby started to give directions of the bird's whereabouts over the CB. Apparently, it had flown into a *Pittosporum* bush in the field in front of me. In spite of this, I was still not exactly sure where. No one near me appeared to be on it either. There were some obvious landmarks in the field, notably a gate, but these did not seem to be getting a mention. I anxiously scanned the hedges and trees in the vague hope that I might chance upon something.

The appearance of a robin in the hedge on the far side of the field provided a couple of heart-stopping moments, but at least it gave me some confidence that I was looking in the right area as Dick had just mentioned it in his commentary. To make matters worse, two Song Thrushes were feeding behind a strip of ferns that ran through the middle of the field. Occasionally, they would appear in the gaps between the ferns. I knew that they were Song Thrushes, but I still had to check. I just couldn't help myself. Suddenly, a small greyish bird hopped into view with its head held upwards at an angle; it was a thrush with grey-brown upperparts, a half-speckled breast and it was tiny. Incredibly, no one said a word as if it wasn't there. Yes, it was the Grey-cheeked Thrush – at last. Cries of delight suddenly started erupting around us, while those unfortunate enough not to be able to see it were pleading for directions. Tom was also on it, so all was well for both of us. It was my first-ever *Catharus* thrush and I was immediately taken by its diminutive size, which was all the more apparent due to the nearby 'monster' Song Thrushes. It was a little cracker. We were able to watch it on and off for at least an hour as it hopped in and out of view allowing us to study it really well. This was what Scilly was all about – mad pager activity, high-speed walks, tense moments and scoring a yank lifer. It does not get any better than this. Well it does as we were about to find out.

We left Borough Farm with just under an hour to make it back to the quay for the last boat back to St. Mary's. We hoped to pick up a few padders along the way which included Black Duck, Pectoral Sandpiper and a few other good 'holiday list' waders. We arrived at the edge of the Great Pool and immediately saw the Pec Sand on the far side of the reed bed. As luck would have it, a Green Sandpiper flew past revealing its characteristic white rump and all dark wings. With time pressing, we quickly moved across to the Abbey Pool where the Black Duck had been showing. We found it sitting resplendently on a rock at the far side of the pool. The bird looked particularly good, catching the light and showing its pale head and contrasting dark body. Again, we quickly moved on and headed back along the far side of the Great Pool only to run into a group of birders watching both the Curlew Sandpiper and the Little Stint. That was it, we had cleared up on the lot – every decent available bird on Tresco had succumbed with little more than a whimper. Neither of us had expected to do it quite so easily, but with birders flooding the island for the thrush, every decent tick seemed to be staked out. The journey back to St. Mary's passed in a flash as we luxuriated in the knowledge that we had just spent a superb two hours on Tresco and finally got Grey-cheeked Thrush on our lists.

Our plan was to head back to the flat to drop off our gear, quickly change and head to the Scillonian Club to watch Turkey versus England in a European Championship qualification match, a crucial game in which England had to get at least a draw to ensure their place in the finals. I was looking forward to a few celebration pints as well. We had literally walked off the quay when Dick Filby's voice crackled over the CB with news.

'A reported Red-eyed Vireo has been seen on the Garrison.'

This was unbelievable, merely three hours earlier we had been bemoaning our luck and now a second American passerine was possibly on the cards. Our chances of seeing the match were seriously in danger but who cared when the yanks were on show. Red-eyed Vireo is an absolutely classic American bird and epitomises what October on Scilly is all about. In my view, there is simply no European bird that remotely compares with a vireo.

The Garrison, as the name implies, is an Elizabethan fortress set up on a round-shaped hill overlooking Hugh Town. It is a short, steep climb no matter which route you take. We immediately set off up the road from the quay, yet again at a very fast pace. On the way Brett Richards, a well-known twitcher, disagreed with me that running up the hill was easier than walking. We left him behind overtaking a number of people and were soon at the Lower Broom platform where the bird had been reported. Only a handful of birders were there. It had apparently been showing just moments before and was definitely a vireo. We assembled along the Garrison wall and waited patiently. It was a very difficult place to get any kind of decent views as the bird had been favouring the elms on the far side of the wall, which was about five feet high. Minutes passed and the ranks of birders were rapidly swelling when a shout went up that it was showing only a few feet to my left. From my position, I could not see it but, suddenly, it hopped into view, partly obscured by leaves. It remained still for a few seconds before hopping onto another branch, offering a brief and tantalising glimpse of its distinctive head pattern before moving out of sight. The head colouring on a Red-eyed Vireo is the colour of 'housewife blue' eye shadow. The white supercilium also borders a black line that looks as if it has been drawn on with eyeliner. Typical of a yank bird to be wearing make-up! We moved further along the wall and after a few minutes the vireo showed again right in front of me. The birder next to me could not contain himself and started shouting that the bird was showing, pointing and waving his hands. Unsurprisingly, it instantly cleared off back amongst the thick foliage. I was really hacked off and could scarcely contain myself. He even tried to briefly engage me in conversation afterwards but I just blanked him. I think he got the message. We decided to head back to the flat following a further fruitless wait. After a quick change we headed to the Bishop & Wolf. Home-made lasagne and chips proved to be a good choice, washed down with Tinners ale. It was a fitting and satisfying end to an excellent day. With such a start, we could not predict what tomorrow would have in store for us, although we still had the Red-rumped Swallow to catch up with. Fortunately, it had hopped islands and was now on St. Mary's.

Sunday morning saw us both making an early start and heading for Buzza Hill in an attempt to see the Red-rumped Swallow. Buzza is supposedly the place to be on St. Mary's if you need to see hirundines as it offers a splendid view in all directions and seems to have a natural attraction for swallows and swifts. It came as some surprise then that there was only one other birder *in situ* when we arrived at 8.00 am in the morning. We passed a pleasant hour seeing good numbers of Barn Swallows and the occasional House Martin, but the Red-rumped failed to put in an appearance. The crucial news eventually came that it had been seen at Porthellick early on, so at least it had not departed overnight. It was time to make a move. We decided to make our way there. We had just got there when the CB crackled into life again.

'Red-rumped Swallow showing well at Higher Newford.'

We headed up there but as we arrived it had again disappeared and been seen at Telegraph. It was turning into a real wild goose chase around the island. This was something that we had discussed earlier and our tactics were very much based upon staying in one spot where the bird was likely to reappear. I was happy that we were now on fairly high ground and had a good all-round view but was slightly concerned that we were site hopping. To compound matters, news came that the bird was showing at Newford Duck Pond, about a five-minutes' walk away. It was too close to miss, so we simply had to go. The sight of birders with raised binoculars usually signifies that a bird is showing, so we were hopeful as we rounded the corner at the pond. We quickly joined them and soon got directions for the bird's location; it was now some considerable distance away, high in the air and flying away from us. We watched what was little more than a fluttering speck disappear over the horizon towards the north of the island. We had seen it, but there was absolutely no way that either of us could justify ticking it on the meagre sighting that we had obtained. It was the dreaded NTV. Tom's bogey bird was not giving up without a fight. The CB was alive with requests for information on the swallow's whereabouts. Very few people had seen it and many were heading towards Newford Duck Pond in the hope that it would reappear. To our incredulity, a well-known female birder announced over the CB.

> 'It had flown high and strongly north,
> heading towards St. Martins.'

She seemed to be insinuating that it had gone for good. It was a somewhat irresponsible message to give out on air, based on conjecture and totally exaggerating the circumstances of what had actually occurred. The fact of the matter was that the bird had flown out of view high to the north along with all the other swallows but with absolutely no evidence to suggest that it had gone to St. Martins or anywhere else for that matter. Somewhat disconsolately, we remained at the scene hoping it would reappear. A string of birders continued to arrive, a number quizzing us to find out what had happened. One of them received a phone call from his friend that a Yellow-browed Warbler was showing near Trenoweth R & D Centre, just a ten-minutes' walk away. Over thirty minutes had elapsed since we had glimpsed the swallow, and other than a Merlin shooting past overhead and a Whinchat perched on a wall, there was little bird activity, so we decided to give up and head to Trenoweth in search of the warbler. Perhaps our fortunes were changing as I found a Black Redstart along the way, perched on the roof of the Centre. As luck would have it, we then saw a Firecrest closely followed by good views of the warbler in the trees nearby. Black Redstart, Firecrest and Yellow-browed Warbler are all classic Scilly birds, padders to be precise, but all worth seeing. I even managed to get the warbler in my scope on a couple of occasions as it flitted about in a beech tree.

We pushed on towards Watermill, one of the most north-easterly points of the island and a particular favourite area of ours, both for birds and its tranquil beauty. News broke again that the swallow was on view from Newford Duck Pond and heading in the direction of Watermill. I kept hearing snippets on the CB, which was not receiving well. Messages were coming through thick and fast, and it appeared that the Swallow had been seen in the Watermill area and also at Telegraph. At this point, I wanted to go back to Newford Duck Pond. I felt this was the best site to see the swallow as it had shown several times there and I was painfully aware that we were chasing it rather than being patient, a total divergence from our original strategy. Tom had different ideas, saying that he wanted to check out Watermill and pretty much headed off down to the cove where the swallow had last been seen. I followed at a slower pace feeling a bit frustrated with Tom as I thought it would be sheer pot luck to see it because Watermill Lane is tree-covered making viewing very difficult. I caught up with Tom at the cove, not in the best of moods. We returned along the lane only to hear on the CB that it was currently over the woods at Watermill, literally above our heads. We could not have been nearer but had no way of seeing it through the trees, an incredibly annoying and ironic situation. This bird was taking the Mickey. Like all sections of society, birding has its fair share of prats. I am probably one of them but I do not think that I am premier league in this respect. At this point we met a title contender who greeted us by smugly shouting.

'It has just flown over your heads.'

He knew full well that we could not possibly have seen the bird from our position. He made no effort to disguise his pathetic pleasure at gripping us off and several others that he met. We moved on up the lane without telling him what we thought of him. I still wanted to head back to Newford and was openly bemoaning our stupidity at site hopping when the decision of what to do next was made for us when a voice over the CB announced:

> 'The Red-rumped Swallow is currently showing well over Newford Duck Pond.'

There was no time to waste. We made our way back to the pond to be greeted by the welcoming sight of birders looking intently above our heads as we rounded the corner. We got into a good vantage point right next to the pond and started scanning the hirundines, which were now feeding low over the trees about seventy yards away. The first few birds were all Barn Swallows and then a pinkish rump flashed past and out of view. It quickly flew round again, the large, pink-washed rump showing clearly and the slower more elastic flight clinched identification beyond doubt. Tom had got it too, so we could now both relax a bit and enjoy the day. We also had the luxury of comparing the bird with both Barn Swallows and House Martins in the same flock. The pursuit of the Red-rumper had taken up most of the day and we decided to head back to Hugh Town and try to see the vireo for a second time which had been showing on and off throughout the day on the Garrison. En route, we stopped at the Longstone Centre for a baked potato with chilli and a pot of tea. We had a browse around the shop and a customary stroke of the cat, which was sleeping in exactly the same chair as it had been the year before. Change is not good. The vireo failed to put in an appearance. The Bishop & Wolf beckoned where we tucked into 'Wolf Burgers' washed down with Tinners ale. Tom had a second lifer in as many days and had moved his list on ahead of mine yet again.

Six days later we were about to go up to the Garrison for a Red-breasted Flycatcher when suddenly the CB crackled into life with the news of a big find on Bryher – a Bobolink, and the third American bird of the week. Boats would be leaving imminently. Our luck and decision making were again proving to be good as we were within a mile of the quay and the pace, although quick, was not too taxing. We were safely on the first boat to Bryher. Dick Filby was the last man allowed on board, but I was pleased to see him as it would be so much easier to see the Bobolink with him and his massive CB around. The trip to Bryher was reasonably uneventful in terms of birds, but I did manage to get one half decent soaking when a large wave splashed over the side of the boat and went straight down the back of my neck. Such drenchings are part and parcel of the inter-island boat experience and it is possible to end up absolutely sodden if you are in the firing line. Our position in the boat entailed that we were amongst the last to disembark. We immediately set off at a brisk pace up to the campsite where the Bobolink was reported to still be showing. As we approached the entrance, Dick Filby signalled for birders to slow down as the assembled throng was within a mere twenty feet of the bird which was in a hedge of bracken and thick brambles. I managed to get in position on the right-hand side of the line of birders, but in spite of directions from the birder next to me, I simply could not get on it even though it was apparently sitting up on one of the fronds of bracken.

More birders arrived, some running the last few steps to get a good position in the crowd. The lack of care and calmness in their approach meant inevitably that it was flushed, affording me only brief and certainly non-tickable flight views as it passed overhead out of sight. I could hardly believe what had taken place; the Bobolink had been showing in front of me, I had missed it and then it had been flushed by rushing birders. Thankfully it was not a lifer, but I was still feeling really fed up and had little hope that it would be relocated in the surrounding fields, which were thick with cover and did not allow the greatest access or visibility. We moved over to the area where the bird had appeared to land and spent the next twenty minutes fruitlessly scanning the surrounding fields. It was beginning to look hopeless and a matter of pure chance for it to be relocated. I think many other birders were feeling the same as quite a few were beginning to drift away. Suddenly, Dick Filby's voice came over the CB announcing that it had returned to its original position. We quickly moved back to the other end of the field, although, as we neared the site, birders again began to run. Desperation to get a good vantage point and panic to see the Bobolink were overcoming any sense of field craft. Unfortunately, such behaviour can be contagious and it was proving to be a scene of utter chaos with people stampeding towards the line of birders. Dick Filby had spotted the on-coming wave of birders and had the good sense to intervene by heading them off and restoring a modicum of order. This piece of foresight almost certainly prevented the bird from being flushed for a second time, which would have been inexcusable.

Both Tom and I were at the front of the group but had not resorted to running, although this had been a close call over the last few yards with people scampering in front of us. We managed to secure front row positions. Within a few seconds, I got onto it as it had fortuitously sat up on a fern, showing in the open for a few seconds before flying up to the right and onto a nearby hedge. This was certainly a nervous and flighty bird, which had no doubt been spooked by the burgeoning crowd of viewers. Luckily a sense of decorum seemed to prevail over the gathered masses following the earlier antics. There was an appropriate veil of silence amongst the assembled group as it was 'touch and go' whether the Bobolink would remain or fly away. Nervous as it undoubtedly was, it was showing exceptionally well in the hedge. I obtained good scope views at this point before it flew again. We were all grateful that it had dropped back into the ferns and bracken that it had been favouring since it was found. There followed a period of about ten minutes when I just could not see the Bobolink but eventually I got it in my scope and was able to track it as it unobtrusively passed low along the hedge. For the next half hour, it fed amongst the grasses and ferns moving in and out of cover. It would occasionally show very well for a matter of seconds before disappearing again only to reappear several feet away. It was a real test of everybody's skill to firstly pick it up in the dense vegetation and then to keep it under observation. I soon became acquainted with every fern, flower and piece of bracken in front of me as the only way to see the Bobolink was to scan backwards and forwards with the telescope.

I had expected the bird to be yellowish in appearance, like the bird that I had seen a couple of years previously at Prawle Point, Devon, but my initial views did not seem to substantiate this. It was only when it returned to the low cover that the colouration and markings started to resemble my recollections. The Bobolink was incredibly intricately marked and quite different from our resident sparrow species. It also behaved far more like a bunting due to its extremely skulking habits and preference for deep cover. As we watched, more people joined the throng, due to the boatloads of birders arriving from Tresco and St. Agnes. I had been concentrating so intently on following it through the hedge that when I looked up I was quite amazed to see how many people were present. A further twenty minutes elapsed and the Bobolink had just simply vanished. It was clearly in the hedge somewhere but no one could locate it. We had both obtained good views and when Filby announced from behind us that both Richard's Pipit and Hawfinch were showing 'on this island', it seemed quite a good cue for us to move on and let other birders come to the front. Big Yankee bird number three in the bag.

Like many birders, I love my bird books. I have loads of them. They are a source of joy to me on all those lonely womanless nights in. Richard Millington's *A Twitcher's Diary* was a particular inspiration to me in the eighties. It is no Pulitzer Prize winner and does not have much of a personal touch to it but he sees some great birds and his illustrations are fantastic. Basically, the book describes Richard's attempt to see as many birds as possible in a calendar year. I got it for Christmas in 1982. When I unwrapped it on Christmas Day, I had to feign great surprise as I had found it on top of Mum and Dad's wardrobe and had already read it cover to cover at least twice. During the year, Richard also has a couple of weeks on Scilly. I remember looking at what he saw and thinking that nothing could be better. I so much wanted to get onto Scilly and emulate his sightings and listing feats. At the time, it felt like the birding pinnacle. I had grown up a bit since the Minsmere holidays and the Scillies were eclipsing it as the place to go for an aspiring sixteen-year-old wannabe twitcher.

The funny thing was in 2003 that we more or less saw all the same birds as Richard did, yet somehow it did not feel quite as good as it should have done. Everyone seemed to be grumbling that the Scillies had had their day. Was it worse or were we simply getting used to rare birds? Just as Richard had done in 1980, on our 2003 trip we saw Red-eyed Vireo,

Pallas's Warbler, Olive-backed Pipit, Isabelline Shrike, Black Duck, Red-rumped Swallow and pretty much all the same padders. Granted, he got Yellow-billed Cuckoo, but we had Grey-cheeked Thrush, Little Crake and Bobolink which is not a bad trade off in anyone's book. So, what had changed? Certainly Red-eyed Vireos and the rest of the American cast were far rarer birds back in the eighties. I just think that the expectations are just too high now. The Scillies enjoyed some unbelievable autumns in the eighties and early nineties when American mega jewels such as Parula Warbler, Black and White Warbler and Philadelphia Vireo were almost 'expected' to turn up. It seems harder to get these birds now, but when you compare Richard's year and our year of 2003 not a lot has changed, yet the euphoria around it clearly has. Back in 1980, I would hazard a guess that Richard would have felt that he came off Scilly with a good haul of birds. Secretly reading his book pre-Christmas in 1981, I would have given my right arm to get those same birds.

Another favourite read of mine is *Going for the Biggy* by the late Stuart Gibson. It is very similar to Richard's book but edges it with the personal touch. The odd reference to girlfriends, bunking off work, gripping off his mates and knocking back pints in the Barlaston Inn just make it a much better read. The Scilly trips that he embarked on are fantastic and his elation at jamming in on a Bobolink really captures the moment. He also gets Myrtle Warbler, Parula Warbler and Red-eyed Vireo on the same day. Halcyon days indeed. Maybe Scilly was better then, but it is still pretty good and 2003 proves the point. It just shows how perceptions seem to have changed when nearly twenty years on Bobolink felt slightly commonplace.

My last trip to Scilly was in 2005 when I substituted Tom for Vicky. It was certainly a bit different having the 'bird' in tow and meant that I had to adapt my dawn to dusk birding approach for a slightly more sedate style. The trip started off badly with our helicopter flights onto Scilly being cancelled due to fog. We had to stay nearby just in case the fog lifted and keep ringing for updates every couple of hours. I did get a Ring-necked Duck near Marazion but this was scarcely a consolation for the two lifers that were sitting taunting me from Scilly. A Sora Rail on St. Mary's was a big bird for me as it was my worst bogey bird by a hefty margin. There was also a Blackpoll Warbler on St Agnes which I needed too. I was a forlorn figure, being so near yet so far away. Both birds were showing and both had the potential to clear off any day soon. I was somewhat hacked off and cursing my luck. Strangely, Vicky seemed less perturbed.

The next day we arrived at the heliport in perfect flying conditions only to find that the battery on the helicopter was flat. Another delay ensued while the reserve chopper was wheeled out. We finally managed to leave Penzance some twenty-six hours late. Great news though – the Sora was still there. We headed off to Lower Moors and spent an hour in the hide before Vicky had to leave as she was bursting for the loo. I felt a bit guilty about letting her walk back alone but the allure of the Sora was too much. I had to stay. It was after all my bogey bird. Following a further hour's wait, it finally gave itself up and scuttled from the reeds in front of the hide before showing well for a good thirty minutes. My bogey bird had been laid to rest. I headed back via a Spotted Sandpiper at Old Town beach which was giving crippling views down to a few feet. On the way, I bumped into Lee Evans who asked me about the two birds. He had obviously just arrived on the islands. It was good to see him and as ever he seemed appreciative of the positive news. The next day Vicky and I headed over to St. Agnes for the Blackpoll. It had gone and the Greenish Warbler that had been around also proved to be incredibly elusive. It was a double dip day; the helicopter problems had cost me big time. The highlight of the day was a couple of pints of Cornish Cream in the Turk's Head and a nice lunch with Vic. I did find a Lapland Bunting which provided excellent views and later caught up with a cracking Long-eared Owl on the Garrison back on St. Mary's.

We had one more full day left on Scilly which proved to be action-packed from the outset. It started with a report of a Blackpoll Warbler from behind the football pitch on the Garrison, quickly followed by a report of a Red-eyed Vireo from the same area. Confusion reigned. No one was sure what was seen where. Cries of 'there it is' went up continuously and groups of birders kept charging en masse from spot to spot. Vic and I got split up in the mayhem and to cap it all neither the vireo nor the warbler was showing. There were even rumours of two vireos being around. Eventually, definitive news came through that the Blackpoll was showing on the Lower Broom platform. I got in position and after about ten minutes it showed well in the trees above my head. A good bird and one that I thought had got away. It transpired that this was the St. Agnes bird which had hopped islands. However, the vireos seemed to have gone to ground. I re-joined Vic and we headed off for a walk on what was a beautiful October day. We stopped for a celebration lunch in the sunshine in the delightful gardens at Juliet's

Cafe overlooking the islands. It was idyllic and the view was fantastic. We had an excellent meal washed down with a great bottle of white wine, so much nicer for being in the fresh air. Birding with 'the bird' was not so bad after all. It was almost romantic, besides the fact that my bins were lying on the table and my scope was propped against my chair. I was beginning to relax and contemplating a second bottle when the pager went again.

> 'Probable Trumpeter Finch on the Garrison,
> drinking from small pool near the football pitch.'

Shit, another lifer, and here I was miles away eating lunch and glugging wine with the missus. What was I playing at? All of a sudden, I was beginning to revise my recently formed opinions of birding with the bird. I called for the bill and settled up as quickly as possible. We headed off at a canter back to Hugh Town with Vic wondering what the hell had hit her. As we got into town, a battered car pulled up. It was Nigel Hudson, a local Scilly birder, asking if I had heard news about the Trumpeter Finch. I replied that it had been paged a couple of times and was on the Garrison. He looked at me and Vicky.

'I can give you a lift if you like but I've only got room for one. I haven't got a back seat,' he said.

Chivalry and lifers are never comfortable bed partners. It was a terrible dilemma for me. Well, it wasn't, but I felt that I should write that for the sake of appearances. Stay with Vic and walk up or take the lift? In a flash, I jumped in and told Vic to meet me on the Garrison and to ring me if she was struggling to find her way. We zoomed off leaving her on her own in the street. I don't think she could quite believe it or maybe she could. At least she was getting a good taste of an October on Scilly. One minute we were sitting having a lovely lunch, drinking good wine and enjoying intimate conversation in an idyllic setting, the next I had left her stranded in the middle of the road having fled the scene with a complete stranger. Some readers will be appalled at this, I know. There will be women out there reading this, shouting at the pages, cursing me for the callous, selfish sod that I am. It barely crossed my mind as being a bad thing to do at the time and, if truth be known, I would do the same again. We were on a birding holiday after all and I wasn't going to miss a Trumpeter Finch, was I?

On the Garrison, things were looking good. The 'Trump' had been visiting a small puddle to drink every hour or so. I was right at the front and in a prime spot. I got the scope set up and waited. A constant stream of birders started to arrive. I was joined by a well-spoken lad in his twenties and got chatting. He was quite funny for a birder and we had a good natter. We waited patiently for about an hour and a half. Vic had been and gone. She was still on the Garrison but had decided to have a stroll rather than stand with me looking at a puddle. You just can't please some people. It was all 'me, me, me'. After a bit, she returned and told me that it was behind me. I looked round to see a group of birders staring at some bushes. They were on the vireo. I was just about to rush over when a washed-out juvenile Greenfinch dropped in. It had a slightly deformed bill which was stained red from berries. I looked at the lad next to me who raised his eyebrows quizzically.

'Call me a cynic but I'm off out of here. It has been nice talking to you.'

He promptly packed up his scope and left in search of the Blackpoll. Every year on Scilly there is either a good hoax bird or a bad misidentification. The 'Trump' was the latter. I cut my losses too and went to look at the vireo. I ended up getting very good views through the scope and Vic got on it, too. Two Yanks in a day, one a lifer, and a big boozy lunch had made it a good day. It was a shame about the 'Trump' though. We decided to have one last look at the Blackpoll which we both saw in deteriorating light. As it hopped out of view, Vic casually mentioned that she had just seen a 'little mouse'. Suspecting it to be something better than a mouse, I asked her to show me where it was. It was scuttling around our feet and proved to be my first-ever Scilly Shrew. Tick number two of the day. It had made a good day into a great day. I got as much enjoyment out of the shrew as I did out of the Blackpoll. It's strange sometimes what lights your flame. My few days on Scilly had been as good as ever. I have not been back. Every year, I get the itch to go down there, particularly when the good birds are on show. I will surely go back some day. No matter what anyone says, the Scillies are still magical, even without birds.

PELAGICS
1998–2003

Sitting on a boat being tossed around in the Atlantic Ocean, with the stink of rotting fish and people throwing up around you, is not everyone's 'cup of tea'. To be honest, it is not mine either, but if you want to see rare seabirds it has to be done. The birding stakes must be high to get seventy-odd birders year after year out there. The Scillonian pelagic was for a while an annual event on the birding calendar. For the uninitiated, the RMV *Scillonian III* is the boat that runs from Penzance to the Scillies. For quite a few years, it was chartered by birders to go out to sea in search of seabirds, for a single day in August. Sadly, this service is no longer running. The ferry operators tried a re-launch in 2010 but due to a lack of numbers the trip was cancelled. It was a shame, but did anyone know about it? I certainly did not until it was too late. In 2002, it was cancelled due to an engine failure and the most recent trips have been blighted by bad weather and few birds. It is also not cheap when you consider the petrol costs of getting to and from Penzance, a minimum of two nights' accommodation and the cost of the trip itself. You do not get much change out of £300. It is also a long, long day. You need to be on the boat before 5am and you do not usually get back until around eight in the evening. Smaller pelagics running out of the Isles of Scilly seem to have completely eclipsed the *Scillonian III*. The birds have been just as good, if not better, and you can get closer to them by all accounts.

The Scillonian pelagic really took hold when Wilson's Petrels were discovered in what became known as the Wilson's Triangle in the Western Approaches off the Cornish coast. Wilson's Petrel was a much sought-after bird to get on one's list and the only guaranteed way of seeing it at the time was by going on the Scillonian pelagic. There was also a host of other goodies on offer, including the big Shearwaters and the chance of a real mega find. It felt a bit like the Scillies on a boat. It was an event with lots of chat, stories and some great birds. It does have its drawbacks and, for many, it is an intestinal endurance test. It is not for nothing that the *Scillonian III* has been renamed the '*Spewlonian III*'. Choppy seas and I are not the best of companions, but I have discovered Stugeron sickness tablets which have been my saviour over the years. I need to pop the pills at regular intervals throughout the day which means putting up with two major side effects, hunger and drowsiness. Both are quite nice as side effects go. Usually, it takes me three to four hours to get my sea legs before I really start to settle, yet even then I still do not enjoy the pelagic experience. For me it is a necessary evil. I enjoy the birds and the laughs. I have never been sick which means that I have emerged unscathed from four pelagics but I have never felt confident that I would not be ill. I am always very glad to get back onto dry land and check the clock constantly on the home run. There is nothing better than walking down that gang plank back onto Penzance quay.

In 1998, Tom and I decided we would book ourselves for our first-ever pelagic trip. The pelagic has a unique atmosphere. It is dark when you get on the boat and there is that very distinct smell of 'boat' which all ferries seem to have. The smell on the Scillonian pelagic is slightly different as the reek of a rotting fish mixture, known as chum, permeates the air. There is also an air of anticipation about the birds and a dread about what the sea might hold for many. It certainly felt different to anything else I had experienced. It was rough as we set off but I had taken precautions with my new best friend, Stugeron. The boat felt packed and there certainly were not too many free seats on the decks. After a couple of hours, we pulled up near a fishing vessel and immediately I hit on two lifers, Storm Petrel and Great Shearwater. Over the next couple of hours, we also got some cracking Sabine's Gulls and more Greats, but the Wilson's was looking dodgy at the triangle. We had dipped and moved on to another area a bit further out. Again, it was looking dodgy and it seemed that we had chosen the first-ever pelagic to miss out on Wilson's. Suddenly one was spotted just as we were about to head back to Penzance, quickly followed by another and possibly a third. The weather had grown warm and the sea was calm. While the boat is chumming, it can be quite disorientating. You spend a lot of time looking through your bins, mostly at Storm Petrels, in the hope that you will pick up a Wilson's. The boat is always moving, so you can come off a bird for a second or two but literally cannot find it moments later. This happened to me several times with the Sabine's Gulls and the Great Shearwaters which were on the sea. The Wilson's seemed to be circling the boat – or was the boat going round in circles? Or was it both? Eventually I got on one and even managed to see it 'paddle' as it danced momentarily on the water with its legs hanging beneath it, its feet touching the waves. I also saw the distinctive wing pattern as one zoomed past. It was a relief rather than a delight as we had nearly run out of both time and chum. I had seen the Wilson's well and was satisfied but the views had all been 'bitty'. Still it was a British tick until, that is, someone later questioned whether we had been outside UK waters because we had gone further out than usual. I decided to ignore the rumour and just bloody tick it anyway. As it transpired, we were still within British waters. It all felt a bit absurd. We were somewhere in the Atlantic off the British coast. Did it really matter whether we were technically half a mile outside a very arbitrary boundary? Not really. One of the highlights of the trip was seeing a pod of Common Dolphins as well as two Pilot Whales and a Sunfish. It all made for a good day. We were satisfied but perhaps slightly disappointed. Maybe we just had unrealistic expectations.

The year 1999 was christened the 'magic pelagic' and quite rightly so. We simply hit the big shearwaters big time, both Cory's and Great. We had seen Cory's the previous day at Porthgwarra but they were very distant and only just identifiable. Still it was a lifer and expectations were high for the pelagic. It did not disappoint. Everybody on board could get spanking views of both big shearwaters and see every plumage feature to their heart's content. The photographers on board had a field day. We got two to three Wilson's Petrels and nine Sabine's Gulls as well. The Wilson's were not quite as good as in 1998 but I think most everyone got onto at least one bird. For many it was the best of the twelve pelagics to date but it was not without controversy. For some of us, the day was blighted by what happened as we approached Land's End. We were still miles out to sea, and for the most part the birds had 'died off'. There were still plenty of Gannets, the odd Storm Petrel and an occasional shearwater. Tom and I were standing on the middle deck at the stern of the boat.

We were still birding as that was pretty much all one could do to pass the time. Besides, that was the whole point of being on the boat in the first place. Lee Evans was on the back of the boat with us. Suddenly, there was a clamour from the lower deck. The call of 'Albatross' went up and pandemonium broke out. The boat was still steaming onwards, oblivious to what was happening. We both looked frantically around. I was checking all the flying birds when someone said, 'it's there on the sea.' I do not know why but I just had not expected it to be sitting on the sea and lost valuable seconds scanning birds in flight. Now, all this time the boat was still going at full steam ahead and hence moving away from the albatross. One of the birders nearby put us onto the bird which was by now quite distant. I saw enough to see a large dark-backed bird with white underparts and head, as well as a pale, carrot-like bill, which was held downwards at an angle. At this point, Lee came rushing over to see what was going on and was asking directions as to where it was. Unusually for him, Lee was rather slow in recognising that something had been seen and I had to come off the bird to tell him where it was, which turned out to be an error. I should have stayed on it. One of the other birders gave him general directions. Having come off it, I struggled to find it again. There were also lots of Gannets on the sea. He looked in the general direction and said,

'It's a bloody Gannet. You're all looking at an immature Gannet.'

I looked again and he was right, there were just Gannets there. I could not see the albatross anywhere. There was another clamour from the deck below that it was now flying. I then picked up a huge bird flying away from the ship. Quite a few other birders saw this flight view as well. Everyone knew that it was a massive bird, but at such a distance was unidentifiable. It just kept going and going until we lost sight of it. The *Scillonian* made a belated attempt to turn round, but it was too little too late. That was it. That was the *Scillonian* albatross sighting. So, what do I think I saw? I actually believe the bird was a Black-browed Albatross and that Lee and many others saw one of the many Gannets that were around. Immature Gannets can superficially look like an albatross, but if you see an actual albatross then I think you would know. I just did not see it well enough for long enough to be one hundred per cent sure. I am still convinced that it was one but would not bet my life on it. Tom and I discussed it incessantly for the rest of the trip and on into the night in the Penzance pubs. In the end, I was not sure whether I had dipped out or dreamt it up. It felt like an hallucination. It is not on my list. Some months later, I was looking through a copy of *Birding World* and there happened to be a picture of a Black-browed Albatross sitting on the sea. I had that same feeling that I had when seeing the Golden Oriole photograph years before after we had seen our mystery bird at Minsmere. My heart sank as it appeared to be the bird that I saw with its dropped carrot of a bill. Alas, it is the one that got away. Afterwards, it was a very hotly discussed bird with two camps – those who saw it and those who did not.

I occasionally see it discussed on Bird Forum and there is still a lot of heat on both sides of the fence sixteen years on!

That autumn, I was at my parent's house in Derbyshire and had been recounting the story to them when my dad happened to say that it reminded him of the *Ancient Mariner* by Samuel Taylor Coleridge. Mum and Dad were outside on the lawn, so I popped into my room and grabbed a copy of *Coleridge's Major Works*. Having got a degree in English, I have always been a big lover of poetry, in particular that of Coleridge. In fact, I wrote my dissertation on Coleridge and the Supernatural, so *The Rhyme of the Ancient Mariner* is a poem I know inside out. In a moment of inspiration, I typed up a spoof of the Ancient Mariner featuring Lee and the Albatross escapade. Mum, Dad and Tom all loved it and told me that I should send it in to one of the birding magazines for publication. I seem to recall that someone else wrote to *Birding World* with a similar version. I could not bring myself to do so as I felt it was somewhat irreverent to Lee. Anyway, here it is many years later:

The Ancient Twitcher

It is an ancient twitcher
And he stoppeth one of three
With gold-dyed hair and glittering eye
He hath the first name Lee.

He holds me with his skinny hand
'There was a ship', quoth he
For seeing Wilson's Petrels
'Twas named the *Scillonian III*.

He holds me with his glittering eye
I cannot choose but hear
And thus spake on that ancient man
The bright-eyed twitcher.

The ship was cheered and Penzance cleared
Merrily did we motion
Out to the sea towards the Scillies
Right out into the ocean.

The Cory's were here, the Greats were there,
Shearwaters all around,
And soon did Wilson's Petrel come
About our boat fly round.

At length some saw an Albatross
Amongst the Gannets they claim
As if it had been a Christian soul
They hailed it in God's name.

God save thee ancient twitcher
From the fiends that plague thee thus,
Why look'st thou so? 'With my Leica bins
I dipped the albatross.'

And I had done a hellish thing
And it would work em woe
For all averred I had dismissed the bird
That made their lists to grow.

Ah wretch! Said they that bird to say
Was no albatross.

Gannets, gannets everywhere
But no albatross to see
Gannets, gannets everywhere
And no Black-browed for Lee.

Sorry Lee! I seriously thought that I had missed my chance of getting the 'biggy' on that albatross pelagic, but little was I to know that in 2001 we were going to hit the jackpot. We had missed out on the pelagic in 2000 as I was in the middle of completing my dissertation for my MBA, so the world of birding had to take a back seat to the world of franchising, unfortunately. This turned out to be a stroke of luck though as it was a generally rubbish trip by all accounts. So much so that it became known as the 'Tragic Pelagic'.

The following year Tom and I met up at Gwennap Head at Porthgwarra with a host of other fellow sea-watchers on a lovely sunny August afternoon. Literally the first bird I saw was a Balearic Shearwater, a tick for me at the time. It was close by and gave cracking views. I saw at least another four as well as loads of Manx and three Sooty Shearwaters. It was one of those days when there were nice steady movements of birds and always enough to keep my interest. A few Great Skuas also drifted past, including a quite rufous individual which showed no white in its wings. There was a bit of discussion about it on the day but we all put it down as an odd Great Skua. I have occasionally thought about that bird and wondered if it was in fact something more special. Another mega tick down the pan, no doubt.

The following day was a massive disappointment weather-wise. It was horrible with a squally wind which was making for a nasty swell on the sea. The visibility was poor as well and there were not many birds. As we headed out of Penzance quay and passed the sea wall, it was obvious that we were in for major fun and games. Of all the *Scillonian* pelagics that I have been on, this had to be the worst in terms of swell and roll. The weather just seemed to get worse as we headed out and the boat started getting slammed by some big waves. I had taken my Stugeron but that did not stop me from feeling very queasy for the first few hours. I was also rather drowsy from the tablets and could barely stay awake. I just sat in my seat drifting in and out of nauseous slumber. Tom was fine and would give me a nudge if there was any activity, but by and large it was quiet. I think I got Sabine's Gull in between dozes but not much else. Unfortunately, after about three hours I had to venture below deck to the toilets. It was carnage in there. All I could see were bodies strewn around the floor. Each cubicle had a pair of legs sticking out of it and the smell of vomit was overpowering. The sound of retching alone was enough to turn your stomach, not to mention the gruesome spectacle of vomit sloshing around the toilet floor. I did my business and returned above deck as fast as I could before I too joined the living dead. On the way upstairs, I could not help clocking more prone bodies lying virtually everywhere and lots of very sick-looking blokes dozing in the seats, just like extras in a zombie horror film. I was feeling rough, but they were in a very bad way. The '*Spewlonian*' was living up to its nick name alright. I was glad to get above deck, though. If I had stayed down there much longer then I would undoubtedly have turned into a zombie too. The mood on the boat was low as there were virtually no birds and well over half the birders on board were very sick.

After about seven or eight hours we were approaching Wilson's Triangle, and the weather seemed to be brightening up. I was still feeling off colour but needed to eat. One of the secrets of staying well is to keep eating regularly. I think many people avoid eating which to my mind exacerbates the sickness. I was right on the verge of either going under or getting through it. My stomach's health was in the balance, so I asked Tom to get me some chips while I stayed in the fresh air. The chips were top notch – salty, piping hot and not too greasy. I forced a couple down, felt better and then scoffed the lot. Magic, I was cured and had my sea legs. My timing was impeccable as the weather was beginning to improve and chumming was about to commence. Tom and I situated ourselves on the steps at the back of the boat above the lower and mid-decks. The chum started to work its own magic, and soon the petrels started to appear out of nowhere, attracted by that oily slick of rotting fish and popcorn. The smell is unpleasant and obviously fishy, but I do not mind it that much. All I can remember was an absolute mass of birds off the stern of the boat with about 200 Storm Petrels and innumerable Gannets. It is often somewhat quiet during that first chumming session apart from the clanking of the boat as everyone is concentrating on the birds. A voice from the lower deck suddenly piped up.

'What's this? What's this?' followed by a scream of, 'SOFT-PLUMAGED PETREL IN THE WAKE!!!!'

For a few seconds, it was absolute bedlam as everyone tried to get onto the bird. Directions were shouted out and then, amazingly, I was onto it almost straight away. It was just to my right. It was the pelagic equivalent of winning the lottery. Tom was onto it, too. We had hit the jackpot! I know we have a bit of friendly rivalry but I do not like him to miss new birds, certainly not this one. It flew around for maybe thirty seconds and then was off. Everybody who had seen it started cheering and clapping Steve Rogers, the finder. Basically, he got a standing ovation for finding that bird. What an atmosphere. It was so tense and exhilarating, but it was also the culmination of fourteen years of pelagics where the really big bird had never materialised. Here we all were making birding history. Well, at this point only some of us were making birding history as at least half the boat must have missed it. There were still half-dead bodies all over the place below deck. There were people at the front of the boat and the sides who had also dipped just by being in the wrong place at the wrong time. There were also a few who had been at the back of the boat who had not seen it. There is a certain amount of 'schadenfreude' when people dip and you succeed. You cannot help but feel a certain smug happiness because you have scored, which is made even better by the fact you are not one of those who has missed out! It was jubilation for the chosen few and misery for the rest. Minutes passed with no further sign of the elusive bird. The *Scillonian III* did a U-turn and headed back to the slick of chum on the sea. It was very, very tense again.

Much to everyone's delight, the bird reappeared. It was at this point that it was identified positively as a Fea's Petrel by better birders than me. Eventually everyone on the boat got to enjoy it. Those of us who had it in the bag were largely those who had not been sick. We all enjoyed the sorry spectacle of those grey faces emerging on deck to see the Fea's. It took some will power, I can tell you, but one by one they all managed to make it up on deck. Ironically, the Fea's was the worst possible thing that could ever have happened to some of them. Still, even they must have thought it was worthwhile to get it on their lists. It stayed with us for a good hour and a half and could be seen in the wake of the boat without any trouble. Tom even got some video footage of the bird. Some of his video 'grabs' were later put on the web which made him particularly proud. A couple of Wilson's Petrels also got in on the act and at times could be picked up in the same binocular view as the Fea's making a classic double bill. There were also three Great Shearwaters just in case one got bored. It was all amazingly exciting. The atmosphere was unbelievable. It was more like a football match than a pelagic. Everyone was rapturous and could not believe what we were witnessing. Grown men were high-fiving and clenching their fists in jubilation. Later, as we approached the mainland, we went up to the top deck to get the last of the evening sunlight. Tom nudged me and pointed at a bike chained to the railings. It was absolutely covered in thick lumps of sick. It made us both giggle but also served as a salutary reminder of how bad it had been for those first few hours. For once, I even managed a couple of ales on the boat. We were not alone as virtually everyone was celebrating. *Scillonian* chips, a pint and Fea's Petrel on my list. Life does not get much better.

The pelagic did not run in 2002 as the boat had an engine failure. Looking back, this was a stroke of luck for me. I had bought a ticket almost as soon as they went on sale. Tom then informed me that he was off to Chile to live there for the next three years and would not be going on the pelagic. That left me in a bit of a quandary as I really did not fancy going on my own. In the end, I decided not to bother and decided to sacrifice the cash. I could not believe my luck when news broke on the pager that it had been cancelled and that I would get a full refund. I was absolutely elated. My last pelagic was in 2003, but it felt like a bit of a non-event after the dizzy heights of 2001. We got Wilson's Petrel but no large shearwaters. Like many other birders, I had had enough of it. It had also burnt a huge hole in my wallet each year. I doubt whether we could ever hit that 2001 high again either. Also, the main thing for me was that it has always been a bit of an endurance test. Once you are aboard, you are a total prisoner on that boat for a long time and if you do not feel well, it is a terrible thing to have to endure. I do not enjoy the sea and you are a hell of a long time out on that boat. I have enjoyed all my pelagics, but it would take a lot of persuasion to go back on one. However, never say never.

In 2009, I did have another cracking seabird moment but this time I was on the ferry between La Gomera and Tenerife in the Canary Islands. I had been over to La Gomera for the day to get the endemic Bolle's and Laurel Pigeons. I had readily found both of my target birds but had completely missed out on any seabirds on the outward crossing. There were Cory's Shearwaters literally everywhere, but I also had high hopes of picking up something more special. With White-faced, Madeiran and Bulwer's Petrels as well as Macronesian Shearwater, I thought that I had some chance of adding to my list. On the way out,

I drew a complete blank and was bitterly disappointed. I did not even get any cetaceans for which the ferry is renowned. The views of Cory's were stupendous though, and memories of the *Scillonian* in 1999 came flooding back. It made me feel a bit lonely standing on the side of the ferry birding on my own, thinking of those Scilly pelagics with Tom. Having had a wash out on the journey to La Gomera, I was not too hopeful for the return. The weather on La Gomera that day was rather bad with a lot of low cloud in the mountains. There was not the greatest variety of birds to see either. I spent a lot of time trying to get decent views of the two pigeons.

I parked up at one of the panoramas on the side of the road overlooking the laurel forest. Within two minutes a pigeon had shot round the corner of the mountain at breakneck speed. I managed to get my bins straight on it. Bang – Bolle's in the bag! It was frantically brief but identifiable. Five minutes later a second pigeon shot out from behind the mountain. I just managed to get onto it in time. It was clearly different. Bang – Laurel's in the bag! Both pigeons were seen within five minutes. Fantastic from a listing point of view but hardly aesthetically satisfying. I had all day left and wanted to get better views of them. Another couple of pigeons shot past but they were tough birds to get onto as they were really moving fast. Then the clouds started to roll in and visibility was lost. I moved on, but to be honest the weather was wrecking the birding.

I tried a few more spots and saw loads of pigeons, but they were literally rocketing over my head. I picked up a few other birds with wonderful views of Tenerife Goldcrest and Canary Island Chiffchaff, but I simply could not emulate my earlier success with the pigeons. I also got some wonderful views of the

Canary Lizard, the La Gomera subspecies no less! Finally, the weather lifted a bit and so I headed back down to my original panorama and set up the scope. Suddenly I was seeing pigeons everywhere and eventually got good views of both Bolle's and Laurel Pigeons. I decided to head back down to civilisation and get some food. Being Sunday, most places were closed apart from a single store near the harbour which sold biscuits, nuts and crisps. I stocked up mainly with nuts and some water and sat in the car listening to the radio commentary featuring Newcastle United getting relegated. It was quite amusing to see the old Geordies dropping down a division and certainly helped me kill a couple of dull hours while I was waiting for the ferry. Middlesbrough crashed out the Premiership as well, so a bad day for the North East all round. The locals were all listening to the Tenerife game who were trying to qualify for the Champions League. A big roar went up around the cars when they went 1:0 up. I was getting bored and was relieved to finally get on the ferry.

The trials and tribulations of the North East's finest had passed a bit of time for me, but I was very bored with sitting around. Back on the boat, I headed upstairs onto the deck. It was not that warm either, but I really wanted to score a decent seabird and so stoically cleaned my bins and wedged myself in between the railings of the upper deck on the starboard side. My expectations were not that high after the blow-out of the first leg. Again, there were Cory's everywhere and I had even better views than in the morning. About half way back, the light was just beginning to go when I picked up a dark bird midway out. It was quite a big bird but not quite as large as Cory's. Gradually, it came a bit closer to the boat and banked, showing brownish carpal patches on the wings. It was a Bulwer's Petrel. Absolutely fantastic! I love my seabirds and it does not get much better than picking up your own Bulwer's amidst hundreds of Cory's Shearwaters. It was decidedly the bird of the trip and probably my bird of the year. Memories of the Fea's came flooding back, but this time I was on my own and had to pick it up with no help. I had worked damned hard for that bird and not given up. You do not always get what you deserve in birding but this time I had been rewarded with a real cracker. It certainly put those pigeons in perspective.

HONG KONG
1988-1995

During my final year of university, I did not have a clue what to do with my life, but I did fancy doing something a little different. Studying English takes you everywhere and nowhere. It is not a vocational degree by any means. After four years of studying English literature, I had to say that I could not have even picked up the Beano without trying to analyse it and look for themes. Studying literature had become a habit and the source of pleasure which reading had always represented was no longer available to me. I struggled badly in my final two years through a lack of motivation, laziness and what had become aimless, meandering study. I really needed something to shake me up, give me some structure and challenge. I had become a lazy slob spending too much time on the ale, birding, playing football and carousing. The only thing that really appealed to me was joining the police. This was largely based on insights from a murder enquiry that had occurred in my home village of Castleton in Derbyshire. Along with every local male over sixteen, I had been interviewed by the police several times. My Dad, who was the local doctor, had certified the body as dead and had been amongst the first on the scene. Eventually a local seventeen-year-old villager was arrested and convicted. The whole case from start to finish had unfolded with me as a suspect. As a result, I had decided to apply to the Metropolitan Police and had been successful with my application. Tom was away working in Nicosia which was quietly inspiring me to get out of the UK and see the world. To be honest it was nice to have a job in the bag but it was not really ticking every box. I was chatting this through with an old schoolmate, Simon Monaghan, when I was back home for the Christmas holidays.

'Have you thought about joining the Hong Kong police?' he asked me.

All I could hear was a penny coin hitting the floor. That was a moment that changed my life. A seminal moment. Cheers Mona. The lights suddenly went on inside my head. As Simon uttered those words, memories of advertisements in *the Sunday Telegraph* magazine with the caption '*Be an Inspector in the Royal Hong Kong Police*' came flooding back to me. I could remember looking at them when I was sixteen and thinking that I fancied joining but was then too young. This was it. This was the job I wanted. I have never been as dedicated in my life to a single aim as I was about joining the Royal Hong Kong Police Force. I studied and prepared myself for that job like nothing else. I was completely set on it. If I had shown the same enthusiasm and drive for my degree then I would have walked away with a first instead of coming in with a 'Desmond' (Student parlance for a 2:2 Honours degree, so called after Despond Tutu).

When I went to the University Careers office and told them about my plan, they gave me short shrift saying that each year a few people applied but nobody ever got in. I walked away feeling very down but as I reflected on it I felt the fight and determination rise in me. Sod them, I was going to do this. At other times in my life I could have been put off, but not this time. That uninspiring woman in the Careers Office inadvertently did me a favour. I had even more resolve and drive than before. I was going to prove her wrong. A whole application process, two interviews, a medical and an unbelievably protracted vetting process (due to having an Irish mother) saw me successfully on the plane out to Hong Kong with eight other recruits. There should have been nine of us but one chap who we never met, a Sergeant from the Manchester Police, had 'torched' his car as part of an insurance scam. In one act of stupidity he became surplus to requirements to both police forces. You could not make it up! It was September the 1st 1988. The day before had seen a China Airlines jet crash at Kai Tak airport in Hong Kong. This meant our flight was severely delayed, but the upside was that we got upgraded to first class. Champagne and caviar were the order of the day as we luxuriated in the high life offered by Cathay Pacific. Desmond Lynam was on the flight with us, probably heading out to the Seoul Olympics. Bizarrely, my friend Simon had also applied for the Royal Hong Kong Police (RHKP) and ended up on the same intake as me and was on the plane, too. We flew out in the lap of luxury, served by exquisite hostesses, who were jaw-droppingly beautiful. This was the life. I was soon brought back to earth with a bump in the weeks to come. Joining the RHKP turned out to be a huge culture shock for me. I had literally stepped off the plane and been dumped into the Police Training School. On my first evening, I was walking up the steps past the Officers Mess when a young Chinese PC slammed his foot down with a crack and came to attention.

'Good evening, Sir!'

He then enacted one of the smartest salutes I have ever seen. I had a quick glance round to see who he was talking to. Apparently it was me. I gave him a rather embarrassed wave of the hand while quietly pinching myself. Literally, a couple of days before I had been signing on the dole in Sheffield and now here I was being saluted by a recruit police constable. All the time you were faced with small but quite unfamiliar events that smacked you in the face. It took me days to get used to leaving air-conditioned buildings into the smothering blanket of humid heat that hit you the moment you stepped outside. It just seemed wrong. It should be freezing when you go outside, surely? It was all strange and different but brilliant at the same time.

On the Wednesday of our first week, the weather was still scorching hot and stickily humid. We had returned to the Mess for morning coffee and the daily perusal of the *South China Morning Post* newspaper. I left the others to pop up to my room for a few minutes. I walked out of the front doors of the Mess and ran up the wide concrete steps that led to Heath House, our accommodation block. I rounded the corner at the top of the stairs and was about to cross to the block's entrance when I caught a movement out of the corner of my eye and stopped stock-still. In front of me was a black snake stalking a large frog, and I was only two or three feet away from them both. Suddenly the snake reared up. Its neck flared. It was a Chinese Cobra. I was head to head with a Cobra. How the hell had this happened? This was not in my script. I did not move a muscle. To be frank, I couldn't move a muscle. The snake and I were both transfixed. It was a standoff. Perhaps one or two seconds passed, but time was standing still – for me at least. All I could do was eyeball the snake. There was no question of flight or fight. I was glued to the spot. We had been warned about snakes, spiders and various bugs, including flying cockroaches, before we came out to Hong Kong, but I had not expected to meet a deadly snake eye to eye so soon. More alarmingly, I could not recall any sound advice about what to do next. I vaguely recollected the recruiting officer recounting some story about one being killed with a boat oar, but that did not seem to be of much practical value under the circumstances. To my relief, the snake obviously decided that I was not worth the bother and recoiled before slithering off towards the side of the building. I instantly legged it hell for leather down the steps back to the Mess in a state of shameless panic before breathlessly announcing there was a cobra outside. Everybody piled out and ran back up to the entrance of Heath House with me. I recounted the story again.

'Here it is!' one of the lads said.

We all instantly whipped around to see Nick Robinson pointing at the frog. It had hopped a few feet away, completely oblivious of the near fatal experience that I had interrupted. I am not sure who had the luckier escape, me or the frog. It was a very close call either way. I was lucky not to have been bitten, which was the likely outcome had I taken another step. Now this did not happen back home in Derbyshire. There, a love bite had been about as dangerous as it had got! A couple of days later the same thing happened to another recruit when he was walking out of Heath House when he had to leap right over the snake to avoid being bitten. This time they saw that it had gone under a pile of old wood which was in the grass right next to the entrance. I do not know what happened to the snake, but the wood was moved the following day.

It is funny looking back on that incident as it was like an out-of-body experience for me. Everything seemed to happen in slow motion. It was as if I was on 'pause' and being played frame by frame. I was there but I was watching it, too. I have had the same thing happen to me a few times when I have had a hyper-adrenaline rush. The first time was when I skidded my car off a cliff, literally weeks before I went out to Hong Kong. As the car went through the fence and flew off the road, I had the same slow-motion experience, as if I was looking on and watching myself. It could only have been fractions of seconds but my recollection is of a long time, moving slowly, ponderously, like a paralysed dream that I was in but also observing at the same time. It is also so focussed. There is just this terrifying scene unravelling in front of you. All the other 'unnecessary' inputs such as noise are eliminated by this incredibly streamlined catalogue of events. I had flashbacks for a long time after the accident. I should have been in a box twelve feet underground. I know that now and I sort of knew that while it was happening. I could tell it was an incredibly bad thing happening to me at the time. My Dad who had seen how far my car had travelled when we surveyed the wreckage kept looking at me for weeks after that as if I was a ghost. The Cobra incident was similar with the slow-motion action and the feeling that I was watching myself. There was nothing else, just me and the snake staring at each other, in that slow, adrenaline-induced time warp.

I had the same thing happen to me again when a year or so later I had my gun drawn while I was lying behind a car waiting for an armed gang to come out of a bank. It turned out to be a hoax call, but the emotions were the same as if it had been a genuine incident. I was about to open fire. Surreal, slow motion, my mind outside my head, tunnel vision, watching myself, an aching feeling at the back of my legs – fear of death is at the root of it all. There is also a sort of shutout of everything else. Everything that does not matter is eliminated. Outside the bank I was not aware of anything else. I cannot even recall what happened to the cars or the people around me. They must have been there, but my memory is of a clear road with no people or traffic. It was Causeway Bay in downtown Hong Kong and mid-afternoon! It must have been packed. The need to drink copious amounts of water after the event is the other common factor. I seem to get the giggles, too. It is quite nice giggling after the event in relative safety.

Snakes aside, I was keen to get my bird list going. I can remember my first Hong Kong tick vividly. Our rooms overlooked a small lawn bordered by a row of shrubs and trees. I was looking out one morning when a beautiful black and white bird appeared on the ground. It was like a cross between a male Pied Flycatcher and a miniature Magpie. It was an absolute beauty. I watched it intently, inspecting all its features. I grabbed my copy of the *Birds of South East Asia* and leafed through the illustrations. I could not find it. I went through it again and again but could not find anything that fitted the bill. I was really hacked off. The guide covered a massive geographical area and a huge number of birds. It was not up to the mark and was a big disappointment. I kept on looking for the bird over the next few days and eventually noticed a bird called a Magpie Robin in the index. I looked it up and there was a black and white illustration of my bird, Oriental Magpie Robin. I picked up quite a few good birds in those bushes, including Yellow-browed Warbler, Japanese White-eye, Chinese Bulbul and Violet Whistling Thrush. The other common Hong Kong bird that I would see on a daily basis was Black-eared Kite. On a good day, these could be seen in their hundreds over the training school grounds. Occasionally there would also be a few Common Buzzards and, even better, the odd White-bellied Sea Eagle, a fantastic bird that I always loved to see.

For the first two months our daily routine was very much set in stone. We had to be in our PT (physical training) kit for roll call at 6.30 each morning. At 8.00am we had to be either on parade for Foot Drill or outside the armoury for Weapons Training. We would then have Cantonese lessons all day until 4.00pm when we would have an hour of PT. I hated Foot Drill at first as I just could not get the hang of it. I always seemed to be out of step or on the wrong foot, 'tick-tocking'. Being inept at drill singled you out for a lot of unwanted attention from the instructors. All I wanted to do was keep my head down but being constantly out of step was putting my head squarely above the parapet. Not good. A lot of the time I was just trying too hard and once I learned to relax I actually found it quite easy.

Anyway, that was how I ended up standing to attention on the drill square at the Police Training School in Wong Chuk Hang wondering what that distant flash of vivid blue was near the nullah. The routine for foot drill was that the squad prefect would march us all down to the drill square a few minutes before the lesson was due to start. We would have the chance to square ourselves off before being called to attention by the prefect when the Instructor showed up. It was our second week, and we were standing on the small drill square awaiting the arrival of Senior Inspector Tommy Poon, our instructor. As it was roasting, even at that time of the morning, we were all topless wearing our police caps, green khaki shorts, white webbing belts and highly bulled black boots. The prefect's raucous shout broke the morning peace.

'Squaad, Aaa tenn Shun.'

This signified that SI Poon was nearby, marching towards us with his stick tucked under his left arm. We all waited nervously for him to begin his inspection. At this early stage in our police careers, we were given some leeway with our turnout, but any error was painstakingly highlighted in front of everyone. Drill is the way that military organisations instil discipline. It is a pain and a massive chance to be punished if you mess up by not following an order or if your turn out is not up to scratch. It gives you lessons that you keep in life; attention to detail, looking after your kit and personal administration. Sometimes you got punished anyway either as an individual or as a group just for the sake of some minor misdemeanour, real or contrived. It was known as a 'beasting' where you would be made to mark time repeatedly lifting your knees to your waist while standing on the spot. Try it if you want to know how knackering it is, especially in the heat and humidity of Hong Kong. I was in the middle rank of three and knew that I was about to endure an intense examination like all the others. The pressure was on. As he progressed towards me he continually probed, picking up on loose threads, fluff attached to caps, peeling belt paint and making adjustments to people's position and posture. At each one of us he would pause, look at us directly in the eye and then slowly begin his scrutiny of our appearance from head to toe. Fortunately, as the weather was still extremely hot and humid we were parading without shirts, so there was one less item of clothing to worry about.

Finally my turn arrived. I focused my eyes on SI Poon's cap badge as we had been taught and tried to stand impassively before him. The people in the front rank could not see what was happening behind nor could you see beyond your peripheral vision to the sides either. All you could do was guess at what was happening and where he was. The heat, the itches and the trickling sweat made it hard work to stand still. Everything itched and tickled. It was incredibly uncomfortable and all you could do was patiently wait, wriggling your toes and rocking gently from side to side to maintain your circulation and imperceptibly shift your weight. Sweat was a constant annoyance as after a few seconds large drops of perspiration would start to drip from under our caps and irritatingly trickle down our faces. At first the impulse to move and wipe it away was irresistible, but SI Poon was rapidly impressing on us that any unscheduled movements on the parade ground were sins of cardinal proportions. The real test of character came when large hornet-like insects would land on us to drink our salty sweat. Trying to stand to attention with a monster wasp crawling down your sweaty back is not fun. When the order came to 'Stand Easy' there would be an instantaneous scene of en masse scratching. It was like a troop of baboons.

I breathed a huge sigh of relief as he walked behind me to check the rear rank. I had passed the examination. While I was waiting for the rear rank to be inspected with nothing other to do than stare ahead at the playing fields, I saw that flash of blue in the distance. I was a bit perplexed as to what bird it might be as there was no obvious water in the area, just a smelly nullah with a trickle running through it. It flew again and was obviously not a small bird. After the lesson, a couple of the guys asked me what the bright blue bird was. I did not know. The mystery was solved a couple of days later though when we were walking past the same area. A White-throated Kingfisher broke cover calling loudly, flashing brown, white and blue. What a cracking bird. Mystery solved. I saw it a few more times from the drill square. We all did. It was one of the few distractions to take our minds off the insects and itches. It was a bizarre way to get a very good bird.

My first sighting of a Greater Coucal has to be one of the weirdest birding experiences of my life. Again, it was shared with my fellow recruits, but this time we were on the shooting range, not the drill square. Now I absolutely loved weapons training. I was a decent shot. The upper range where we did all our shooting was located near the entrance of the school and was basically a bowl cut out of the hillside. It was surrounded by rich vegetation on three sides with sloping hills of jungle all around. It was a beautiful spot. This may be a funny thing to say about a firing range, but it was also a very peaceful place. It was a sort of oasis of tranquillity. Occasionally, you would get lumbered with guard duty for the night. It meant doing patrols and signing check point books. Every time that I checked the range I would stand there for a few minutes soaking up the peace and tranquillity of the place in the pitch darkness. During the day, the noise of the cicadas from the surrounding jungle was deafening, but that just added to the atmosphere. They would usually be going full tilt when we got up there but suddenly, as if someone had flicked a switch, they would stop. I loved setting up the range with the lads. We would hoist the red flag to indicate live firing was in progress, set up wooden posts, paste on paper targets with silhouettes of a person on them and put out wooden trays with our guns and ammunition. We would then stand in a line and practice various shooting drills. The noise of the guns, the smell of cordite and the surroundings created a surreal experience. I could not believe that I was there actually firing real guns. This was exactly what I had joined for. It was hot, it was humid and it was exciting. I loved it. I was like a little boy again playing soldiers in the garden. I was 8,000 miles from home, blasting away at a paper target and training to be a police officer. It was quite an adventure. It beat being in the Met hands down.

On this occasion, we were free firing when suddenly a loud 'kworrhhh' noise erupted from the bushes to our left. It sounded a bit like a coffee percolator, only much louder. You may remember that shockingly bad advert where the man is pretending to percolate coffee in the kitchen while making up a cup of disgusting blended instant. As if you cannot tell the difference!? What are we supposed to think? He is just a cheapskate, or his wife is so stupid that she thinks instant coffee tastes like real coffee? Anyhow, the noise was reminiscent of that advert, only louder. We all looked at each other wondering what the hell it was. Over the next ten minutes or so the 'kworrhhh' noise kept on repeating itself. Just when you thought it had stopped, another coffee percolator would go off deep in the bushes. It was a really weird sound and we all had the giggles. You could see people's shoulders shaking up and down as they were trying to fire. Our instructor, Inspector Cliff Chow, was a bit perplexed, too. It was rather off-putting and impossible to ignore. Suddenly a massive black and brown bird broke cover and swept across the range in front of us. It certainly was a weird-looking thing. This was the culprit all right. It landed deep in cover on the other side of the range letting rip with a final 'kworrhhh'. Again, I had no idea what it was. It had a huge tapered tail and looked more like a pheasant in flight than anything else. A ripple of 'that's it' went through our group. Nobody was firing as we were all looking at the bird. Cliff very quickly warned us to buck up our ideas.

'Men concentrate on your firing. Never mind the bird.'

As we marched back to the Mess, we still had the giggles. There is something about being in a disciplined environment where you are supposed to be serious all the time that makes daft things even funnier. Once you get the giggles, it is very hard to stop. Cliff went lightly on us that day as I think he knew that we could not help it. I think he was struggling a bit with the comedy of it all, too.

Despite their size, I only saw a few coucals in Hong Kong. That first one was a cracker. The lads used to refer to it as the 'Gwork Bird' after that. Coucals are sometimes referred to as Crow Pheasants and that is exactly what they look like, half crow, half pheasant. I saw one recently in Borneo from a boat on the Kinabatangan River. I had forgotten how big they were and how unobtrusive they are for such thumping big birds. It stirred great memories of days on the firing range and married two episodes of fantastic birding over twenty years apart.

Those two sightings proved to me what great birding habitat the Police Training School was. It had thick jungle growth running down from the surrounding hills but also had unique open grassy areas in the form of the football pitches and the cricket pitch. Such habitat is at a premium in Hong Kong, as you can imagine. I picked up a lot of Hong Kong ticks with several Sunday morning sorties around the grounds when there were no instructors or groups of marching recruits. Invariably, I would have a monster hangover picked up in the bars of Wanchai or Lang Kwai Fong the night before but, somehow, I managed to force myself out of bed. I was a bit of a Wanchai lad. It was seedier than the more refined Lang Kwai Fong. There was one particular club called Pussycats that I loved. It had a waterfall and a fish pond just at the entrance as you went up the stairs. We used to flash our warrant cards and get in for free. The club was a complete dive, but I loved it. I think I thought it was sophisticated because of the waterfall. I ignored the thread bare carpet with its horrible sticky patches. The owner was a massive triad, too. I later got friendly with him. I never knew his real name and just referred to him as 'Tony the Triad'!

Anyway, my Sunday morning birding sessions were made in spite of Pussycats. I managed about five Sunday outings in nine months! The flat grass was great for pipits as I picked up Olive-backed, Red-throated and Richard's as well as a good selection of herons, waders and pigeons. The rarest bird that I saw there was a Small Turtle Dove, the only one I ever saw in Hong Kong. Like many of the birds I found there, it was on the cricket pitch attracted by the wet-cropped grass. I also saw Wood Sandpiper and Little Ringed Plover there on the same day. I got amazingly close to the plover and had some belting photographs of it. The most stunning bird around the school was Blue Magpie, an exotic-looking bird that always reminded me that I was miles away from home. One bird that took me ages to get to grips with was the Asian Koel, a dark black cuckoo-type bird. It had a distinctive far-reaching call. That call had been haunting me for some weeks, but I never managed to clap eyes on the culprit. I had a fair idea that it was a Koel from the description in the Hong Kong field guide. I eventually got my first one in odd circumstances. I was queuing outside one of the classrooms to go into a law exam. While we were waiting, a Koel struck up calling. I had a quick glance out of the window and to my surprise there it was sitting in the top of a tree near the parade ground. At last, that haunting call and the bird were as one. There is nothing quite like a lifer before a traffic exam. I passed the exam too, so a good day all round.

Having been out in Hong Kong for just under two years, a mate of mine, Dave Stanfield, suggested that we go out to Nepal to do some trekking. It was not primarily a birding trip but there was obviously a lot of opportunities to add to the list. This was a holiday that completely did not go to plan. The whole experience was quite weird, and I had one of the scariest moments of my life there. Our original intention was to fly into Kathmandu, get the necessary visas for internal travel on our first day, fly to Lukla and then trek up to the Everest Base Camp before retracing our steps back to Kathmandu. We had about ten days to turn it all round which was a tight schedule. We should have known that Nepal was not your run-of-the-mill country when we jumped in a taxi at the airport. On the way into Kathmandu, the taxi driver dropped his friend off. As he reversed the car to turn round he backed straight into a wall. He hit it with quite a thump, certainly enough to give us a good jolt. Dave and I made a few noises of concern from the back but the taxi driver just said in a comically strong Indian accent, 'Don't worry, Sirs. It's a very old taxi!'

It set the tone for the holiday. We did not have a hotel booked, so the taxi driver dropped us off at one in central Kathmandu. It was nothing special but it was clean and reasonably well maintained. We decided to go out for a beer and something to eat. I do not know what Kathmandu is like today but back then it was a very dark city at night with only occasional street lights. We both remarked on how quiet it was. There was literally no one on the streets but we did not think it was that strange. We just thought that everyone went to bed early. As we rounded a corner we were confronted by a group of militia armed with huge sticks. They came straight towards us. We really did not know what was happening. As they approached they obviously realised we were tourists and just let us go by without saying anything. We eventually found a café bar and got some much-needed food and a beer. It was totally empty in there. The owner seemed surprised to see us but did not say anything. We returned to the hotel without any further incident. The concierge was aghast as we walked in.

'Gentlemen, where have you been? You should not be out. No one is allowed out tonight. There has been bad, bad trouble. Very bad trouble.'

He pointed at the TV as scenes of riots were being shown on the local news.

'Some people are dead. Very bad. Very, very bad.'

No wonder it had been quiet. The army had imposed a curfew after a day of trouble on the streets. About fifty people had been killed during the riots. That explained the militia that we had met. We had been totally oblivious to it all.

The following day was a beautiful, crisp sunny day. There was no sign of any trouble or even a hint of the tragic scenes of the previous day. We headed off to the Visa office to get our passports sorted out before booking a flight for the following morning to Lukla. We were on the third flight of the day. Later we retrieved our passports complete with our full-page travel permit. Everywhere we walked people kept sidling up to us offering us drugs, mainly marijuana but also heroin. It was a bit of an eye-opener and something, as police officers, we were clearly not used to. In parts of the town you really could not walk twenty feet without somebody muttering the words 'hashish' or 'marijuana' to you. There were a lot of 'travellers' in town, so there was a ready-made clientele for the drug pedlars.

The next morning saw us at the airport in high anticipation for our flight to Lukla. Things did not look good when the second flight of the day was cancelled. Then our flight was cancelled. There appeared to be no apparent reason. All we could do was book for the next day, but we had at least managed to get on to the second flight and felt we had a reasonable chance of making it to Lukla. It was a precious day wasted unfortunately. We headed back to town for some lunch and a stroll around the town. Things went from bad to worse the next day when our flight was cancelled yet again. Our trekking expedition to Lukla was in serious jeopardy as time was now against us. Any altitude sickness and we were going to struggle as there would be no time to acclimatise. We decided to have one last try and booked onto the first flight out of Kathmandu to Lukla. Day three of our holiday saw us back at the airport. We were confident and things looked good when we were told to go through to departures. We had to have a pat-down search by a soldier and he made me put my Swiss army knife in my rucksack which was going in the hold. Later, when I got my pack back, I found it had been nicked. We then saw our bags go out to the plane. Game on. This was surely it and we would be on our way. No this was Nepal. We watched while our bags sat on the runway. We then watched while our bags were wheeled back into the airport. They had cancelled the bloody flight again! Our trekking trip was down the pan. In desperation, we headed to the bus station with our gear to see if we could somehow get up to Lukla and salvage something of the holiday which was now in tatters. We spoke to the manager about the bus. In the same comical-Indian accent as the taxi driver, he dissuaded us from taking the bus

'No Sir, you will have to go with all the local people. It takes many hours and it is no good for you. There it is now. Look!'

He pointed at a rickety old bus stuffed with people, chickens and livestock. There were people on the roof and clinging to the sides. It was chaos. Neither of us fancied sharing a bus seat with a pig and a wicker cage of ducks for fifteen hours! We decided against it and headed back to the hotel where we rebooked into our room for the fourth time in four days. We needed a drastic change of plan as Kathmandu was getting boring. We had a look in one of the local travel agents and noticed that there were some good jungle trips in Chitwan on the Indian border. Dave hit on the idea of hiring motorbikes and riding down there. There was one major flaw in his plan in that I could not ride a motor bike. No matter, Dave insisted that I could go on the back of his bike. All we had to do was travel light. In the end, we shared a rucksack which I wore on my back. The journey was an amazing experience but did not half set the nerves jingling. The road out of Kathmandu is similar to the one in *The Italian Job*. It is steep, high and twists down to the valley below with unbelievable sheer drops inches from the road. It also had some huge wagons on it. At times, we were perilously close to massive juggernauts on one side and inches from plummeting to certain death on the other. We were both scared as hell but it was also strangely exhilarating. I clung on hard during that descent. We were both pouring with sweat at the end, more because of nerves than the heat.

Our road troubles were not over when we hit the valley below. Every time we approached a village all the locals would run out to try and stop the bike. In quite a few places they would pull a rope across the road to try and pull us off the bike. It was like we had swapped films from *The Italian Job* to *The Great Escape*. In most of the villages we shouted at the kids to get out the way and managed to get through unmolested. The ropes, however, were a different kettle of fish. The first one we somehow managed to get round but in one of the last villages we hit one head on. Unlike in *The Great Escape*, we were not hauled off the bike by Nepal's answer to Steve McQueen. Fortunately, the rope snapped and we speeded on our way unharmed and still on the bike. We had a much-needed stop after this incident in some quiet countryside. It was a beautiful and peaceful place where a troop of monkeys fed in the fields next to the road. It felt very special. Chitwan was not far away. We had only travelled seventy miles or so but it felt like a lot more. It had been an exhilarating, dangerous and very different journey. We were both caked in dust and ready for a cold beer.

That night we were settled into our wooden hut accommodation on the edge of the river sipping a couple of local beers and enjoying watching the sun go down. It was like a scene out of a nature documentary with the pinkish red sun dropping low over the river and covering the grasslands beyond with a reddish hue. It was simply a magnificent spectacle to behold. The guides suddenly jumped up shouting 'Rhino!' In the dull last shards of daylight, the distant shapes of two Indian Rhinoceroses could be made out in the long grass on the far side of the river. It was an exquisite moment. It made me feel good to be alive. Darkness swept down on the camp. We could do little but retire to bed with our oil lamps. The staff at the camp were insistent that we did not wander round at night. They claimed that the rhinos occasionally came into the camp and that it was very dangerous. Both Dave and I were up in the night when the beers took hold. It was pitch black out there with a lot of strange noises. We were both too alpha male to admit it to each other, but it felt bloody great to get back into the safety of the hut. I cannot recall darkness like this except when the lights have been turned off in the caverns of Castleton, back home in Derbyshire. Mind you there weren't any rhinos down there.

The next day dawned and we were treated to a canoe trip down the river followed by a jungle walk. The trip was fantastic. There were egrets everywhere and I managed to get my best-ever photograph of a Little Egret perched on a floating log. It was beautifully framed and showed the plumes off to a tee. We landed on the far side of the river and started our jungle walk. A lot of it was through Elephant Grass and to be honest we did not see that much. All we saw really was a pile of rather old rhino dung. There were only four of us on the walk, a German couple, Dave and I as well as our two guides. The guides were well armed with a wooden stick apiece. Chitwan is tiger country and it felt quite awe inspiring to be out and about on foot. As it turned out, tigers were the least of our worries.

After about thirty minutes we approached a small wooded area and once again the guides pointed out some rhino dung. This time it was wet and practically steaming. I am no tracker but even I knew that they must be close. We entered the wood and moved slowly along a path. Suddenly a loud snort came from the undergrowth nearby. The guides started to get excited if not a little panicked. We were far too close to the rhino. It had sensed us and was snorting its displeasure. One of the guides told me to get in a tree. It was not much of a tree actually. It was dead, about twelve feet high and rickety. From all the snorting, there was clearly more than one rhino near us. They had got wind of our presence, and we could hear their irate snorting continually coming from inside the bushes. We could not see them, but they were very close, maybe twenty yards away. The guides were busy getting the rest of the team to safety in trees. They were clearly worried and were showing it. It was like walking into an ambush. It was all a bit too hectic for my liking. After a few minutes I noticed the guides waving at me. I could see that they, the Germans and Dave were all in a huge tree something akin to Robin Hood's oak. They were as safe as houses. My situation was rather different. There I was very near them in my dead sapling with my feet about five feet off the ground. The bushes were starting to rustle from where the rhinos were as they were obviously getting more and more distressed at our presence. We had walked straight into their afternoon nap.

Meanwhile the guides were frantically waving at me trying to get me to join them. I signalled back that I was okay, even though my tree was unfortunately a lot closer to the rhinos than their Sherwood oak. Dave was half shouting to me to get down as well. There was nothing for it but to get down out of my excuse for a tree and leg it across to the safety of the 'oak'. The situation was nerve racking and I had to summon up a fair amount of courage to leave the tree and forego its safety. It had all happened very quickly. I was absolutely 'bricking' it. If the rhinos stirred and charged while I was on the ground I had no chance. All these thoughts had passed through my head as I dropped to the floor and legged it across to the merry men in the oak. I leapt up into the tree and got hauled up by Dave and one of the guides. I was completely breathless from nerves and was shaking from the adrenalin surge. I was safe, but my God it had scared me. I have crashed my car off a thirty-foot-high cliff, nearly stepped on a cobra, fallen down a sheer cliff at night and had drawn my gun as a police officer on the streets of Hong Kong, but nothing compared with this moment for sheer raw nerves and fear. I am getting butterflies now just writing about it. It is funny how some things just press your buttons and others don't. It felt like a bad day in Jurassic Park. I know the others did not feel it like I did, but none of them had been perched in a shrub while everyone else was sitting pretty in the oldest and biggest tree in the forest.

There was more to come though. The rhinos were clearly agitated and looked like they were about to move on. We all got out of the tree and made a big circle around them before clambering into another substantial tree. Unbelievably, the rhinos walked right beneath us. I had an 800mm mirror lens to the camera. They were so close that their heads filled the

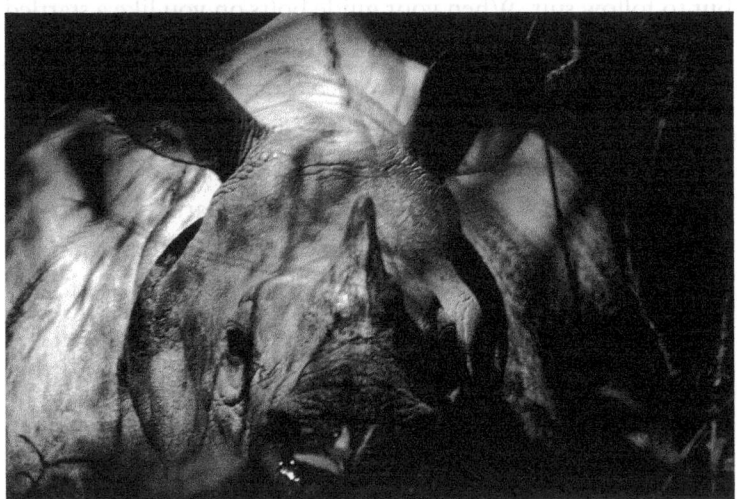

The rhinoceros that chased us

viewfinder. The photographs are amazing as all you can see are nostrils, eyes and horns.

It was the most incredible experience being so close to these enormous primeval animals. We were very much on their turf. We did one more loop round and got more fantastic views. Somehow, we had managed to get separated from the Germans and one of the guides. The rhinos were still agitated and were crashing around the wood. It was time to get out of there while the going was good. We sneaked out of the wood behind the rhinos. We could not see them and they could not see us. We both knew each other was there though. We had just got into the grassland on the edge of the woodland when we heard the noise of crashing trees and bushes. It sounded like a stampede and we were now out in the open. The guide took one look at us, dropped his stick and shouted, 'Run'! He then fled the scene. He went off like Usain Bolt. There was nothing for it but to follow suit. When your guide bolts on you like a startled rabbit you know that you are in trouble. We sprinted for our lives. I cannot remember how far we ran but it was probably about fifty yards or so. We all stopped and looked behind us. Nothing. No rhinoceroses, just grass and dust in the air. We were in the clear. Dave, the guide and I all started laughing. It was adrenaline-fuelled laughter, though. Nerves, danger, flight and relief. I guess it was quite comical really. It was also totally bizarre and the whole event is etched on my memory. I can still visualise that piece of woodland with my little tree and that gigantic 'oak' as if it was yesterday. On the way home I saw Purple Sunbird and Crested Serpent Eagle, but for once the birding was taking a back seat. Not much was going to eclipse those two rhinos.

Hong Kong – 1988-1995 | 197

The comedy element of the day did not quite end there. We were sitting having a beer when we heard a terrible squawking noise from the 'kitchen'. I looked around to see a headless chicken running round before promptly dying in front of me. Predictably, we had chicken for dinner that night. By the time we got our dinner we were famished. I took one bite and hit the equivalent of rubber bands. It was like chewing on a car tyre.

'I can't eat this,' I said to Dave. 'Have you tried it yet? It's dead rubbery.'

'Get it down your neck and stop being a girl. I've had tough chicken before.'

'No, it is – honestly.'

'Get on with you. If you're hungry enough then you'll eat it. I've had worse when I was on exercise back in the mob.'

The 'mob' was Dave's way of referring to the RAF, which he had left after failing to make the grade as a pilot. He still had a bit of that RAF arrogance about him at times which occasionally rankle badly. I thought to myself, '*Just you f***ing try it then. Then we'll see what you think.*' Dave took a bite and I saw his jaws go into overdrive for a few seconds before spitting out a piece of chicken into his hand.

'Yeah, I see what you mean about that chicken, John.'

I gave him dog's abuse about it for the rest of the night. In all, I spent just under seven years out in Hong Kong. I probably did not do as much birding as I should have done, largely because I was just having too good a time. There was a hell of a social life which was irresistible to us as single, young men in our twenties. I also spent a lot of time playing rugby and football which, combined with a six-day working week, left little time for birding. I did manage several trips to Mai Po marshes and have a fantastic waders list. The highlights included finding my own Spoon-billed Sandpipers amongst hundreds of Red-necked Stints and picking out a single Nordmann's Greenshank in a huge flock of roosting Common Greenshanks. The hide was packed at the time with a visiting party of British birders and their guide. I announced the Nordmann's and put the whole hide onto the bird. It was a very appreciative audience, including the guide. I also competed in the annual sponsored bird watch which was a magic way to spend twenty-four hours trying to observe as many species as possible.

One great birding opportunity that presented itself was working on the Hong Kong/Sino border. With the approach of the handover of Hong Kong to China in 1997, preparations were underway to withdraw the military. As a result, many of the duties that the army previously undertook were passed onto the RHKP. In my final year of my first contract, I joined the Police Tactical Unit (PTU), which in layman's terms is the Riot Police. It was a standard choice for anyone in uniform and at times unavoidable for some. It was an enjoyable attachment with quite a lot of training and had a bit of prestige to it as well. Unlike the rest of the Force, the PTU Companies all wore berets. The berets that we were issued with were like large blue Naan breads and certainly not fit for public consumption. All of us would buy our own berets, shrink them, shape them and try to look ultra-cool with little more than a postage stamp on our heads while patrolling the streets. It may have been vain but it was a lot better than looking like a French onion seller.

Trying to look macho during patrol duty at the Hong Kong / Sino border.

The RHKP had developed a very strong Internal Security capability following the riots in the late 1960s when the force was awarded its Royal title. At the time I joined the PTU in 1990, my company was among the first to take over border patrol from the army. The border itself was divided into three sections; we had the most easterly section based in a small town called Sha Tao Kok. The town actually straddled the border, so parts of it were British and parts Chinese. Virtually the whole border area was totally unspoilt countryside. It was a fantastic place. We had two main tasks: the first was to patrol the fence line and stop illegal immigrants from entering the Territory; the second was not to get involved with the Chinese in any way and avoid any kind of political incident. This last point was rammed down our throats. It also meant that we were unarmed on the border, save for a light stick. The last thing that both sides wanted was a shootout across the wire. Mind you, that did not stop the Chinese being armed to the teeth.

It was therefore with much amusement that we learned that the very first RHKP company to patrol the border fell foul of rule two when the Company Orderly walked down the wrong street in Sha Tao Kok and was promptly arrested by the Red Army. Not a proud moment for 'Asia's Finest' as we were known (largely by ourselves). The Force attracted some total nutcases, a lot of eccentrics and some brilliant lads. 'Asia's Funniest' was probably a more suitable epitaph from my own experience and one that we used to go under when we were on a rugby or football tour somewhere. The actual border itself consisted of a single road with a fence either side; there were a couple of border crossings but these were only open to the peasant villagers who worked around the area. The road followed a little river which was in effect the border demarcation line. At some point, you were literally a yard or two from the dividing line and at one crossing you could see the Chinese sentry post just a few yards away. It was a weird place. On the Hong Kong side of the road was beautiful hilly countryside. Parts of it were riddled with slit trenches from the Second World War. They were so well dug that you could still hop into them in places. I dread to think what had happened in those trenches when we were fighting the Japanese fifty years earlier.

The whole area was very well preserved and an absolute wildlife haven. I saw some great birds but my most memorable sighting was not of a bird. One day, I had been walking along a stretch of the border with the Chief Inspector, Ken Reid. It had been a good day as I had gone off the road to explore a culvert and found that a small tunnel had been made under the road, a sure sign that illegal immigrants were using it to sneak across the border into Hong Kong. We were miles away from our Command Post, so we had radioed for a vehicle to come and pick us up. One of my PCs who did not have the greatest command of English was on board. He was a cracking lad who loved having a chat with me but it would often be a case of 'gai tung ab gong' which literally translates as 'a goose chatting with a duck'. Anyway, he told me that they had caught a special animal trapped in the fence. When I asked what it was, he replied 'Chuen Saan Gap' but was unable to elaborate much more. He and the driver did their best to translate and after a lot of conferring he triumphantly came up with the English translation that would enlighten me 'Through mountain go'. I was absolutely none the wiser. They had possibly caught a cave troll, but I had my doubts. When we arrived at the Command

Post, I headed straight into the Ops Room where I was greeted by the sight of a Chinese Pangolin trotting around. To my dismay, the boys told me that they were going to eat it! I got hold of Ken and told him that we would need to get that little animal out of here before it was taken down to the kitchen, to get a vehicle and, in the meantime, I would tell them that it was a protected species and that they could not cook it!

Ken got straight on the phone, while I tried to catch the Pangolin. He was a lovely, friendly little fellow. If you touched him at all, he would immediately curl up into a little ball. A few seconds later he would uncurl himself when he thought the coast was clear and go in search of termites around the Ops Room. The only thing that I could find to put him in was a big yellow bucket. The lads were fed up with me and there was a lot of muttering about 'ah Sir' accompanied by the odd profanity or two. I had just spoiled a rare feast. As the saying goes 'If it has got its back to the sun, then they will eat it'. Being *persona non grata* with all of my platoon, I quickly touched the little Pangolin near his nose to make him curl up, picked him up and popped him in the bucket. Ken and I then made a beeline for the awaiting Police transit van before we got lynched by the mutinous mob. I did not dare open a desk drawer for months afterwards in case I got 'fragged'! (This is when someone puts a hand grenade booby trap in your desk drawer and it explodes when you open it! The phrase derives from the time of the Vietnam War when soldiers murdered their senior officers.)

The main problem was keeping the Pangolin in the bucket. He was such an inquisitive creature and had lost all fear of me. In the end, I turned the bucket on top of him and leant on it with all my weight. In spite of this, he was so strong that he would just get his claws underneath and force his way out. No wonder they called him 'Through Mountain go!' I had to keep tapping his nose to make him curl up and get the bucket back on top of him. After a few seconds the claws would reappear at a point of the bucket where I did not have my weight on and out would pop that little snout. He was magic and very strong. Even when I put all my weight and force on the bucket I still could not keep him in. Eventually, we arrived at a nice part of the border, near to where he got trapped in the fence. This was a bit damaged and I released him underneath it away from the road. He ambled off without a care in the world, never knowing how close he had come to being stir-fried pangolin with ginger and garlic. It was a privilege to meet him. My orderly, Ben, caught a Ferret Badger at the same spot about a week later, again tangled in the wire. This time, he did not want to eat it but to keep it as a pet in his tiny flat. Fortunately, I managed to talk Ben out of it and we released it back into the wild. I may have a place in animal heaven yet!

My favourite oriental birding moment was on a birding holiday to China. Five of us had headed off for a week to the Guan Shang Nature Reserve in the Jin Ling Shan mountains of Jiangxi Province. The primary target was Elliot's Pheasant which has a very restricted range. There was also an outside chance of seeing the rarer Koklass Pheasant, which if you have a puerile schoolboy sense of humour, is, not surprisingly, uncommon due to its inability to breed. I was by far the most inexperienced birder out of the group in Asian terms. All of them had done many more hours in the field than I had, including many birding trips around Asia and China. I was also the youngest by a long chalk. The reserve was great though, and we were well looked after throughout. The accommodation was rudimentary to say the least, with no running water. If you wanted a wash you had to ask for two buckets of water at the kitchen. Armed with one bucket of boiling water and one bucket of icy stream water, the only place to strip off in private was in a stone hen house with an internal door latch. There was chicken shit all over the floor and it was pitch black inside save for the light coming from the gap around the door. It did feel like back to basics though, and I thoroughly enjoyed roughing it.

By about the Thursday of the week I was desperate for a shave. I like a bit of stubble but get fed up when it starts to itch around my neck. I ordered up a couple of buckets and stripped down to the waist outside our rooms. I lathered up and soon had the whole village assembled watching me. I say it was the whole village, but it was just the men from the village. The women were obviously doing menial chores like cooking, cleaning and looking after the kids. Meanwhile the blokes were doing something worthwhile, edifying and educational in watching me remove hair from my chin. I sometimes wonder how we (men) have managed to get it so wrong in Britain. Basically, wherever you go abroad, the men seem to have the life of Riley, doing absolutely bugger all, other than standing in the town square playing giant chess under the shade of a leafy tree, sitting in a nice bar having a well-earned coffee at 11.00am or an evening aperitif at 6.00pm. Whatever, they are not working, and it is the women that seem to be in the fields picking rice and lugging water round. It's the bloody opposite over here. Drive past any school at just gone nine in the morning and all you will see is a gaggle of nattering women.

Drive past again at 9.30am and they are still there. By ten they are all having a coffee and a piece of cake somewhere warm. Shopping, lunch, nails if it's a Thursday, and a dash to school for 3.00pm for more gossiping neatly brings the day's slog to an end. How did we men let it all slip through our fingers? I sometimes reflect on this state of affairs as I cook tea or do the ironing. Mind you, I'm not much of a chess player!

Maybe my shaving was simply a sight that the ladies of the village really did not want to see. Reality is a bitter pill to swallow sometimes. Having an audience was a bizarre experience though. I could speak Cantonese but scarcely a word of Mandarin, so I had not got a clue what they were saying. Throughout my ablutions, there was a constant commentary accompanied with nodding of heads and various gesticulations. Quite what you could find to say about this at such length is beyond me. I was clearly the highlight of the year for the assembled male throng. They probably still talk about me now. Meanwhile various Chinese wives no doubt rolled their eyes and shook their heads, cursing me and their lot.

The other semi-public experience involved the local latrines. The toilets had to be seen to be believed. Basically, they were like a cow shed with brick petition walls forming sort of open cubicles. They were of the communal 'squat and drop' variety. At the back of the cubicle was a hole which led to a ten foot drop to a sort of concrete drain. It was a particularly unpleasant sight below. I think all of us had tried to avoid using that toilet but eventually it had to be done. I put it off somehow for nearly three days. An hour or so after I had paid my first visit, one of my companions, Pete Stevens, queried who had dropped 'the baby's arm?' I owned up. He gave me a quizzical look before adding that he had just met Norris McWhirter from the *Guinness Book of Records* with a tape measure! The sanitation side of things may have been basic but the food we were served was fantastic. It was spicy, fresh and varied. A lot of it was vegetarian but that somehow made it even better. The bean curd there was to die for. The beer was good, too. Our poor hosts were always replenishing supplies. Every morning we awoke with thick heads requiring copious amounts of Chinese tea.

On our first morning there, we headed up onto a high forest trail in search of Elliot's Pheasants. One of our group located a male deep in the undergrowth in the ravine below, but the rest of us could not see it. However, I did observe my first Silver Pheasants feeding discretely amongst the bamboo fronds beneath us. It was a quite magical moment. In Britain, you simply see Common Pheasants everywhere. They are semi-tame birds, more often than not reared and released for shooting. Their behaviour is unlike their wild cousins in Asia, which are timid and stealthy. There is little that matches the excitement of birding in a Chinese forest and hearing the gentle rustle of leaves nearby and waiting patiently for your quarry to perhaps reveal itself. Sometimes you are lucky and they appear for a few moments, sometimes they waft by unseen. The Elliot's Pheasant proved to be a formidable adversary all week. Every evening I would go up onto that high forest path with one or two of the others and try bagging one. We had no luck. My hip flask probably did not help as we would swig neat malt from it until it was empty and we would end up slightly giddy before departing as the evening light dimmed. We had some good laughs up there, though. On the final morning, I decided to have a last throw of the dice and went up to the track alone. As I neared the top of the tree belt, I flushed a pair of brown pheasants from the ferns at about thirty yards. I had noted where they landed but had not seen them well. I was sure that they were Elliot's, but my views had been limited in the trees. I headed stealthily further up the track and flushed them again. They were incredibly flighty birds, not allowing me to approach close at all. This time I completely lost them from view. I know that they were Elliot's but just could not quite nail that clinching ID. They remain unticked and off my list. It was a close one.

The lack of Elliot's may have been disappointing but it was made up for with other great birds. During the first couple of days, I seemed to have developed the knack of missing forktails. The Forktail genus is a fast-river-dwelling bird, a little bit like a wagtail but with a forked tail (predictably enough). They are stunning and enigmatic birds, so I was keen to catch up with one. The rest of the group seemed to be picking them up easily enough, but I was having a run of being in the wrong place at the wrong time. One afternoon, I decided to make a concerted effort to see one, so I found a nice quiet spot overlooking one of the rivers and settled down to see what turned up. I did not have the greatest of expectations but you never know what is in store. It was a warm and pleasant spot and I was perfectly at home in the peaceful solitude of it all. I sat quietly and soon birds started to emerge, feeding on the plentiful flies and insects in the trees. A stream of Mugimaki Flycatchers, Red-flanked Bluetails, Pallas's Warblers, Yellow-browed Warblers and Rufous-faced Warblers helped me pass an easy hour. I was happy and at peace, enjoying the serenity and the birds.

Momentarily, I glimpsed movement on the riverbed below me. There was an exquisite Slaty-backed Forktail flicking its tail and feeding amongst the stones. Then it was gone. It was such a beautiful fleeting moment. I had been calm, motionless and quiet save for the raising of my binoculars. Birds had come and gone in little droves and finally my goal had appeared before me. It felt like a reward, not for my effort but for enjoying the moment, being at one with my environment and appreciating the beautiful natural world on offer. I felt so accepted and part of that Chinese forest, thousands of miles from my home and my family. It was the closest I have ever come to inner peace and understanding what life is all about. It was a truly poignant interlude given to me by birds and my love of birding. Nature is such a beautiful gift and I am privileged to have had such experiences. How could one want any more?

CUBA
APRIL 2004

Every so often you get a year that is totally life changing. 2004 was one of those years. It started off with the news that my girlfriend, Vicky, was pregnant. We technically found out at the end of 2003 but most of the pregnancy, and obviously the birth, was in 2004. I actually knew before she did. She just thought that she was being sick every morning from her love of red wine, but I had a policeman's hunch that something was afoot inside her. Having both come to terms with this unexpected news, we had the rather weird job of breaking the news to her seven-year-old daughter, Molly. She did not believe us. This was followed by breaking the news to our respective parents. They did believe us. My Mum and Dad were shocked but chuffed, it would be fair to say. At the time, they had never even met Vicky so it was all a bit sudden and rushed. Anyway, introductions were made and Vicky went down a treat with them both.

Everything seemed to be going well until March when I went to watch Rugby Union World Cup winners England take on Ireland at Twickenham. I was staying at Tom's house in Shepperton and all was set for a great day. Dad had been complaining of blind spots in his vision and had been in for a scan. I had been over for a meal on the Wednesday night and he did not seem too concerned by it all. He thought that he had a small blood clot that was causing it. This may have lured me into a false sense of security at the weekend. Tom by nature is a bit more of a worrier than I am, and he was concerned why our parents had not rung to tell us about the results of the scan. Tom gave them a bell to see how Dad had gone on. My Mum was a bit evasive on the phone and Tom, smelling a rat, pushed her for the truth. I sat listening to the conversation in his living room and, although I could only hear Tom talking, it became obvious that Mum was very upset. Clearly, something was amiss and so it proved. Mum and Dad had not wanted to tell us the news, so it would not spoil our day at the rugby. Tom put the phone down and broke the news. It was as bad as it could be. Dad had three advanced cancerous tumours in his brain. It was only a matter of time. I knew immediately that it was curtains for him. There is no coming back from secondary tumours. Three months later he was dead. He went from being a picture of health to his grave in no time at all. I went into the bedroom and had a cry. I rang Vic and broke the news but struggled to keep it together. The only good thing was that Tom and I were together and drew a lot of comfort from each other. We chatted it through all day. It was cathartic and helped us both get our heads around the news. England lost to Ireland 13:19 to cap a particularly bad day.

Prior to Dad's news, Vicky and I had planned to have a grown-ups-only holiday somewhere hot before we had a baby on our hands. We had briefly talked about a few destinations but had not really made our minds up. I came back from work one day to Vicky's house to find her looking a bit sheepish. Being a Derbyshire lad, this might have been a turn on, but the truth is that she had been on the internet booking a holiday.

'I've booked a holiday but I'm not sure you'll like it.'

'Go on then. Where to?'

'Cuba!'

I would never have picked Cuba in a million years but I was really chuffed with it. Cuba was just hitting the market as a tourist destination. It was well-priced and looked excellent value with four nights in Havana and ten on the island of Cayo Coco. The news of my Dad's condition nearly led us to cancel, but we decided to go in the end. Dad was still in quite good health at the time and would have been narked with me if I had decided not to go. It was also the last chance saloon for Vicky and me to have a holiday together with no kids apart from the one forming inside her. My life was changing massively around me. My girlfriend was pregnant, Dad was dying and, to make matters worse, work was acting up and I was being made to apply for my own job. I had a lot to cope with at work at the time. Fortunately, I had just managed to recruit a lad called Andy. We had about a week together before I departed on holiday, leaving him to hold the fort.

It was a massively stressful time. Just to throw more fuel on the fire, we were also refurbishing my house for us to move into. Vic did nearly all of it, but even on the morning of our holiday I was off buying an oak beam to put in the kitchen and running around like a blue-arsed fly making sure everything was ready for the builders. My house was stuffed with white goods for the new kitchen as well as tiles and sinks for the bathroom. Needless to say, the builders did sod all while we were away, so all the rushing around at high speed was in vain. For once I really needed a holiday. Cuba was just the ticket, but it was also going to change my perspective on birding forever.

The flight there was a bit of a monster, with an hour's touchdown at Holguin. Fortunately, we had upgraded to first class for an extra £300. It was not quite first class as you would expect, but the extra leg room was welcome and so was the very nice Hine Cognac. Vicky and I spent the first couple of days in the wonderful city of Havana. It is like nowhere else with its crumbling buildings, 1950s-hand-painted cars, cold war history, music and colourful people. Everything was different and interesting. We had a great tour of the old town in a pony and trap with a guide called Tom who could speak virtually no English. It was brilliant. It was probably all the more enjoyable for this as we could enjoy the sights without the usual drab tourist commentary. He even stopped and got Vicky a rose and gave me a 'lucky' coin with Che Guevara on the back. Yes, he was obviously after a tip, but it was a nice touch nevertheless. He was a pleasant bloke who scored points with Vic for the way he cared for his horse. I kept the coin as I felt that I needed all the luck I could get the way things were going. For once, we both really enjoyed the sightseeing and I loved all the Castro revolutionary history. I think we both felt relaxed and happy. It was a wonderful place and experience and we really enjoyed it all. Well, I say we enjoyed it all. Actually I did not enjoy all of it as I got severely embarrassed over the misidentification of Turkey Vulture in the hotel that first evening. Basically, Turkey Vultures are regular sights in the skies of Cuba but I was not that familiar with them. To be honest, a silhouette of a Turkey Vulture would not make you think of a Vulture in the Eurasian sense. They are long tailed and slim winged as vultures go, more like an oversized Harrier to my eye than a Vulture.

I had not done too much swatting up on Cuban birding, so I was not too sure what I might see where. I simply had not had the time and there was not that much information to be had on it either. My British list has always been king when it came to birding which meant that birding abroad was a bit of a poor relation. I therefore had a rather casual approach to what I might see. I had no hit list and no gen on sites. Rather than chase anything in particular, I was just going to search, find and tick. After all, I was not at all bothered about my world list. I did have the foresight to get hold of *Birds of Cuba* which was not a bad field guide; most birds were accurately described and depicted, but it did have one or two weaknesses, particularly some of the plates. I have used far worse guides. Cuba has a fair selection of raptors, most of which I was not familiar with. Anyway, when I was confronted with large birds of prey wheeling high over Havana I turned to the guide and immediately found that I was struggling to identify them. I kept looking at the illustration of Common Black Hawk and thinking 'that is not right'. The Vulture 'penny' had just not dropped. I had very much ignored the illustrations of both Black and Turkey Vultures. I mentioned to Vicky that I was a bit puzzled. She had a look at a couple of the birds through the binoculars and started looking at the guide too. She then immediately pointed to the flight illustration of Turkey Vulture and calmly said, 'that's it'. When I saw the picture I knew that she was right. I felt a right chump. Here was a girl who scarcely looked at a bird from one day to another and there she was identifying Turkey Vulture while I was messing around wondering whether they were Black Hawks. It was very humiliating stuff to be honest. Top shot birder John outgunned by his novice girlfriend. She was cock-a-hoop. I never heard the end of it all holiday.

'You just leave the identification to me.' 'Get in there, top twitcher Vicky!' 'You and your expensive binoculars and you can't even identify a vulture.'

It never stopped. It was also accompanied by a variety of football-style celebrations, such as stirring an imaginary pot and a fair amount of hip waggling. Turkey Vulture was on the list but at what price? It did teach me a salutary lesson though. I needed to look at the birds properly, get the features and stop messing around. Vic had simply looked at the bird, remembered what she had seen and found it in the guide. Simple. Meanwhile, I was using my so-called experience to eliminate birds on grounds of behaviour and jizz and was not looking at the field guide intently. Humble pie or what?

After a couple of days in Havana, we had a short transit flight to Cayo Coco. It was April and Vic mentioned that the clocks were due to change and that we should check if it was also the case in Cuba. I was not aware that anyone other than us Brits did the annual flick from GMT to BST and I strongly doubted that there was a Cuban equivalent. I completely pooh-poohed the idea and did not bother to check with the hotel. Our pick up was at 6.00am the next morning. I set my phone alarm and off we went to bed. You can guess what is coming next. Vic who was sleeping badly owing to her pregnancy with our son Jack noticed the time. It was quarter to seven and my phone alarm had not gone off. I had not bothered changing the time on my mobile from GMT to Cuban time and had just calculated the difference in my head. Maths was never my strong point. I had got it wrong by an hour. Error number one and my fault. We hightailed it down to reception with our bags, checked out and waited for our pick up. We waited and waited. Vic insisted that I checked with reception. I refused to budge, assuring her that the pickup would be there any minute. Error number two and my fault. After around an hour I capitulated and headed off to reception. They pointed out that the clocks had changed and it was now well after eight o'clock. Error number three and again my fault. A pattern was emerging. We had just under an hour to get our flight. We rushed outside and grabbed a taxi. Fortunately, the driver had the good sense to check our tickets as Havana actually has three airports. He shook his head when he saw the flight time and gave us a car-mechanic-style deep intake of breath and then shook his head again. That man did us proud. Havana traffic can be bad at times. He took some great detours for us, including driving across a railway line and a couple of fields. Vic and I kept looking at each other in astonishment and disbelief. He made Hackney Cab drivers look like schoolboys. All the time he was chuntering on to us in Spanish and laughing away. We made it with ten minutes to go. I shoved a wad of US dollars into his hands and scuttled into the departures hall. Meanwhile he went off and purchased a new house. The airport check-in area was deserted other than for a handful of officials.

'We are late.'

They all looked at us seriously for a moment.

'Yes, you are,' one of them replied with a half-smile.

Without much ado, they calmly checked our bags in and issued us boarding cards.

'Don't worry. You do not need to rush.'

We followed a lady up a long corridor to security. We still felt the need to half-run. Vic got waved through while I got thoroughly searched. It was not quite the rubber gloves treatment but surely methodical nonetheless. In the end, I got a dressing down for having a pair of nail scissors in my hand luggage. I would not have minded but they were Vic's. I did not even know they were there. She had just slipped them in – not into her luggage but into mine! This was before the time of small plastic see-through bags for toiletries and the like. It was also an internal flight which in my experience meant zero security. The lady relented and let me keep the scissors, warning me not to do it again. I was having one of those days.

We walked through into the departure lounge. I call it a lounge but it was really a sort of covered extension of the runway and was to all intents and purposes open air. We looked out onto the tarmac to views of our plane, a turboprop, with a gaggle of men with enormous spanners working on the engine. We were clearly in for a fair old wait. We were both starving and there was not much in the way of refreshments available other than a small kiosk selling some rather dodgy-looking snacks. Vic did a reconnaissance mission and came back armed with the information that it was due to open at nine. She had also spied two bumper bags of crisps, which appeared to be the only edible thing on the menu as far as we were concerned. We planned our tactics to the second. Vic got in prime position and was first in the queue.

Minutes later we were the proud owners of two very odd-tasting bags of crisps and two bottles of water. The crisps were not really crisps. They were a bit like bacon frazzles – those things that you pretended to like as a kid because they were advertised on telly but were rather rank when you came to eat them. You saw the advert, got your mum to buy them, found they tasted horrible, ate half a bag and went back to Golden Wonder. Foreign crisps are always a bit different and never that nice. They tend to be sold in massive bags too, which are full of air and generally impossible to open. Crisps are one of the few areas that British cuisine truly excels. We are certainly a global leader in the field and can hold our heads high against the competition. We should make more of it as a nation. Anyway, we devoured those 'frazzles' as if they were packets of Sea Salt & Cider Vinegar Kettle Chips. Normally they would have been in the bin after a few mouthfuls. Vic did especially well, bearing in mind she was five months pregnant and literally anything could bring on a bout of nausea. She had experienced a bad one the night before at La Floridita, a much vaunted, posh restaurant of Hemmingway fame, where we were having a romantic meal for two. It was romantic until she bolted to the toilet in the middle of it all to be sick. I did enjoy the remainder of her meal though but was cheated of a dessert and nightcap due to her ongoing sickness. In spite of the Turkey Vulture ignominy, I was sympathetic and made all the appropriate signs of concern which were actually genuine – well mostly. The Turkey Vulture incident did still rankle.

Anyway, back to the crisps and Havana's third airport. The crisps were a small distraction from the four-hour wait that we endured at the airport. I think I had a couple of cups of coffee as well but it was an arduous sojourn. Eventually, our plane was ready. We had watched and watched them tinkering with the engine. They had also put it through its paces to make sure it was okay. At last we all clambered aboard, clipped on our seat belts and sat ready to depart. That was until we were all told to get off again as there was another problem. This time we were taken to the VIP lounge – actually a terrace with tables and chairs interspersed among the palm trees. As we sat in the sun, I clocked a bird dart into the leaves of a palm tree. I kept my eye on it and soon it flew out again before returning a few minutes later. It was clearly a swift, in fact an Antillean Palm Swift. Not only that, it was flying into a palm tree where it had a nest. What better identification clincher do you need? I am looking at a swift. I am in the Antilles. It has flown into a palm tree. Put them together and what have you got? An Antillean Palm Swift. What a great tick. After ten minutes, and with the APS firmly on my list, we were ushered back to the plane. I must confess that I was not feeling entirely confident about the plane nor the journey ahead. We were in Cuba; we had just watched the mechanics working on it for several hours with hammers and giant spanners; we had been on it already and had had to get off and, finally, we were having a 'funny' sort of day. Certainly, everything that I had touched or done had turned to mush. We got on, took off and had a great flight.

The baggage collection point at Cayo Coco airport was brand new and tiny. The baggage conveyor belt was about ten feet long. Still they had made an effort. Even I could not argue with that. Instead of passing the bags to us they put it on the moving belt. It travelled three feet and we lifted the bags off. It was quick though. Outside I saw a Cattle Egret while clambering on the bus to our hotel. The Hotel Melia proved to be just the ticket after a long and arduous day. We were all-inclusive and really looking forward to ten days of relaxing in the sun. Our room was like a mini apartment. We were on the first floor and overlooked a conservation area of trees and bushes. It looked promising and I was chuffed at the prospect of birding from the balcony. On arrival, we were ravenous as the sustaining quality of the frazzles had long since disappeared. We asked a member of staff for directions and headed off to the beach restaurant. I have to class the meal that followed as one of my all-time best 'feeds'.

The restaurant was on stilts and located in shady trees and undergrowth between the hotel and the beach. We soon learned that the best food was invariably the fresh fish, meat and rice. Anything that was more 'western' was pretty much average, particularly the potatoes which were black and looked and tasted like coal. We gorged ourselves on paella and grilled prawns as well as most of the rest of the buffet. It was just what the doctor had ordered after a very long and tiring morning. While I was going down to the paella and prawns bar, I caught sight of a small brown warbler. It was a disappointing and nondescript bird but it was obviously an American warbler. Its only feature was a single white wing notch. Without the field guide, I did not have a clue. I had not even got my binoculars with me, so I was relying on fairly decent naked eye views. My first American warbler and it was not much brighter than a Chiffchaff. Most American warblers are quite garish and colourful. I had no idea what this one was. When I got back to the room much later on, I had a scour through my copy of *Birds of Cuba*. I was not that hopeful of identifying the mystery warbler to be honest as all I had seen of note was that solitary wing bar. To my amazement, there it was, a female Black-throated Blue Warbler. No trouble. Why could it not have been a male? They are simply stunning.

The following morning, I sat out on the balcony with my bins while Vic was in the bathroom. I knew that I had at least thirty minutes of peace and quiet (and that was on a quick day). What better way to while away the time than with a bit of deckchair birding from the balcony. I was not expecting too much when suddenly a warbler hopped into view, low in the bushes beneath me. It was a little cracker. I sucked in all the exquisite colours and features. It was like a hail of lemon zest darting in front of me. A single yellow wing bar, yellow half outer tail feathers and a beautiful dollop of lemon on the breast were all very much on show. I knew instantly what it was. A female American Redstart. It was simply beautiful; I was ecstatic. This was a seminal birding moment for me too, although I did not know it at the time. With that single sighting, I was off. The American warblers are something to behold. Having seen that first American Redstart, I just wanted to see more. My *Birds of Cuba* guide was stuffed with illustrations of all the passage warblers. It was April and they were all pretty much en route, via Cuba, back to their breeding grounds in the States. Not many Americans visit Cuba but their birds certainly do, as I was to find out. It was also dawning on me how good birding abroad could be. This first American Redstart was sowing those seeds.

My British List was starting to take second place. I loved that balcony and ended up spending almost every spare minute on it. It was most productive first thing in the morning but sometimes there would be 'rushes' of birds in mixed flocks at odd times of the day. This would instil panic in me as there would be an invasion of birds and I would have to sift through the flock, see each bird and put a name to it. I would be frantically looking at them and then scouring the guide. I certainly missed a few species from simply not having done my homework. It was magic fun though. It was like being a novice again. I never knew what I might see or whether I would have time and get good enough views of a particular bird to establish a definite identification. It was also providing me with a break from the realities of Dad's illness, becoming a Dad myself and the problems with my job. When I was watching those flocks of warblers, I was completely removed from all my worries and fears. I realised that it was simply a matter of time for Dad. The clock was ticking and in Dad's case it was ticking very fast. Nobody knew just how fast. While I was in Cuba though, he was still in good shape. Having been brought up in a medical household with my Dad working as a General Practitioner and my Mum as a former nurse, both Tom and I were well aware of the reality of illness, probably more than most. It is surprising what you absorb when you are a kid. I had overheard countless conversations, telephone calls from patients when Mum or Dad were on the phone and had myself taken messages from patients.

As an adult, I had spent many a night sharing a glass of malt with Dad while he recounted stories of his general practice days. Through all this, medicine and general practice was a very big part of our lives. However, even this did not prepare me for the rapidity of his death. Yet, the speed of it all was also a blessing. He did not suffer too badly as some people do. It was mercifully quick. When he finally died it felt like a deliverance. The last few days of his life were traumatic. He seemed to be in pain and he was confused and anxious. As a son, it was hard to come to terms with watching someone you loved dearly and have known for so long in such pain and enduring such suffering. This was my Dad I was watching. What could be worse? Dad died early on Monday morning on 21st June 2004 at home with Mum, Tom and I at his bedside. Over the weekend he had steadily deteriorated, culminating on Saturday night when he had to have a morphine injection.

His former practice partner, Dr. David Moseley, was fantastic as were all the people that treated and cared for him. The injection did the trick and gradually Dad's pain eased and his body relaxed. He woke from a coma-like sleep the next day and had a small drink of water. I knew that Dad as we had known him had gone from us at that point. All I wanted was for it to be over for him. Sometimes now, I wish that he could have seen my son, Jack, and that they had been able to spend time with each other. They would have got on great. It never happened. They missed each other by a couple of months. It is a fanciful notion for me to consider. I have to remind myself of those last few days and how I felt when he breathed his last breath. I would not have wished him to go on for a second longer or suffer any more. If it was hard for me to watch, God knows how my Mum felt. Yes, it was a deliverance for Dad and for all of us. Banal as it may seem, birding gave me a break from the worry of what was to come. It took me away from it all. It helped and it made me happy. It still does. That American Redstart fluttered into my view and helped my life in a way that it could never possibly comprehend. So did all the other birds that holiday. If there was ever a reason to be a birder then that was it. Dad gave me a gift which ultimately helped me cope with his loss. That is a big part of why I am a 'tweeter' still. It gives me pleasure and helps me deal with the adversity that life throws at me from time to time.

That first morning in Cuba dictated a ritual that I was to assiduously follow for every day of the holiday. Vic would go in the bathroom while I would bird from the balcony. We would then go for breakfast which gave rise to another ritual that Vicky came to hate. This was basically my need to go for a number two in the middle of breakfast every day. Cuban coffee seemed to have a very strong liberating effect on my bowels. Each day I would have to excuse myself from the breakfast table and trot back to the room, leaving her alone in the restaurant. She began taking a magazine with her after a couple of days. Lucky girl, I say! I often took the chance to do a spot of sneaky birding, never on the way to the room though – always on the way back. That was just too risky. I was always walking like a penguin by the time I got to the room anyway. I did manage to pick up Cuban Emerald, a hummingbird, my first-ever 'hummer', and Common Yellowthroat on these toilet sorties to and from breakfast. She often used to ask why I refused to use the restaurant toilets. Subterfuge was required, so I pretended that they were not that clean and often had no toilet roll. I think she began to get suspicious when I started carrying my bins with me, including on the way to the toilets.

The best thing about the hotel was a thick patch of bushes separating the hotel grounds from the beach. To get to the beach you had to negotiate sandy paths through the shady alleyways of bushes and trees. After a day or two, we noticed that these bushes were packed with warblers. It became known to us both as 'warbler alley'. Even Vic got the bug for the warblers. She also loved the Cuban Emerald. On one day we had fantastic close-up views of one perched a few feet away. We could even see its tongue darting in and out of its beak. On another day, she shouted at me to look at a warbler, but I was following another bird. I never saw the bird which she was looking at. She asked for the guide and finally pointed to a Blue-winged Warbler. I never saw one all holiday. She was and still is adamant that this was the correct identification. She takes great pleasure in reminding me of it, too. I know better. It was never a Blue-winged. In true Lee-Evans-UK-400-Club style, I have not 'accepted' it as a confirmed sighting, largely on the grounds that I had missed it! That was another one that got away, but I saw a bag full of other warbler species in 'warbler alley', including Northern Parula, Palm, Cape May, Yellow-throated, Worm-eating, Prairie, Black-throated Blue and my personal favourite, the flying humbug itself, Black and White Warbler. I perfected the art of 'pishing' (making a funny noise that attracts small birds) and could soon have a flock of twenty birds buzzing around me.

One particular bird really perplexed me. I watched it at close range on several different days. Most of the warblers were in pristine plumage, but this individual was a right scruffy little thing. No matter how closely I looked, I could not put a name to it. I kept running through all the salient features and it did not fit any of the warblers in the guide. On the final day of our stay, I got on to my mystery warbler again and watched it intently. It was a distinctive bird and easy to pick out. It was such a grotty thing that it was very noticeable. It was clearly different, but I could not name it. This was my last chance. I started scrutinising the bird, knowing that if I did not nail it there and then, it would be a mystery until I went to my grave. While I was watching, it acrobatically flipped upside down on a branch. As it did so, I noticed a few flecks of lemon yellow on the rump, a feature that I had not previously noticed. I looked even harder and managed to see the yellow on the rump again. Armed with this new piece of the jigsaw puzzle, I returned to Vicky who was sunbathing on the beach. I grabbed the field guide out of the bag and started looking at all the warblers with yellow rumps and then I stumbled on my bird, Magnolia Warbler. That was clearly it. The picture showed a bright yellow rump which my bird barely had. In the text I noted that they were highly variable in plumage. It now all made sense. I was elated having solved the mystery.

Ovenbird will always have a special place in my heart. Not because of the bird, although they are little stunners, but because of a case for just desserts and a little bit of summary justice for my then wife-to-be. Well, that is my version. Vicky's is quite different. Even though she was nearly five months pregnant, we had decided to hire a couple of mopeds for the day. We set off on a beautiful morning and headed up the coast to Flamingo Beach. There were American Kestrels on the wires overhead and, as we sped up the road, I caught sight of a large thrush-sized, green-coloured bird fly across the road into the trees. It was a glimpse and I was not sure at all about it.

When we got to the beach there was not a soul in sight. We had one of the most exquisite beaches and lagoons imaginable entirely to ourselves. There are people who would have paid thousands for the experience of having that idyllic beach all to themselves. We headed out into the turquoise waters which were gorgeously warm. You could wade about fifty or sixty yards out and the water would only come up to your chest. It was wonderful. As the water got deeper, we approached a wall of seaweed. All of a sudden, Vic got the panics and rushed back ashore. She just did not fancy being near whatever might be lurking in that weed. It certainly put an end to living the dream. It was a shame really, but afterwards she was quite happy to have a doze and lie in the morning sun. I headed off into the woods at the back of the beach and started pishing. Five Cuban Vireos popped out of nowhere. It was like being a magician pulling rabbits out of a hat. They came within a couple of feet and sat looking at me, cocking their heads on one side. They were very cute. That is how to score an endemic. I also had my first Ovenbird of the day, creeping through the undergrowth near my feet. The mosquitoes were getting a bit heavy, so I decided to head back to Vic and see if she was ready to make a move. We had no real plan but decided to pack up and head on up the road. When we returned to the bikes Vicky realised she had forgotten her sunglasses, so in keeping with the natural order of things I was sent back to get them. As she was heavily pregnant, I did not mind but somehow got the feeling that I would have been sent to get them even if she had not been carrying our child. It was a bit of a needle in a haystack job, but eventually I found them lying in the sand.

When I got back to Vic, she had seen three Cuban Green Woodpeckers near one of the parked cars. I could not believe it. Fortunately, they reappeared and I got good views and was also thereby able to put a name to the mystery bird that had flown across the road earlier. Another Cuban endemic in the bag. We set off heading towards Cayo Guillermo, an island attached to Cayo Coco, where one of our friends had stayed. The only bird of note was a female Merlin which seemed slightly incongruous sitting in a tree in Cuban mixed woodland. I was far more used to seeing them in bleaker habitat on the moors back home. We had a stop at a sort of visitor centre but decided to push on and find somewhere to eat. We just kept riding along the road for miles. After a while we decided to turn round and head back. It was rather a pointless trip but we were both hungry, it was getting hot and Vic was pregnant. It seemed stupid to simply keep pushing on. After a few miles, I spotted a ranch on the right. I drove slightly past it and pulled over onto the side of the road to wait for Vic and see if she fancied trying it for some food. She agreed to give it a go and spun her bike round and waited for me in the entrance. I was messing about a bit with my bike but eventually turned it around in a long arc onto the wrong side of the road which was on the same side as the entrance.

The road had been quiet all day and I had not really bothered to look. The next thing I heard was the deep sound of a horn. I looked up to see a huge coach bearing down on me at breakneck speed. I had seconds to get out of the way. I just managed to get my bike onto the verge, hitting a wooden post in the process and grazing my leg as I crashed to the floor in a heap. It was a close-run thing and I was quite shaken up. The coach roared past and I survived in the nick of time. How the hell it all happened, I do not know. One minute I was doing a leisurely arc on my bike and the next thing this huge coach had appeared from nowhere about to mow me down. I picked my bike up along with my nerves – and my pride – and rode over to Vic. She was in hysterics of uncontrollable laughter. I was not amused. She just kept on laughing and laughing. It got so bad that she started wheezing and coughing. I had nearly been wiped out by a bus and could not see the funny side. I still cannot to this day. After several minutes of listening to Vic laughing, we headed into the ranch. Suddenly a man leapt out onto the road in front of us. He was just wearing shorts and a Stetson, and as we slowed, he menacingly drew a machete. He was clearly a psychotic killer. This was turning out to be a bad five minutes. I was about to lurch from one near-death experience to the next – not good. He then produced a big smile and waved us through the gates with his machete. It was apparently all part of the ranch welcome act. The good news was that they served food. It turned out to be quite a nice little place and we sat outside with cold drinks while chicken and rice were cooked for me, and fish and rice for Vicky. All this time Vic never really stopped laughing. The only time she did stop was to wipe the tears from her eyes before starting again. It came out in wheezy uncontrollable gasps and sobs, half crying and half laughing. I was starting to get rather sick of it. By this point, I was sulking and not speaking.

Our meals arrived and we tucked in. The food was rustic fare but delicious. The chicken was wonderful and gamey, nothing like the tasteless stuff that we get in the UK, courtesy of the Supermarkets. In the middle of it all, divine retribution came to my rescue. Not only had our food been served, but revenge was also on the menu. Vic was hit by one of her nausea attacks and could not carry on eating. She took herself off to the side and was badly sick. I was so fed up with her that I just kept on eating. In fact, I finished off her fish which was also delicious. One of the women working there went over to see if she was okay and sat down with her arm around her shoulders. She must have thought that I was a callous, uncaring man. Anyway, she looked at me in total disgust for leaving my poor pregnant partner to be sick while I consumed her dinner. She was right of course; it wasn't my finest hour. I really had the hump though. It was at this point that an Ovenbird appeared and proceeded to feed right under my table. I was feeling much better with a full belly, my nerves restored, a bit of summary justice for my gloating girlfriend, and a delightful Ovenbird feeding around my feet. Mind you, Vicky still gets the giggles whenever she recounts the story now and I still get the hump. At least I made her happy, I guess.

This incident aside, Cuba was a great holiday from every perspective. We both had a fantastic time in spite of events back home with my Dad. I also bagged some great birds, especially the Yankee warblers which included Yellow and Prothonotary Warblers. One of my favourite birds of the holiday was a Yellow-bellied Sapsucker which had a favourite tree right outside our room. One day we were unlocking the door when I caught a movement out the corner of my eye. I had a second look and could make out a bird on the tree trunk. It had to be a woodpecker of some sort. I rushed inside for my bins and very soon was treated to exquisite views of the sapsucker drinking sap from the lines of drilled holes on one of its feeding trees. For many British birders, it is an iconic bird as 'arguably' the discovery of a female on Tresco by David Hunt in September 1975 put Scilly on the birding map. I have read and reread many accounts of rarities that were found over the years but that Tresco Sapsucker is one of the best. For many years after, the drill holes were still visible on several trees on Tresco. I enjoyed that Cuban Sapsucker immensely. It was such a quiet and unobtrusive bird. We must have walked past it countless times and it was only a sheer fluke that I noticed it at all. It was interesting and very different; after all there are not too many creatures that drill holes in trees and live off the sap that oozes out – and, additionally, it had that tremendous iconic context in British Birding history. Another great bird.

All too soon, we had to return to Havana for our final night. We had a wonderful room in the hotel high up on the top floor with unbelievable views across the city. Our flight back home was late at night, so we paid a small surcharge to keep the room for an extra few hours. Thank God, we did, as Vic had a nasty bleed. I was extremely worried that she was going to have a miscarriage. She did the right thing and just rested. As the time approached for us to go, the problem seemed to ease slightly and over the next hour or so it totally abated. Fortunately, it came to nothing but it was a nasty scare for both of us.

While we were walking near the hotel earlier in the afternoon, I caught sight of a small bird. It was a mixture of black and fiery red stripes, a superb male American Redstart. It somehow felt apt that I should be departing on this note. It was a lovely bird to finish on and it was also the one that had really started our 'birding holiday' off. Cuba had done us proud – as both a holiday and birding destination. It had also transformed me from being a British obsessed lister to a World obsessed lister. Not quite a coup d'état, but my British list crown was close to being deposed. I had finally got the bug for foreign birds and had thrown off the constraining shackles of the UK borders. I was off and I have not looked back. Unfortunately for Vic, this means that every time we are away on holiday she now has to endure my need to pursue new birds. She has certainly changed my life for the better in more ways than one, although I think on occasions she wishes that it would be nice to have a holiday without birds. As I see it, that will never happen and she has only herself to blame!

CANARIES AND SPAIN
2006-2009

The Cuba experience was the catalyst for several birding holidays abroad. Scilly has firmly taken a back seat, possibly permanently, but I guess only time will tell. It is outrageously expensive, both to get and to stay there, and to be honest my birding horizons have moved on. The whole birding scene on Scilly seems to have lurched into terminal decline. Budget airfares, great food and wine, not to mention great birds, make it difficult for Scilly to compete with Spain these days. In 2006, I took my first birding trip there with Tom. Spain is a giant of a country when it comes to European birding. It has fantastic birds and large parts of interior Spain are unspoilt and with their traditional farming methods it plays host to huge numbers of birds, many of which were once common sights in our own British countryside. Spain has quantity and quality when it comes to birding. That first holiday, we headed off to the Spanish Pyrenees in search of two truly iconic birds, Wallcreeper and Lammergeier. You could not get two more different species but they would both be high on anyone's 'most wanted' list. Wallcreepers are simply stunning enigmatic whirls of grey and purple, living on inaccessible rock faces in the high European mountain ranges. They are also tiny. Lammergeiers by way of contrast are bone-eating vultures with a cascade of orange and brown hues, all set off with an amazing diamond-shaped tail. No other bird eats bones, so it is rather special. There is a David Attenborough film of them dropping bones from a great height onto rocks to break them up, which many people will have seen.

Tom had more Spanish birding experience than me as he had been on quite a few holidays there over the years and had got most of the raptors under his belt as well as the much sought-after White-rumped Swift. By comparison, I had hardly done any and was not that familiar with many of the commoner species. I had a 'hit list' of Griffon Vulture, Egyptian Vulture, Bonelli's Eagle, Short-toed Eagle, Booted Eagle, Rock Sparrow, Citril Finch and Black Woodpecker, to name but a few.

With a decent target list and a sound plan, we embarked on our first-ever joint euro-birding trip, flying from Stanstead to Bilbao. We were a bit late in the season as it was the end of June. Basically, I finished work, had a Chinese take away, kissed Vic, Jack & Molly goodbye, drove 180 miles down to our hotel near Stanstead Airport, met Tom, had a pint and went to bed. It was a knackering start. The following morning, we both stood at some ridiculously early hour in the Departure Hall surrounded by police and England fans bound for the World Cup in Germany. We must have been the only two blokes there that were not travelling out for the football. There were massive queues and literally everyone was getting searched. England had topped the group and were facing Ecuador in the

Canaries and Spain – 2006-2009 | 233

next round. They had not played that well and had no strikers, with Owen out of the tournament and Rooney still recovering from a metatarsal fracture. Still, spirits were high and the air was optimistic and upbeat.

Fortunately, our flights to Bilbao meant that we got through security a lot quicker than they did. It was good to get away from them to be honest. I used to be football mad but have gone off it over the last few years. Sheffield United was for me the 'be-all and end-all'. For a few years they took a back seat, but as my son Jack has got into football we are now both big Blades fans. I do not quite have the old passion of my youth but still get a buzz from a big away day or a big game at Bramall Lane. I still like to see them doing well and am a happy man when Leeds or Sheffield Wednesday are suffering. I even have a '100% Blade' tattoo on my right shoulder, like the actor Sean Bean. I was quite worse for wear when I had it done and '100% Bladdered' would have been a more accurate epithet. Anyway, birding is now king and football is number two on my list of priorities. So it was the Spanish Pyrenees rather than Stuttgart for Tom and I. Having got the hire car and a couple of ridiculously small bottles of water from a vending machine, we set off on the long drive to Hecho Valley. We stopped at a service station for a coffee and a bite of lunch. We had steak baguettes which were fantastic. Freshly cooked and reasonably priced, neither Tom nor I could believe that we were actually eating at a service station. The coffee was great as well. It put our own pre-packed, microwaved, additive-stuffed, overpriced junk that our own British service stations pass off as food completely to shame. I have to say that when you are away from the tourist resorts, Spanish cuisine always delivers.

We hit the road again, thoroughly impressed and satiated, and soon saw Griffon Vultures circling overhead. I could see them but only fleetingly as I was driving. I could not really tick them from these views but knew that there would be plenty more to see at my leisure during this trip. The weather was hot and our little car did not have the best air conditioning. On stopping later on, I noticed that the back of my shirt was absolutely soaked with perspiration. I had not really had much to drink other than the coffee and that tiny bottle of water. I felt okay at the time but I was stupid not to have stopped to obtain a further bottle of water or two. Finally, after several hours of driving, we hit the turn-off for the Hecho Valley in the Pyrenees. Almost immediately we started seeing a mixture of Red and Black Kites, getting some wonderful views of birds perched on the overhead telephone wires. We then spotted a superb hovering Short-toed Eagle, quickly followed by three Egyptian Vultures. These incongruous vultures are predominantly white and black, looking more like inland Gannets than a raptor. They are also described in one of the field guides as 'regularly being known to feed on faeces'. I think I would rather be a Lammergeier any day! Egyptian Vultures or 'Gypos', as we called them, are truly beautiful birds, belying their dubious tastes. In a matter of minutes, I had got two ticks as well as confirming Griffon Vulture as a rock-solid tick.

A simply stunning male Cirl Bunting also dropped on to the road in front of the car. Cirl Buntings are very much confined to Devon in England but they should be far more widespread. In Italy and Spain, you can see them all over the place. Their range in the UK has contracted hugely. It just shows how intensive farming and probably climate change has impacted the British countryside. It is a shame because Cirl Buntings are beautiful birds and our countryside deserves them as part of it. As we drove higher and higher, it dawned on me that I did not have any exact directions for the Hotel Rural Uson where we were staying. I had done copious amounts of research via the internet trying to get Wallcreeper sites and birding gen but had forgotten to get directions off the internet for the hotel. Tom ended up calling his girlfriend who was able to get us the directions we required. We need not have worried as in the end we found it easily. Our room was basic but clean. It was a typical Spanish room with dark wood-panelled walls and a tiled floor. We soon headed straight out up to the Gabaradito refuge, which was our prime site for Wallcreeper and offered a fair chance of Lammergeier, too. By the time we had parked the car, it was already late afternoon and still very hot. We set straight off up the track from the field centre to the Wallcreeper location. There was absolutely no one around. The directions given in the field guide were good but were of the type where you cannot be a hundred per cent certain that you have got the right spot.

'Take the obvious track for two miles up through the pine trees. As you emerge from the woods, there will be a steep rocky gully on your left and the cliff face will be on your right. After about a mile you will go around three obvious bends and see a single pine on your right. The cliff buttress opens out. Search the buttress for the Wallcreepers which breed high up on the cliff. Watch out for Black Redstart, too.'

I was quite sure that we had found the correct location but always had a nagging doubt at the back of my mind. The sun was glaring down and the whole rock face was smothered in sunlight. We sat there patiently scanning the cliff for a couple of hours. Nothing. I kept reading and re-reading the directions. Were we really in the right spot? We could be sitting in slightly the wrong place and easily miss the bird. Eventually, I caught a glimpse of something flit round the corner of the cliff and out of sight. We got up and headed up the track. Again, nothing. We kept walking and the cliff to our right got further away from the track. Surely, we had been at the right place but the nagging doubt was still there all the same. All this time we had not had a drink as we had no water with us. I was starting to feel a bit dehydrated. My shirt had been soaked in the car when I was driving and I had just spent two hours sitting in the sun looking at a cliff. I don't think having a salty Chinese takeaway and a pint the night before had helped much either. I always have to drink lots of water after a Chinese. Reluctantly, we had to accept that we were going to dip out on the Wallcreeper. I must say I was glad to be heading back. As we trudged downhill, I glanced at a vulture that had just gone overhead. I had not really clocked it properly and so I casually put my bins up, expecting it to be just another Griffon, when I was suddenly confronted by a diamond-shaped tail and an array of orange and russet hues. Lammergeier! I shouted to Tom who was some way behind me on the path. He did not seem to comprehend what I was saying and looked at the wrong bird, a Griffon. I shouted 'Lammergeier!' again and suddenly the penny seemed to drop with him. He came bounding down the track towards me shouting 'where? where?' All this time, the bird was flying away from us. I had got spectacular views but came off the bird almost instantly to alert Tom. Eventually he got onto it but it was by that time quite distant. He was unconvinced as he had not seen it at all well. It spoiled the whole sighting for me. Gone were the old Minsmere days when I enjoyed the elation over Tom missing a rare bird. We still have a friendly rivalry over our British lists but not to the extent that we want each other to miss seeing new birds. We trudged back down the track to the car, me with a banging headache and Tom disconsolate due to a double dip. It was just as well that we left when we did as it absolutely poured with rain just as we arrived at the car. That night at the hotel we were treated to a spectacular thunder storm across the mountains.

The next day saw us back at the Gabaradito Refuge. It was a beautiful day and I was feeling a lot better having spent most of the previous evening glugging bottles of water. In spite of everything, I still managed a couple of glasses of a fantastic Crianza. We even had food with us this time, courtesy of the hotel's packed lunches. Bizarrely, the sandwiches were made from English-style white sliced bread rather than the fantastic rustic bread we had with our breakfast. A shame but they had obviously fed us like the English generally like to be fed. We were not grumbling when we tucked in later. This was just as well as there were not too many shops around. We retraced our footsteps up the trail. I meticulously checked our progress against the site directions and we ended up at exactly the same spot as the day before. It had to be right.

We plonked ourselves at the foot of the cliff and set ourselves for a long vigil. We had two Black Redstarts in the area but the prize bird, Wallcreeper, was not showing. The problem was that we were sat at the foot of a large, grey cliff and Wallcreepers are predominantly tiny, grey birds. After nearly two hours, we became aware of the occasional high-pitched whistle from high up the cliff. It was hard to hear with the breeze blowing and was barely discernible. It sounded like a distant kettle whistling. Knowing our luck, it was a goat herder brewing up high on the meadows above! Anyway, our hopes were raised but still the bird was not showing. We simultaneously saw a movement in a long crevice of a rock that ran vertically high to our left. The rock face in question was like a giant, crooked chimney. All we had seen was something dropping straight down the chimney and out of view. We scanned and scanned the area and then there was another movement. The tenseness of the situation was unbelievable. All we could see were vague wraith-like movements high up above our heads. It felt like our quarry was close to giving itself up but with such a rare and fantastic-looking bird we were desperate that it did not to slip through our fingers. I was sweating again but not from just the heat this time. The tension was palpable. I was desperate that these glimpsed, vague movements would not simply evaporate into nothing. This bird could easily slip away unseen in the bat of an eyelid.

The seconds ticked past and then a Wallcreeper just materialised on the rock above our heads. It was high up and gradually working its way down, occasionally going out of sight, only to re-emerge a few feet lower. After twenty minutes or so, it perched with a butterfly in its bill, sitting still in the sunlight. Both of us had questioned whether it was worth trudging up there with our telescopes and tripods. Thank God, we did. Unbelievably, we were able to grill this little cracker of a bird at 60x magnification. What an exquisite gem, a real beauty.

Every tense minute of waiting had been worth it. There was absolutely no sense of anti-climax as sometimes there can be when expectations are high. Wallcreeper for my money lived up to all of my expectations. As a bird, it has the lot; fantastic colouring, character, rarity and it inhabits dramatic, high and inaccessible cliffs. It looks like nothing else and is like nothing else. To make things even better, we also got on to two Lammergeiers in the valley behind us. One of them even landed enabling us to get reasonable scope views. Both birds were in the bag. It felt good to be doing some top birding in incredible surroundings.

The next day England beat Ecuador, but we did not even bother holing up in a bar to watch the match. We spent the morning down in the lowlands away from the mountains in the towns of Riglos and Aguero. I grabbed a couple of ticks in the form of Spotless Starling and Blue Rock Thrush. On the whole, it was a bit disappointing but we did end up with a few decent padders, including Golden Oriole, bee-eater and Melodious Warbler. I had really been after Black Wheatear and Rock Bunting.

We decided to head back up the Gabaradito refuge to see if we could unearth Citril Finch, which had so far eluded us on our two previous visits. The day was hot and balmy, so we had the windows open. As we drove up the access road, we heard the unmistakeable call of a Black Woodpecker from the pine woods to our right. This was number three on our hit list. Fortunately, I could park the car up nearby and we scrambled over the fence into the thick pine woods. The Black Woodpecker was calling regularly and was quite close, about thirty yards downhill. We edged closer downwards but kept getting stuck in the impenetrable undergrowth. We were conscious of making noise and flushing the bird, so were being ultra-careful. Eventually, we managed to find a route. It was calling periodically and then suddenly – silence. We had taken too long or perhaps it had sensed our presence. Either way, we had dipped. We had been so bloody close. I was absolutely gutted. Black Woodpecker was always going to be a long shot; to get one calling nearby and just miss it was mentally crippling. Neither of us could quite comprehend how we had missed it. From our vantage point it seemed impossible that we would not have seen it fly. Sometimes birds vanish. They play with you, tantalise you and vanish. Now that is birding. One day you are up and the next you come crashing back down to earth with a bump. So near, yet so far. The highs of a Wallcreeper were soon negated by the lows of a dipped Black Woodpecker.

We got back in the car and headed up to the car park, feeling very hacked off. As we approached, I noticed a couple of finches feeding on the grass. Binoculars up and there we were looking at a pair of Citril Finches. The disappointment of the Black Wood was put to the back of our minds, not completely but for a few moments at least. I would have traded the woodpecker for the finches any day, but a tick is a tick and Citril Finch is a nice bird. This basically completed the 'alpine set' as I had already seen Alpine Accentor and Snowfinch while skiing in the Alps and Pyrenees. The Accentor had been a wonderful find, perched on the roof of a mountain peak restaurant in Flaine. I had heard an unfamiliar song, and as any song was a rare occurrence that high up, it had to be one of the alpine specialties. I have seen Snow Finches a few times, including a small flock right next to a drag lift in Austria. Gyr Falcon, Alpine Chough, Ptarmigan, Red Crossbill, Great Grey Shrike, Ring Ouzel, Ibex and Snow Vole have all been ticked while skiing.

The next day we unfortunately had to head for home but still enjoyed a good day spotting raptors with Golden and Booted Eagles seen around Hecho. The finale came at a small picnic site on the way back where we saw Short-toed Treecreeper and had two Short-toed Eagles fly low past us over the fields. The eagles were a magnificent sight and brought closure on a great trip. Spain had delivered. We simply had to go back.

I have mentioned that I like to do copious amounts of research before going on a birding trip. This inevitably involves buying all the relevant books, particularly site guides, as well as trawling the internet for trip reports. I have spent a small fortune on these books over the years – hence the bulging book cases on my landing. I absolutely love this research phase of holiday planning. I get a right old kick out of all the planning, working out routes, finding flights, compiling target lists, identifying birding hot spots down to the final yard, not to mention alternative sites just in case, finding accommodation and even getting the car rental sorted out. Meanwhile Vic always makes out that I leave the planning to her and that she does everything when it comes to family trips or holidays. To an extent, that is true but when it comes to birding there is no stopping me. PRINCE2 and all the other available project management courses can't hold a candle to me when it comes to sorting out a birding trip. I find it all incredibly motivating. As I plan and research, I get more and more excited about the forthcoming

Preparing for a birding trip

trip. It's almost as if I am eking extra value out of the whole thing. I feel like I am getting my money's worth, that's for sure. Tom has always remarked on how well prepared I am. But this is because I come equipped with all the best trip reports, maps and most of the core knowledge stored in my head as I have been through it so many times.

Following on from our success in the Pyrenees, we decided to go on a second trip to Spain the year after. This time it was planned for the last week of April. My original idea was to fly to Seville, bird the Coto Doñana area before heading up to central Spain to Extremadura. I got the dates sorted with Tom and we both booked leave, from Wednesday to Wednesday, to take advantage of the cheapest airfares. I booked flights to Seville with Ryanair, literally the day the schedule was published on their website. I left it a couple of months before confirming the hotels and car hire. I knew the Coto Doñana area inside out in my head and had a great itinerary planned. You cannot believe my anger and frustration when the day after I booked the hire car Ryanair e-mailed me to notify me of a change to the air schedule. The flight had moved from Wednesday to Friday. Great!

Our leave dates were quite fixed and it was just a non-starter to accept the new flights and schedule. We were stuffed and my plans were in tatters. To make matters worse, the weblink on the e-mail to cancel the flights was broken and I actually had to put pen to paper to redeem the flight costs.

Whatever trip that I planned afterwards, there was absolutely no way it was going to be with Ryanair. In a pique of temper and moral indignity, I made a mental pledge never to fly with them again, which being a shallow soul I have since broken many times as they are simply the best budget air-line around. I also had to cancel my car hire and the hotels. It was time for plan B. I did not actually have a plan B, so I had to devise one otherwise it was going to be a poor do. I started my research over again and eventually stumbled on the alternative. We had both fancied trying to see another iconic bird, like Wallcreeper or Lammergeier, but there were no obvious candidates. While I had been staying with Tom, he had put on the *Finding Birds in North Spain* video depicting Sheffield birder Dave Gosney's attempts to catch up with various much sought-after Spanish birds. The video is far from Oscar winning but is quite watchable if you're a birder. You won't get it on Netflix though!

There is a scene where he and the crew try to see and film the near mythical Dupont's Lark, a bird that is unbelievably hard to see. In Gosney's case, it was nigh on impossible to see. Eventually, they manage to get a few dodgy flight shots of it disappearing into the distance. Larks are not the most stunning birds to look at but they have a certain mystique. Our own Skylark is a fantastic little bird when you hear it singing and then eventually spot it sixty feet up in the air twittering away. When you see it on the ground it is a nondescript, streaky little brown job. All the larks are great songsters and have some amazing display flights. The Gosney video certainly inspired us to go for Dupont's Lark as it fitted the bill and certainly had iconic target bird status. The main site for it was in the north of Spain, miles from Extremadura. However, we were both set on the idea of going to the Extremadura area for the array of good birds to be found there, including the huge Black Vulture, Black Shouldered Kite, Spanish Imperial Eagle, Bustards and Sandgrouse. There was an absolute bag full of ticks on hand for both of us. We also only had a week to play with, so doing loads of travelling was not really on our agenda. I know a lot of birders are happy to spend hours travelling to boost their lists, but quite frankly I would rather be out in the field enjoying the birds than sitting in a Fiat Punto for a week not enjoying the road ahead!

Finding a suitable Dupont's site was proving to be a tough task. We needed reasonably up-to-date information and some ground directions if we were to have any chance of connecting. The main Dupont's Lark site was pretty much out of the question unless we wanted to waste an entire day driving. I could not really see how we were going to try and re-enact

Gosney's trip in the limited time available. Extremadura was a must, so it had to be in striking distance of a day's travel. I spent hours scrutinising various possibilities and eventually landed on a less well-known Dupont's Lark site near the town of Sepúlveda, a couple of hours drive north of Madrid. It seemed rather hit and miss as far as finding the bird was concerned as the quality of the information was limited. I had read dozens of birding trip reports to Spain to unearth this site. I love a good, well-written trip report which has a bit of character. Unfortunately, they tend to be few and far between. Most of them are really very dull and bland with no sense of humour. When you read a good one that captures the mood of the country or some of the fun, they really stand out head and shoulders above the rest. One of my favourites is *The Magnificent Marshside Seven do España*. It is full of tacky Spanish puns and very loosely based on the theme of the *Magnificent Seven* film. It is also very funny and had a piece on Dupont's Lark echoing that of Gosney's film as well as capturing the enigma that surrounds the bird:

By mid-afternoon we were bumping along the sandy track from *Villaseca* to the 'Ermita de San Frutos', our stomachs churning, not because of the road surface but in dreaded anticipation of what was to come. The previous year, three of our magnificent seven had been well and truly destroyed in a duel with the 'diablo', which had cruelly tormented them for ten hours, until one by one their minds, bodies and spirits had been broken. Only one had managed a brief glimpse, which only made the other tortured souls even more dispirited.

We decide on a more pragmatic approach to the problem and spent the first 40 minutes overlooking the tremendous grand canyon of the Duraton gorge spread out before us. Parties of Choughs, displaying Peregrines and vultures galore helped to calm our nerves as we prepared for the showdown in the bad-lands that awaited us.

We trudged off towards our potential nemesis, after all Dupont's Lark was the main reason for the trip in the first place. Supplications were offered to any god that might be listening and I seriously considered the ritual sacrifice of my troublesome telescope, in return for decent views of the devil bird, by offering to hurl it over the precipice into the river many miles below us… but the omens looked very bad.

Not only were we not seeing the bird, but we weren't hearing it either. On the previous trip our compadres had heard Dupont's constantly in the area we were scanning. El Drivero y El Belchio decided to walk ahead for about 250 yards and after some initial hesitancy had a Diablo singing quite close to the road. We signalled to our other crew members and within five minutes we were all listening intently to his haunting "weeee. weeeio" song. Actually seeing 'el diablo' was another matter of course, but by standing on a roadside rock, El Belchio managed to surprise him out in the open.

To the eternal thanks of his friends for life, we all had repeated good views of the apparently well behaved and obviously much maligned Dupont's Lark. What was all the fuss about? But disaster, our leader El Padrone, couldn't see what we all enthusing about.

In a final cruel twist of fate, El Diablo had somehow blinded him; had made his hands shake uncontrollably; had chilled him to the bone; surely this wasn't happening. We rallied round, found him gloves, targeted El Diablo, reminded him it wasn't a bird at all, but a rat-like creature that scurried from bush to bush, and sure enough, after what seemed like an eternity, he sighed with enormous relief…he was actually watching El Diablo.

That was it. It had to be El Diablo, I mean Dupont's. We finally had a bird to compete with Wallcreeper and Lammergeier. It was game on and what an adversary. The plan was to have a couple of days trying for Dupont's, head over the Sierra de Gredos mountains and drop into Extremadura. EasyJet had flights to Madrid. We were all set. There was another snag though. Tom had developed chronic back problems and had been really suffering all year. He is a bit of a hypochondriac too, if truth be known. By way of a strange coincidence, I had also done my back in the week before. Vic and I had decided to take an impromptu Easter family holiday to Estepoña in early April with some friends at their time share flat. I felt my own back pull as we were moving bags to the car on the final day of the holiday. I say 'we' but I really mean 'I' as there are never too many willing hands when it comes to loading or unloading the car. It is just one of those tasks that is male only. It is sort of preordained by our wives, mothers and girlfriends. It is the same with supermarket shopping as well. Women seem to think that they can just bugger off out of sight as soon as there is a bag to be moved out of the car boot. That is probably why most men try to carry as many bags as possible all at once. Many a time I have lost all sensation in my fingers trying to carry a whole boot's worth of shopping in one go. Estepoña was no different. I single-handedly ended up lugging all our bags around like a pack mule. No sign of Vic whatsoever. I noticed a bit of a pull when I was moving one particularly heavy bag. I think it was Vic's make-up bag to be honest. I was in some discomfort at the airport and was really struggling when we arrived at Liverpool. I was creased in two by the time we got home. This was the only time that I have ever watched Vic unload the car at the end of a holiday. Usually there is mass exodus to get inside and the magic elf, that is me, is left to it.

The next day, I could not make it into work. It did not matter what I moved, it made my back shoot with pain. The only things that I could move painlessly were my eyes. I rang the doctor and was told to take Ibuprofen and Paracetamol and was given some exercises to do. I ended up having the whole week off but was just about recovered by the following Wednesday when we were due to head out to Madrid. I am sure my boss was not that impressed with me having a week on holiday, a week off sick, two days at work, followed by another week on holiday. It was the only sick leave that I had in nine years with Britannia, so they could not really grumble. It was also genuine. It had been a somewhat unpleasant week and I would have been gutted to miss the birding trip with Tom, which was touch and go. My back seemed to loosen up in the day and then completely seize up again at night. I also dreaded sneezing or laughing as this would make me wince with pain. Tom was actually in worse nick than me. We were a right pair of crocks. Still we both made the flight.

We left Liverpool airport in magnificent sunshine, only to arrive at a rain-swept Madrid. It rained more or less all the way to Sepúlveda. We did manage to tick Southern Grey Shrike en route but things were looking rather desperate in terms of the weather. After checking in at the hotel, we popped over to the Hoces del Rio Duratón to get the lie of the land for the Dupont's. We had four species of lark, including Calandra Lark, which was a good tick. Calandra Lark is a real lump of a bird and has occasionally turned up in Britain where it has mega-rarity status. Seeing them in their home territory, singing and displaying, was just amazing. We only had two days to get the Dupont's and I had not really planned or allowed for bad weather in our schedule. What was already a tough ask had just got a whole lot tougher. The following day dawned overcast and far from ideal birding conditions. There was nothing for it but to get out there in the field and see how we could make out. We ended up birding from the car in mixed weather, mainly light drizzle, which was more reminiscent of a British April's day than a Spanish one. In spite of this we had a reasonable haul of birds, including the beautiful Azure-winged Magpie, which is near enough an Iberian endemic other than a small population in China, bizarrely enough. We also saw Black-eared Wheatear and a few other decent odds and sods. As the morning progressed, the rain steadily got worse and looked set in by the time we hit the Dupont's site.

In the finest tradition of resolute birders, we headed back to town for a fantastic lunch at a restaurant washed down with a cracking bottle of local red wine. I could have stayed there to be fair. The restaurant proved to be an excellent decision because the bad weather started to improve as we came out. The clouds had lifted and the drizzle abated. There was nothing for it but to try the Hoces del Rio Duratón again for 'El Diablo' itself.

Our hopes were not high as we had lost so much time. However, the weather was really improving and we were even seeing a bit of blue sky and sunlight. We stopped about half way along the road in what we thought was likely habitat. There were larks singing everywhere as if it was a second dawn. The morning rain had obviously kept the birds down but they seemed to be taking advantage of the afternoon sunshine and warmth to have a song blast. In fact, many birds were now singing and displaying in the cool afternoon sunshine. The noise was phenomenal with the plains full of lark song. It was as if dawn had come several hours too late. Conditions were near perfect, but could we find the bird? At this point, we decided to take a risk and split up. I dropped Tom off and drove up the road, stopping periodically to have a scan and listen. This was a high-risk strategy as it meant that potentially one of us might miss the bird while the other got it, but at least we were covering more ground this way. Tom phoned:

'I think I might have heard a Dupont's.'

'Okay, are you sure?'

'No, but it probably was. I can't hear it now.'

'Right. I'll see you in a bit.'

At the end of the call, I was not that convinced whether he had heard one or not, so I kept on birding and listening out for Dupont's where I was. Ten minutes later I got a text.

'Defo Dupont's.'

I was about a hundred yards up the road and he was onto one of the most elusive birds in Europe. I reversed back up the road as fast as possible. I could not be bothered doing a fifty point turn on the narrow road. I got to Tom who was about twenty yards off the side of the road. I phoned him:

'Where the chuffin' hell is it?'

'It's somewhere to my right and singing pretty regularly.'

'Have you seen it then?'

'No, it's just been singing.'

'Shit, right, I'll get my scope up. How far is it in?'

'Not too far. You should be able to hear it okay from where you are.'

I hung up and grabbed the tripod and scope, as much in hope as anything. Within seconds, I heard the unmistakeable fluty song of the Dupont's. We were close and literally seconds later I spotted it sitting on a rock. Il Diablo! It was an absolute piece of cake. I rang Tom again:

'I've got it.'

'What, singing?'

'No, it's sat on a rock to your right. I've got it in the scope. Get over here quick.'

I was then able to watch the rather amusing spectacle of Tom scuttling across the rocks with his scope. I also kept a good eye on the Dupont's. His back did not seem quite so debilitating now Il Diablo had put in an appearance. The healing powers of Il Diablo are as yet undocumented by modern science but there is research to be done. Mind you there is nothing worse in terms of birding pressure than when a rare bird is showing and you know it may disappear at any second before you get to it. It has happened to everyone who has ever picked up a pair of bins. Yes, that dreaded greeting 'it's just gone out of view, mate', 'you should have been here five minutes ago' or 'I've just lost it'. It is absolutely gutting to miss a bird by seconds. Dupont's was also the sort of bird that was not that likely to reappear. It was now or never for my brother. Fortunately for Tom this Dupont's stayed put and we watched it on and off for the next thirty minutes. Occasionally, it would sit up on a rock and give belting scope views before scuttling off amongst the rocks to feed. A second bird also started singing from the other side of the road.

A Swiss birder joined us and was absolutely elated to jam in on it. He was ecstatic. We later bumped into two Belgian birders who had driven past us and had simply missed it. They mentioned that they had seen us but had not bothered to stop. I guess that's the difference between the two countries right there: Swiss efficiency and fantastic watches versus overrated chocolate and the self-acclaimed inventors of 'frites'! It must have been very obvious what we were looking at in that habitat. El Diablo had fallen very easily in the end. The weather, which had seemingly been our enemy in the morning, had proven critical. The sunny afternoon spell had got everything up singing and feeding. It was a brilliant afternoon. To cap it all, we had a quick roadside stop near Villaseca on the way to the hotel where we got onto a mixed group of raptors. Amongst the many Griffon Vultures, we had fantastic views of an immature Golden Eagle, a Booted Eagle and a Short-toed Eagle, all in the evening sunlight. We had seen six species of lark and ten species of raptor, as well as a host of other classic Spanish birds. It was a simply magical birding day.

The next few days in Extremadura were just as successful. We left Sepúlveda in torrential rain. It slammed down all the way to Monfragüe which put pay to my chances of picking up a couple of ticks en route. This meant that I missed out on Rock Thrush and Pied Wheatear.

We birded Monfragüe for a couple of hours in mixed weather but had some good birds, including Red-rumped Swallow and Black Vulture, before heading off to the much vaunted

Finca Santa Marta, our accommodation for the next five nights. It was about seven o'clock in the evening when we got there and both of us were ravenous. I enquired about dinner only to find that they could not provide it as we needed to book. We could simply not believe our ears. I had exchanged multiple e-mails with them about our arrival time and our booking. The requirement to pre-book meals had never merited a mention by them. It was not as if it was an open restaurant for all comers but rather was purely for paying residents such as ourselves. What kind of establishment allows their paying guests to turn up mid-evening without giving them the opportunity to book a meal? It was as if they just did not give a damn. Instead, we were directed to a restaurant a couple of miles down the road. It was a rather odd place as it was in the middle of nowhere, had a huge dining room and was almost empty. It surpassed all expectations with great rustic food and wine. The wine did not even have a label on the bottle. It was sumptuous though. I had a superb dish of fried potatoes mixed with eggs in a huge tureen. Even better, two British birders showed up and gave us a load of gen, particularly for Black-shouldered Kite and Red-necked Nightjar, for which there were no longer too many reliable sites. I had my maps in the car so we could get pinpoint locations and great directions.

We returned to the Finca Santa Marta satiated and pleased with our luck. I ordered a couple of packed lunches for the following day at the exorbitant price of €12 a head, so was expecting something a bit spectacular. The next morning at breakfast I enquired where the lunches had got to, expecting to see a couple of laden hampers, only to be told that we had to make our own from the remains of the buffet breakfast. Being birders, we would have done that anyway for nothing. I could not believe it. For €12 we were being told to make our own packed lunch out of leftovers. As a rule, I do not like complaining but for once I kicked up a stink. We made our lunches taking phenomenal amounts of food out of spite more than anything. To be fair, they had the decency not to charge us when the bill for our stay arrived. However, as a result, we refused to eat there anymore and went out to the odd restaurant down the road for dinner and skipped breakfast as this used up quality birding time anyway. So much for the vaunted Finca Santa Marta. It was a rip off; the one breakfast we had was average, our room was not that clean and their customer service was poor. On the plus side, there are some decent birds to be seen around the grounds.

We ended up clearing up on nearly all of our target birds around Monfragüe, which included some special sightings. Probably my favourite was Eurasian Eagle Owl, which nests on the cliffs at the Portilla del Tiétar, a huge bush-covered rock face. You really need to know where the nest is to have any chance of finding the owls. Fortunately for us, we met an English couple who pointed out the chicks at the nest on the cliff face. We got the scopes on them when one of the adults suddenly appeared out of the bushes behind and then flew down across the cliff face. What a bonus to see an adult bird. We had also been given precise directions from the birders that we had met in the restaurant for a Black-winged Kite stake-out near Madrigalejo, involving lines of Eucalyptus trees, ponds and finally a stand of Holm Oaks where the birds were nesting. Without that information, we would never have seen them. We got there early in the morning and were treated to stunning views of a pair of birds guarding their territory, looking like two miniature Barn Owls as they hunted and fended off Red Kites. We also picked up bee-eaters, Rollers and Gull-billed Terns. It proved to be a fantastic birding site.

The other memorable moment was after a long hard and hot day in the field looking for Bustards and Sandgrouse on the plains near Santa Marta de Magasca. We had started off well with a distant Little Bustard but afterwards had struggled in the hazy heat. I had quite luckily stumbled on a large flock of Black-bellied Sandgrouse. They were absolutely miles away and the heat haze was badly distorting our views. I could tell they were Sandgrouse, but only just. I could not pin them down to one of the two possible species in the area. We stayed with them for over an hour. Eventually, a little bit of cloud caused the haze to dissipate slightly and, as luck would have it, a couple of the birds were just close enough to show their diagnostic features. I had my scope on 60x magnification and was mightily relieved to clinch the identification. We spent much of the afternoon aimlessly looking for Great Bustard which eventually just appeared out of nowhere in a field. We met a few birders but nobody seemed to have caught up with our final target bird, Pin-tailed Sandgrouse. As evening approached, we decided to make our way back along the crumbling road that leads through the plains. We played the CDs of the calls in the car which proved to be very useful as we picked up more Black-bellied Sandgrouse on call before eventually getting good views. About ten minutes later, I remarked to Tom that we could just do with a bit of luck on the bloody Pin-taileds.

The words had scarcely left my mouth when two of them flew past the car. It was a crazy coincidental moment, signifying that when your luck is in it is most definitely in. We stopped nearby and then had great views of four more birds, calling like Jackdaws as they flew past. This was followed by more Great and Little Bustards as well as a superb Stone Curlew, many Montagu's Harriers and a distant Imperial Eagle. We had wrapped up again. It was another cracking day. I enjoyed that day's birding a lot. I had never seen bustards or Sandgrouse before. Both are a bit different and really have the 'feel' of being exotic foreign birds. Bustards are big birds, almost too big. They are quite incongruous, almost like a European version of an Ostrich. I liked them and they had given me a taste of something special and I fancied more of the same.

In many ways, our success on that holiday meant that mainland Spain only held a handful of birds left for me to see, all of which were mainly in the south but nothing in the league of Dupont's Lark, Lammergeier or Wallcreeper. I did toy with the idea of a third trip to get White-headed Duck, Red-knobbed Coot, White-rumped Swift and a few other species that I needed, but they did not have anything like the allure of the big three. However, there was a bird that I desperately wanted to see, Houbara Bustard, which was not present on the Spanish mainland but could be found on the Canary Islands. An idea for another trip with a single iconic target was hatching in my mind. Any British twitcher from the 1960s or 70s will hold Houbara Bustard in a legendary light. Only a handful of birders have it on their British list from a single bird that appeared in Suffolk in late 1962. It has never been recorded in Britain since. There are some famous grainy black and white photographs of it that the renowned bird photographer, Eric Hosking, took through his car window. Every British twitcher worth his salt knows about the Suffolk Houbara. It was perhaps the bird that started twitching as we now know it. Sadly in my eyes, Houbara Bustard has now been reclassified as two separate species, MacQueen's and Houbara Bustards. The Suffolk bird is of the MacQueen's species and technically should no longer be referred to as a Houbara. MacQueen's just does not have the same ring to as it as Houbara. It also dents the legend. To me and many others, it will always be a Houbara and not a MacQueen's – despite the scientific reclassification to the contrary. Being fickle, I would be more than happy to tick them both as separate species, but in terms of the legend I like Houbara most. The Great and Little Bustards of Extremadura had whetted my appetite. I also wanted to see a legend and so I began plotting another birding trip with Houbara Bustard very much in my thoughts. The Canary Island birds are actually Houbara Bustards ironically enough. What I did not know was that I was going to embark on one of the most embarrassing and disastrous birding episodes of my life and it would all be because of my quest to see the Houbara Bustard.

Unlike my previous two Spanish escapades, Tom was not coming along. His replacement was Vicky who had vehemently promised not to get in the way of my birding. In return, she got a free 'holiday' and the pleasure of my company. I was more than happy to have her along though and knew that I would have a much better time with her than being on my own. It was a twin centre trip with three days on Fuerteventura and three on Tenerife. I spent hours reading trip reports and came up with a hit list including twenty-two lifers of which ten were endemics. I had no chance of bagging them all, but top of the pile were the Houbara and Cream-coloured Courser on Fuerteventura, with Blue Chaffinch and Atlantic Canary on Tenerife. I was also keen to see both endemic Pigeon species, Bolle's & Laurel.

The holiday was doomed from the start. Our Thomas Cook flight was delayed by six and a half hours, meaning that my planned afternoon of birding, searching for Houbaras on the plains of Costa Calma, were in tatters. I ended up spending a small fortune on clothes in Fatface and on the quiz machine at Manchester Airport while we waited. We landed just before 10.00pm and only just made it to the Hertz desk for the hire car. God knows what would have happened if we had missed it. Fortunately, our little apartment was okay and we even managed to get a half decent meal just around the corner. The next morning, I was up at first light and found that we were right on the doorstep of the Bustard area. I headed off in the car out onto the tracks that criss-crossed the arid plains. In no time at all I scored with a Spectacled Warbler and Stone Curlew in the early morning half-light. I found a good track which seemed to take me into the middle of the plains but it petered out at a rocky ridge line. I did get my first lifer there though, a Berthelot's Pipit, which allowed great close-up views. One down and twenty-one to go.

Behind me, I could hear the occasional lark-like 'chirrup' but there was no sign of any birds. A sort of sixth sense told me to check out a small shady gully just out of view. There I found the culprits, ten Lesser Short-toed Larks, another lifer. I went for a drive round and picked up a couple of Hoopoes and a Southern Grey Shrike but was unable to find a decent way through the maze of tracks. Eventually, I returned to my original spot and spent ages scanning the plains with my scope but could not pull out a Houbara. I picked up the call of Black-bellied Sandgrouse but failed to see them at all. There was a fair old breeze which was making it hard to hear the calls and get any bearing on the birds. After a couple of hours, the heat was starting to build and the birding was literally dead. I did not fancy travelling too far on foot in the heat, so I retraced my steps back to the car. I had a closer look at the ridge and noticed a bit of a track which looked just about passable in the car. Further along it joined a really good track. I decided to go for it and negotiated the car up the ridge, avoiding a couple of prominent rocks and across a bit of light sand on a rock base. I made it without a hitch and was able to continue birding. I call it birding in the loosest possible sense as I saw absolutely bugger all. I eventually turned the car round and decided to head for home. I sent Vic a text to say I was on my way and would be back within the hour.

On a whim, I decided to take a different route back and turned left at a fork in the track. As the track sloped downwards I could see some sand ahead. Buoyed by my earlier success on the ridge, I cavalierly ploughed the car downhill. It shifted to the left as it hit the sand and promptly became stuck. I was on a downwards slope and in front of me was about 15 yards of sandy track before the road became solid again. With some digging, I managed to get a bit further down the track before getting well and truly stuck again. My near-side wheel was in a big drift of sand which I could not dig out as it just kept refilling with sand. Reality was dawning on me. I had got the car stuck and the chances were that it was not going to come out easily. I was miles from anywhere with no spade, no water and no one in sight. The air temperature was also boiling hot. I started wedging rocks under the tyres but it was useless. I tried everything. I had the car mats out under the tyres and stacks of stones but nothing was working. I even jacked the car up so I could get more rocks underneath but the sand was just too deep. The more I dug sand away, the more it started to refill with loose sand from the side of the hole.

Distant memories from Hong Kong came flooding back to me when I was in charge of our command car in the Emergency (999) Unit. Early one morning when working a night shift, we had been looking for illegal immigrants at a beach on the south side of Hong Kong Island. Without warning, the driver drove straight out onto the sandy beach and promptly got stuck. It took the four of us in the vehicle and another van crew about an hour to get us back on *terra firma*. I was particularly unnerved by the possibility of the press turning up and taking a photograph. It would have been a front-page picture no doubt. I could just see it on the front page of the South China Morning Post and imagine the ensuing ribbing I would have to endure from my mates and countless others. It did not bear thinking about. Fortunately, it was too early in the morning and no one was about.

Back in Fuerteventura, I was completely on my own without any police colleagues to help out and it wasn't looking good. As I dug and moved rocks, I heard a 'kee kee kee' call from close by. There in front of me perched on a rock was a fantastic juvenile Barbary Falcon. Unbelievably, an adult bird arrived as well but promptly shot off when it spied me standing there covered in sweat and sand. At any other time, I would have revelled in this sighting, a lifer as well, but I just could not enjoy it because of my predicament. I threw in one final monstrous effort by piling loads of rocks beneath the wheels and digging a beach full of sand away. I even built a mini road of stones and car mats in front. It looked good. I clambered into the driver's seat, turned on the engine and gently engaged the accelerator. I gunned the engine, the car lurched forward an inch, rocks fired off at all angles and I finally came to terms with the inevitable conclusion: the car was not going anywhere and that I was an inept, stupid imbecile.

Time was also pushing on and eventually I decided to make the dreaded call to Vic. This was probably the worst of it all for me. I could cope with being covered in sand, parched, being stuck in the middle of nowhere and dying in the desert of heat exhaustion. It was the prospect of humiliation and oncoming ignominy that was really upsetting me. I knew there was a good story in it, a story where I starred as the prize clown. I would look like a complete tit. It was going to be public news. I could envisage her drunkenly recounting it to friends and guffawing with laughter as she did so. Jesus, I had to face reality. There was no chance of getting away with it like I had in Hong Kong. I pressed the green phone button on my mobile:

'Hiya – it's me again.'

'Oh good, are you coming back soon. I'm starving.'

Well, I've had a bit of a problem. Uh, I've got the car stuck in the sand...'

'What are you?'

The answer was 'a complete tit', but I didn't respond. I was totally hacked off. I had dipped on Houbara and got the bloody car stuck in the bloody desert. There was nothing for it but to walk back to town. On the walk back, I noticed my fingers and hands starting to stiffen as if I was losing the sensation in them. The dehydration was kicking in. An hour later I was back in our apartment, feeling very hot, grumpy and desperate for a drink. I was praying that Vic had been to the supermarket and had stocked up on water. She had not. She poured me a glass of tepid tap water which was undrinkable in spite of my hour of need. I am not even sure that Fuerteventura tap water is potable. My feelings of humiliation were exacerbated by Vicky's look of disdainful disbelief. To be fair to her, she did not say too much.

After a shower, we headed to the supermarket where I drank bottles of cold water like a man who had been out in the desert for too long. In fact, I was a man who had been out in the desert for too long! It tasted so good. The afternoon was spent arranging to get the car towed out. Eventually, a couple of expats turned up in a 4x4 with a tow rope. I was sat in the back with a limited view and was struggling to pick out the track that I had taken earlier. I got them to take the long way round via La Pared where I finally got my bearings and located the car. We soon had the rope attached to the two vehicles and my car came out no problem at all. My relief was short-lived when it came to detaching the rope. The nylon rope had pulled the knots so taut that we could not untie them from the cars. This was just getting stupid. Fortunately, one of the vehicles had a tow hook rather than a loop and after much cajoling I managed to get the rope off otherwise I would have been walking back to town again for a knife. It cost me €50 for the tow out which I could have done without but it felt cheap enough considering my predicament. To cap it all, I left my binoculars in my rescuer's car and had to call him back after he had gone. I felt like I was starring in 'Holidays from Hell'. That evening, I tried again for the Houbara but, true to form, dipped again. I still had one full day left on Fuerteventura before island hopping to Tenerife. I was determined to get the Houbara come what may.

I set the alarm on my phone early for a dawn start the next morning but awoke late to broad sunlight streaming in the bedroom window. The alarm had been set to weekdays only and had not gone off, it being a Saturday. I legged it out of the apartment and hit the same tracks as the day before but was considerably more circumspect with my driving. As I approached the ridge, I saw a large bird on the plains in front of me. This was it, my luck had changed and here was the Houbara at last. I stopped the car in an instant, put up my bins and started to 'grill' the Houbara. I could not believe my eyes as I was looking at an adult Yellow-legged Gull. How could this be? It was like a mirage. I still could not believe it. It had been there, hadn't it? I looked again. It was still a gull and not a Houbara. Maybe I was hallucinating after the previous night's goat kid stew. I can honestly say that I have never been so fed up in all my birding life as at that moment. I had glimpsed that gull and, in my haste and excitement, just assumed I had hit the jackpot. What an absolute sickener. I kept looking at it and the surrounding area to make sure. No matter how I tried, it remained a Yellow-legged Gull. I parked up feeling absolutely gutted and set off on foot. I was beginning to feel cursed.

There was nothing doing apart from the odd rabbit or goat. After an hour or so I was getting seriously fed up as there were just no birds at all. I changed tactics and decided to get on to some high ground. As I broke the sky line, I saw the silhouette of a long-necked bird walking away from me. It was too small for a Houbara but proved to be a beautiful Cream-coloured Courser. It was one of a pair and they both gave me stunning views. They were so tame and fearless. There was also a flyover Barbary Falcon, probably the same juvenile bird from the day before. This time I was more appreciative. I had expected it to be a very tough bird to get. There was also a Lesser Short-toed Lark and a surreal Stone Curlew standing statuesquely among the rocks. It proved to be a fantastic detour but alas no Houbara. I went back to Vic, pleased with the courser but still desperate for the bustard.

Unlike me, Vic had experienced quite a chilled – if not slightly boring – 24 hours and was unusually up for a day out birding with me. I had to chivvy her to get a move on as she was oblivious to the fact that I needed to get out and make the most of the coolness of the morning. We headed for La Lajita, a good site for the endemic Fuerteventura Chat, Laughing Dove and Barbary Partridge. When we got there, I was not too impressed with the habitat. There were also a lot of tourists waiting to go on camel rides. All I got in the end were two naturalised escapees in the form of Monk Parakeet and Common Myna. I am not into this plastic fantastic lark and was more than ready to move on. We continued up the coast to just south of the airport to Barranco de la Torre, which is a well-known site for the chat.

We got there about midday and it was becoming hot, far from ideal birding conditions. Still I had no choice and headed off down the valley. Vic inexplicably decided to remain at the car reading her book in the shade. A Sardinian Warbler flitted in front of me, giving me some hope that birds might be active. I headed towards some palm trees to get shade and cover when a flock of Plain Swifts appeared overhead, providing another lifer for my list. I made my way to the shade of the cliff at the bottom of the Barranco where I flushed a pair of Egyptian Vultures, both affording me fantastic close-range views. I moved away quickly, suspecting that they might be a breeding pair and not wishing to disturb them further. Still there was no sign of the chat. It was looking poor for passerines in the afternoon heat and another dip appeared to be on the cards. I decided to have a quick scan around a grassy goat field and, suddenly, my luck changed as I flushed a flurry of birds. Berthelot's Pipit was the first, quickly followed by an immature Fuerteventura Chat and then a nice adult. As I watched the chats fly, I noticed two birds unobtrusively feeding a few feet away. These turned out to be a pair of Trumpeter Finches and another lifer. What is it about Trumpeter Finches and birding with Vic? It was good, albeit hot, birding but at least some of my targets had fallen. It was time to get back to the car for water and some food.

Over a lunch of Calamari and chips, Vic seemed surprised to hear that I was not done for the day. I broke the news that we were heading for La Oliva, a well-known Houbara stake-out. We spent the next three to four hours driving up and down the road interspersed with many stops for me to scan the plains for the Houbara Bustard. Cream-coloured Courser, Lesser Short-toed Larks, more Egyptian Vultures, and a *dacotiae* race Kestrel were scant reward for the effort. I would have waited until dusk and probably should have, but Vic was at the end of her patience. It had been a long and fruitless vigil. The whole Houbara saga had been a calamitous disaster. From getting the car stuck, hallucinating over a Yellow-legged Gull and spending hours scanning barren desert. What a sad experience. I guess Houbara Bustard was not to be. I had failed and missed out on a legend. I have not been back to Spain or the Canaries since. The pain of that dip remains. I need to exorcise the demon. In the words of Arnold Schwarzenegger, 'I'll be back!'

HITTING 400
2013-2014

If any half decent birder or twitcher worth his salt was to look at my birding statistics they would not be overly impressed. When Jack was born, my listing took a bit of a back seat and for a couple of years my British List barely moved. It was meandering around the 370 mark. Some of the top twitchers are not far off 600 which puts my list in perspective. Mind you, I do not include Ireland and they do, so that brings their totals down a bit. I just do not quite get how Eire has conveniently slipped onto many birders British lists. Where do you stop? Calais? Agincourt? Hitting 400 used to be a twitching landmark and it is still not a bad achievement, but for a few years I could see little prospect of uncorking the bubbly. There is even a club called the 'UK 400' run by Lee Evans, one of Britain's leading twitchers. I guess seeing 500 birds in the UK is the new benchmark, but 400 still takes serious effort.

Sometimes in life events beyond your control have unforeseeable ramifications. In 2009, I changed job and moved to a company called Vaultex as their Head of Security & Safety. Britannia Building Society, where I had happily worked for nine years, had 'merged' with the Co-op Bank. We had all received the usual reassurances that we would be treated fairly and that it was not a takeover, but everyone could see it was all just corporate spin. The place was in mayhem, so I made up my mind to get out early. I do not know exactly what the redundancy count is since the Co-op got its hands on Britannia but it is probably not far short of a thousand. I managed to secure a cracking job with Vaultex as well as walk away with a nice fat cheque as part of a tidy redundancy package courtesy of the shambolic company that I was leaving behind.

The new job proved to be just the ticket in terms of career motivation – interesting, challenging and good people to work with. It also meant that I had to travel the country which in itself offered opportunities for birding and twitching. To be fair, I had been there about eighteen months before I really started to consider the possibility of adding to my list. The first time I gave it a shot was when I had scheduled a trip to Colchester to visit one of our centres and, as luck would have it, a Short-toed Treecreeper had turned up at Landguard Point in Suffolk. I got up ridiculously early and nailed the bird first thing before heading off to Colchester for the day. I did feel a bit naughty and slightly duplicitous as if I was a kid smoking behind the bike shed. That feeling did not last too long. A very tough tick had been chalked up and the guilt had most certainly faded by the time I got to Colchester. My British list was moving again. Since then I managed quite a few decent ticks through job-related travelling. If there was something about en route then I got up ridiculously early and hit the road. Greater Yellowlegs, Little Bittern, Bonaparte's Gull, Savi's Warbler, Stilt Sandpiper, Sandhill Crane, Siberian Stonechat, Spectacled

Warbler, Penduline Tit, Short-toed Eagle and Myrtle Warbler have all been successfully bagged on work trips. Work simply put me in the right place at the right time, more or less. Admittedly the detours for rare birds did get longer!

I have had also some horrendous misses, though. Both Desert Warbler and Pacific Swift had both been seen the day before I was due to travel to sites nearby. Tom got both birds on a famous Norfolk trip back in 1993, along with Oriental Pratincole. He rang me in the middle of the night when I was in Hong Kong to regale me with his sightings. I was knackered and could not get him off the phone as he described each sighting in minute detail. It was reminiscent of that Curlew Sandpiper at Minsmere all those years before. He never did consider the time difference when he called me. If the phone went at 3.00am then I knew it was him ringing me about birding or Sheffield United, or both. I always answered just in case it was bad news about Mum or Dad. It was quite a relief to find that he was just ringing me to 'share the joy' about his latest tick. I always felt a tinge of guilt if I went birding on work days, but it was largely overshadowed by the thought of getting something back on work time. New birds felt better if I was at work! It was like a corporate bonus to me. I worked hard and had my fair share of inhospitable hours, nights away from home and hours spent on the motorway, not to mention calls in the middle of the night. I guess it is called bird / work life balance, or have I got that wrong?

Anyway, my job meant that I had managed to get my British list rolling again and that 400 was becoming a real possibility. In 2014, I set myself some personal targets. This was something that I had never really done before but I felt that

I needed some kind of catalyst in life. I am an odd person in that I can be incredibly motivated or incredibly lazy at times. I don't even understand the paradox myself of how I can be so different. Once I have made up my mind to do something though, I bloody well do it. When I gave up smoking, I just did it – that was it for me. I did not need e-cigarettes or any of that nonsense. So, the goals were probably a good thing for me. It meant that I would deliver. There were only two that I could think of that I really wanted to do. How crass is that? I can only come up with two goals! They were both about birding too. Anyway, one was to hit 400 species in the UK and the other was to write this book and get it published. If I wasn't so shallow then I would feel guilty about my lack of altruism towards dedicating my goals to a good cause. Hardly inspirational, but that is me. Other more decent people go and run a marathon or swim the channel and raise money for charity, do voluntary work or put something back into society. What do I do? I go birding and write a book about birding. I go and do stuff for me, not anyone less fortunate or in need. It says a lot about me. The charge to 400 British ticks was on though and my mind was set.

For Tom's fiftieth birthday, I had suggested that we had a week's birding together on Fair Isle, which is part of the Shetland Isles. Neither of us had ever been there before. We had done Scilly to death and, to be honest, I was starting to turn over the same rare species year in, year out. I have now seen several Pied Wheatears, Red-eyed Vireos, Rustic Buntings, Olive-backed Pipits and Isabelline Shrikes there – all great birds, but they were not doing my life list much good. It was time for a change. As it was his birthday and a big one at that, I had paid for the airfare to Shetland for him. Fair Isle has a reputation for rare birds like no other. It is the mecca for rarities in the British Isles, and September/October is the ultimate time to go. Prior to our departure, the winds had been blowing strongly from the east for days, so the chances of a Siberian rarity were looking good. I met up with Tom at a Birmingham airport hotel the night before our flight. The plan was to fly to Aberdeen, get the connecting flight to Sumburgh on mainland Shetland and head up to Tingwall Airfield using public transport. It was a full day of travelling, involving three flights, a bus ride, a walk and a taxi. And we would still be in Britain at the end of it all! Despite the quality look of the winds, good birds were few and far between on Fair Isle. The prevailing theory seemed to be that the wind was too strong and that birds were shooting straight over. I had hardly looked at what was on Shetland mainland because I did not think we would have any birding time there and that we would be stretched to make it up to Tingwall for the flight. All my thoughts had been focussed on Fair Isle, so I had not really got much of a clue about birding mainland Shetland at all.

The night before flying, Tom mentioned that there was a Pechora Pipit at a place called Levenwick and thought that it might be worth a shot en route to Lerwick. I was slightly sceptical but tentatively agreed to consider it if the Pipit was available the next day. We checked out the map and it looked feasible. Our plans of catching the bus from Sumburgh to Lerwick were well and truly shredded when the pager went off at Aberdeen airport announcing that the Pechora was still around. Now, Pechora Pipit is a true Shetland speciality with hardly any seen on the British mainland. Along with Lanceolated and

Pallas's Grashopper Warblers, Pechora Pipit is right up there as a bird that every birder goes to Shetland for. It was also a lifer for both of us. On the flight, we discussed our options and decided that we would grab a taxi at the airport and head to Levenwick. Fifty odd quid lighter, we pulled up in our taxi at Levenwick. The taxi meter was running, so the pressure was on to get on the bird before we blew too much more money. Speed was of the essence as money and time were ticking by – literally. Fortunately, a birder was present as we arrived and he told us to walk through some grass where the bird had flown into. Minutes later it flushed, flew up and landed in front of us. In the bright light, I could make out the diagnostic zebra stripes on the mantle. It was a little cracker. Pechora Pipit was in the bag. I got dazzling scope views in fantastic light. We were ecstatic but had no time to waste as we needed to kill off that taxi bill, so we piled back into the cab and headed to the Queen's Head in Lerwick for a celebration pint of Belhaven Black and a bite of lunch.

We then had to find another twelve quid for the taxi bus up to Tingwall airport. As we arrived, the weather was beautiful with bright blue skies but with a fair wind blowing. We were greeted with the news that our flights to Fair Isle would not be going as it was too breezy for the small plane to land safely there. This was a major blow to our plans. We had no alternative but to find some digs in Lerwick. The next day, it hammered down with rain and blew a howler, meaning that our flights were off yet again. We were nevertheless summoned to the airport to have it confirmed that the flights were cancelled with more taxi money going down the pan. We salvaged something of the day by doing a bit of birding locally in Lerwick, but it was 'Monsoon' birding. On the Friday, we made the now familiar journey to the airport and spent most of the day sitting in the waiting room watching *Cash in the Attic* and various other mind-numbing daytime TV programmes. We were told that a go / no go decision would be made at 3.00pm. By this time, we were both getting hacked off and could see our holiday evaporating before our eyes. Nearly three days had flashed by and we had not been anywhere and had hardly raised our binoculars. Thank God we had seen the pipit. There was only so much more of that bloody waiting room that I could stand – not to mention yet another episode of *Homes Under the Hammer*!

Just before three o'clock, the pager bleeped into life with the Mega alert going crazy carrying the news of a Thick-billed Warbler at Geosetter, about twenty miles away. Thick-billed Warbler is seriously rare and up to this point had been nigh on impossible to see in Britain. Suddenly, getting on to Fair Isle was not looking so attractive. I turned to Tom.

'I think we might as well sack Fair Isle and stay on Shetland. What do you reckon to hiring a car and staying on?'

'That's exactly what I was thinking too. I didn't want to say this as you had put so much effort into trying to get us on Fair Isle. Do you think we can get to see the Thick-billed?'

'Too right. I really can't be bothered with Fair Isle now; we're just wasting our holiday. Let's get out of here as soon as we can.'

Within the next few minutes, confirmation came that there would be no flights to Fair Isle and that we should try again tomorrow. Bugger that! I told the lady that we were no longer interested in flying to Fair Isle and to strike us off the list. There was no way that we were going to spend a single minute more in that waiting room, wasting our precious time. I took a final glance at the TV; Jasmine Harman clonking round a Spanish villa in high heels in yet another re-run of *Home in the Sun* on the TV. It was no contest. We walked out. The Thick-billed Warbler had won hands down. We took yet another taxi and headed off to get the hire car. Within an hour, we were on our way to Geosetter and had managed to book back in at the Braeview Guest House in Lerwick for the remaining nights of our stay.

Naturally, the Thick-billed was not showing when we arrived. It was holed up in a field of oats. We had a fair vantage point. Minutes ticked by, fifteen, thirty, when suddenly a bird broke cover, flew a short distance and dropped back into the oats. This happened a couple more times. Everyone kept getting terrible views. As soon as you got your bins on it, the bird would drop back into the oats. I could tell it was something odd and could see that it had a fair old-sized tail but that was about it. Eventually, it flushed out of the oats and went deep into cover in an adjacent shrub-filled gully. The assembled throng panicked and charged en masse towards the area. It was like being in a herd of stampeding wildebeest! A metaphorical wild goose chase then ensued as rumour control went into overdrive. We rushed again en masse up the gully in pursuit of something or possibly nothing. No one seemed sure where it had gone or what we were looking for. To further mix metaphors, we were like sheep in a flock, mindless and as one, following something, desperately sticking together, not wanting to miss out. It was purely a safety in numbers exercise and nothing else. As we headed back down the ravine, there was a confirmed sighting back where we had all started! We packed the side of the gully in a mass body of binoculars and green coats, silent, expectant, and all desperately anxious. It must have been a tick for everyone there. This time it flew right over my head. I could hardly focus on it as I desperately twisted my neck to see it better. I had seen enough to tick it though – just. A list blocker if ever there was one. The next day we went back to have another look. As luck would have it, the bird was still there. I ended up getting at least three good flight views, one of which was with it flying directly at me from across the oat

Tom happy after seeing a Thick-billed Warbler

field. It was at eye level and just seemed to be looking at me as it flew. One of the toughest birds to see in Britain had fallen.

Over the next few days that remained, we kept picking up very good birds. I added Eastern Olivaceous Warbler, Eastern Subalpine Warbler and Blyth's Reed Warbler to my British list. We also both fell in love with the island of Unst, which is the most northerly place in the British Isles and more or less on a line with Stavanger in Norway. We headed up there on a particularly foul day hoping to get the Blyth's Reed that had been there for a few days. The forecast was horrendous throughout the day across Shetland. However, the weather gods smiled upon us on arrival as we hit a little break in the weather front. There were birds everywhere and they were taking advantage of the dry weather to feed and dry off. We had also hit a 'fall'. Literally, as we stopped the car, Tom spotted a very white finch-like bird sitting in a tree. I told him to stay on it while I got the scope up. It proved to be the feathered snowball itself, a Hornemann's Arctic Redpoll. What is more, it was our own find and a little stunner. Sadly, it flew off after less than a minute never to be seen again. What a bird though. Our spirits were up and we were convinced that there were other rare birds to be found. There were Blackcaps everywhere; every time I looked, I seemed to find them.

There are certain birds that you just seem to have an eye for. Blackcap is a very common species but I see too many of them. Don't get me wrong, there is nothing wrong with Blackcaps, but if there is one around then I will spot it, usually before anyone else. When I am in a migration hot spot like the Scillies or Shetland, it can get frustrating on seeing fifty per cent more Blackcaps than anyone else. The phrase 'not another chuffing

Blackcap' is something that I repeatedly mutter to myself. It was Tom that first noticed it some years back on Scilly and since then I have become painfully aware of it. I will see a movement in a likely bush for a scarce migrant and it will be a Blackcap. The leaves move, a new bird is appearing and, lo and behold, you've guessed it: Blackcap. There are also some birds that you seem to be just plain lucky with. Others may struggle but I seem to get them. Waxwing is the one for me. I am good at finding them and running into them. You just cannot see enough Waxwings as they are scarce and stunning looking. My run on Waxwings started back in 1992, when Tom and I were on our way to watch the mighty Blades take on Luton Town in the FA Cup. We had parked the car outside a pub called The Stag's Head about a mile from the ground, where we had stopped for a couple of pre-match pints. As we left, we saw a few birders with telescopes looking into the trees. We went over and asked if we could have a look. They (the birders) were a bit wary at first, probably because they thought we were football hooligans taking the Mickey. We explained that we were that rare breed, football-supporting birders on the way to the match. They looked a bit dubious but I guess they had a right to be a bit circumspect when birding near Bramall Lane. Waxwing was a lifer for Tom so he was ecstatic. United won 4:0, making it a perfect day. Football, beer and birding – now that's the way to go! I also got chatted up by a beautiful lady Blade while standing in the pie queue at the match. Okay, that actually never happened but it should have!

In 1996, I remember sitting in Tom's flat in Hampton when he was at work. There was a Rowan tree outside laden with berries and I thought to myself that it looked just right for a Waxwing. About half an hour later, I glanced out the window and there were five Waxwings in the tree, feeding away! Every now and then those mental predictions just come true. Since then I have found Waxwings while at work in the Britannia offices in Leek and twice in my garden. The second time I was replenishing the feeders when a flock of about twenty flew right over my head. My luck does not just lie with Bohemian Waxwing (the species most often seen in the UK) either. In 1996, I had set out on a 'double strike' twitch with Black-throated Thrush and Cedar Waxwing as the targets. I got the thrush feeding on someone's drive near Peterborough in the morning and hightailed back up to Nottingham for the Cedar Waxwing. As I was looking for the right spot, I spied a group of birders with binoculars and scopes pointing upwards at a berry-clad Rowan tree. I jumped out of the car and peered through someone's scope where I was greeted with crippling, but momentary, views of the Cedar Waxwing. At this point the whole flock took off. Nobody connected with it over the rest of the day and it proves to be a very elusive bird at times. Cedar Waxwing was – and still is – an exceptionally rare bird in the UK with only a handful of records.

Anyway, back to sorting through our 'fall' on Unst. I found a very strange-looking Lesser Whitethroat, one of the eastern forms. It looked nothing like any 'Lesserthroat' that I had ever seen before. We then found a Hawfinch that had been reported there – closely followed by another one. The second bird was very grotty indeed. There were some weird-looking Chiffchaffs to be seen too. One of them was a grey bird with black secondaries and primaries on the wing and again was probably some kind of eastern form. I hold my hands up and agree that I am just not good enough at birding to pin these birds down to a particular race. I'm just happy to get the species right! This felt as if we were birding in a different league. It was like playing in the Champions League for the first time and finding that you were a bit out of your depth. Manchester City fans will know what I mean by this. We had to be on our mettle as we could easily mess up on a mega with all these strange eastern forms of the commoner species. There were just so many birds, mainly Blackcaps and Chiffchaffs, but also good numbers of Bramblings and at least five Yellow-browed Warblers. Best of all, we flushed a Long-eared Owl from a pine tree. I had a brilliant view of its angry orange eyes staring down at me later on when it had returned to its favourite roost, which happened to be in the only pine tree for miles around. The whole experience was magical.

We found the Blyth's Reed Warbler site and spent an hour or so staking it out without success before the weather deteriorated. Those few hours on Unst are right up there with my best birding moments ever. We had found a British rarity, seen some great birds and lots of eastern types in amongst them. However, I did come to hate the little patch of bushes where the Blyth's Reed Warbler had been seen. We went back there on our last day and spent literally all day staking it out, seeing nothing. We had both had just about enough and were ready for home when we agreed to give it one last try. The weather had been a bit mixed – with rain on and off all day. It was approaching 5.00pm as we walked up to the bushes at the top of a small hill. The sun chose that moment to break through and out of the brambles a small, greyish brown warbler emerged. It moved right in front of us giving momentary but ID-clinching views. I had scored the Blyth's Reed at last! My fifth lifer of the week. I had also fallen back in love with Unst which I was starting to despise in spite of the magic earlier in the week. I am certainly fickle, if nothing else. I celebrated with arms raised, boxer style, as the rain set in. The Shetland holiday had brought me up to 391. I could smell the magical 400 wafting tantalising in front of me.

Being so close to 400, I knew I had to do a bit of twitching and probably return to Shetland if I was to succeed in my goal. 2014 started well, including the additions of Buff-bellied Pipit, Hume's Warbler and a very out-of-season and out-of-place Myrtle Warbler to my list. Myrtle is an American Warbler so quite what this bird was doing feeding on a coconut on a Durham housing estate in February, I do not know. It should have been in Central America somewhere. I did miss the long-staying White-billed Diver at Brixham in Devon, which was a major blow. I had been working in Bristol and stayed overnight with a couple of lads from work. We had gone out for a curry and watched Sheffield United knock Fulham out of the FA cup. It was an away replay and I had not expected the Blades to do it on what was a horrendously rainy night with gale force winds. I had been to the away league game at Crewe on the Saturday and seen them get completely turned over 3:0 in what was an abject performance. Anyway, with the Blades turning up a cup shock and the diver showing at Brixham, the omens looked well set for a solid tick the next day. The diver had been showing brilliantly, just swimming round the harbour, down to a few feet at times. There were severe weather warnings all over the south-west and most of Somerset was already under water. Ian Hallam who worked for me at the time described it well when he recounted the events of the next day. If you can imagine a Mancunian accent for a moment:

'I was driving home back up the M5 along with everyone else and this daft bugger is going in the opposite direction to see a bird. He must have been bloody mad. We all thought it. It had to be the worst weather for years and everything you heard on the radio was saying just don't go there. Let's be having it right you just don't do that and nobody was. Apart from him of course!'

Ian does have a good point. As it turned out, the weather was 'birdable' – just. The only problem was that the White-billed Diver had listened to the weather warnings too and cleared off somewhere drier and more clement with the rest of sensible Britain! It was a bad dip and I was absolutely gutted. I still am.

I had a poor Spring in terms of my British list, largely because I spent most of April on holiday in New York and Costa Rica. I am not grumbling though, for, as you've rightly guessed, I spent copious amounts of time birding. I did manage to pick up a fantastic Spectacled Warbler in Norfolk, again en route to Colchester. Well, it's not really en route at all but in fact a huge deviation; this, however, is the rhetoric of the obsessive birder in 'justifying' the detour! The bird was simply stunning and I very much enjoyed it, mainly because I had a two-hour window before partaking in a conference call. It was about 30 minutes' walk to the bird from the car and the same back (obviously). I did not particularly want to take the call from the beach and anyway needed my lap top to access various documents. I also did not fancy the prospect of squatting in the sand dunes with the noise of Avocets and Redshanks piping overhead with the boss on the other end of the blower! It felt like a bit of a giveaway. As I arrived at the site, I could see a crowd of birders looking at nothing in particular. It was the usual scene of birders listlessly standing there chatting and not really bothering to look. I saw a movement in a bush just feet away and thought to myself that I had better check it out. Thank goodness I did, as it burst into song and gave me exquisite views from feet away. I had ticked the Spectacled Warbler within seconds of arrival. I watched it for a further ten minutes getting amazing close-up views in great light before hot-footing it back to the car for my conference call. Now that's how to twitch! It was some form of catharsis for the White-billed wounds and I was feeling back on track at last.

A month or so later, a Short-toed Eagle had been haunting the south-east counties. Eventually, it settled in Ashdown Forest in East Sussex and could be seen daily hunting for snakes. It was a huge 'blocker' (a birding term for a bird that blocks a gap on your list) for anyone who had not graced Scilly in 1999 when the first UK specimen was seen. Tom had banged on about it for years, along with the haul of Megas that he got (and that I did not) that fateful year when I was on my MBA course and hence not on Scilly. The STE is a spectacular bird. I like them a lot, having seen them in Spain. I had a scheduled visit planned in Tonbridge to attend our centre there and meet up with the police for a theft case that I was investigating. It was only a few miles from Ashdown, and what is more the STE was performing like clockwork. The local birders reckoned you could set your watch by it, so predictable was its routine. I checked the bird news avidly in the days preceding my visit. Each day it was showing like a dream. Stage Entry

Left: John Lee. I had done my usual and got up at an ungodly hour and for once had a great journey down to the south-east. The weather was beautiful, I had found the site with ease and there were plenty of birders on hand to help spot it. The only problem was that the eagle had not landed. It had eloped back to Dorset where it had first been seen. I could not believe it. I went to work in a foul and ugly mood. I had dipped on what most considered to be the bird of the year. Virtually every twitcher in Britain had seen it, apart from one. The next day, while I was with the police, Tom texted me:

'The STE is showing back at Ashdown now. Can you get there?'

I couldn't. I was dealing with a complex and large theft case and had no way out. The afternoon passed into evening with the local CID. They had turned up late for our appointment and had taken their time on site. The Tonbridge centre is notorious as being the site of the largest heist ever to take place in Europe – £53 million pounds to be precise. The police officers were keen to chat to me about it and look around the centre. Time just ticked by. My chance had gone. The bird showed well throughout the evening, but not for me. The next morning, I decided it was worth one last shot on the way back up north. When I got there, the news was not good. No pager news and no bird. I had just started chatting to two local birders who were both postmen when I saw a large raptor some way off.

'Hang on, what's this?'

It started to hover and dropped its legs beneath it in a classic pose. It was not so much pleasure as huge relief. The magical Short-toed Snake Eagle had stopped toying with me at last. Bird number 397.

In late September, Tom and I were back on Shetland. This time I had decided to take the car and get the ferry over rather than fly and hire. When we arrived at the ferry pier in Aberdeen, I pulled up behind a car full of blokes. One of them was clearly mad and was trying to catch my eye while frantically gesticulating at me. The other guys looked normal enough. The psychotic one proceeded to come over to my window, which I half wound down with an element of caution.

'We're all Blades too, mate – apart from him but at least he isn't a pig (a Wednesday fan). I just saw that dangling down and just had to say hello.'

He pointed at the Sheffield United air freshener hanging from my mirror. I had forgotten it was even there. I am not a big one of having football paraphernalia in my car as it is likely to prompt some moron from Leeds to key your vehicle or find it covered in Wednesdayite spit. Jack had bought it for me for my birthday so I had to have it hanging up in the car. I use the term 'bought' lightly as he borrowed the money off me and 'forgot' to pay me back. He's his mother's son!

'Bloody hell, what's the chances of that. I didn't know what you were pointing at mate, sorry. I just thought you were a nutter!'

After he had returned to his car, I caught sight of a pair of binoculars and a tripod. They were birders and Blades! Jesus, there were others out there. I had always felt like I was the only member of my species up to that point (other than Tom, but he didn't really count). The last of the dinosaurs as it were. I got out and introduced myself properly, explaining that we too were birding. For the week that followed, birding and the Blades would develop into a strangely symbiotic world as if the normal part of my life, football, and the geeky part of my life, birding, were natural bed partners. It was like a kind of mutating virus whereby two incredibly discrete entities had suddenly merged. This super bug would, unbeknown to me, have ramifications that I could never have predicted.

The crossing was very rough but we had had the foresight to book a cabin and I therefore slept through the pitching and tossing that hit the boat in the early hours. I had downed about seven pints of 'Corncrake' ale too, which was not the best idea but the social scene had been good in the bar with the 'Birding Blades' as we had collectively become known. Apparently, there were four more due to arrive the following day bringing us up to a total of nine. The crowds at Bramall Lane would be down! We had a good laugh with them for the rest of the week. I almost got to know one of them, Nick Addey, quite intimately after sending him a text that was meant for Vic! Fortunately for me it was clean. I did send him a 'witty' hoax one (pretending it was to Vicky) full of filth and innuendo after the holiday which his wife read out while he was driving. I think it mentioned nipples, crocodile clips, jump leads and whips! As Vicky often says following my moments of bad behaviour, 'John, you do let yourself down...' I really do not want our respective wives ever to meet up.

Moving back to slightly more mundane matters, we were all set for our big week on Shetland, but there was not that much about as the winds had moved from east to west. There had also been a bit of a clear-out, so the only bird really worth getting was a Hornemann's Arctic Redpoll which we connected with straight after arrival. We also picked up a couple of nice padders in the form of a Yellow-browed Warbler and a

Red-breasted Flycatcher in Cunningsborough, near our cabin where we were staying. That night, news came of a female King Eider on Yell. It was a lifer for Tom but not for me. I had seen several in my Aberdeen University days. Naturally, the following day we had to go for it. The conditions were tough in that we were looking directly into the light and the wind was strong causing the scope to rock around on the tripod. I caught a glimpse of a possible candidate but lost it in the waves and wind. By dipping, I knew we would be back and have to endure the experience again. Well, Tom had certainly put in the hours with me for the Blyth's Reed the previous year, so I could hardly grumble. As we left the site, Mega Alert pager news came from Unst – a Swainson's Thrush had been found. Bloody hell, those westerly gales had brought something in after all. Swainson's is an American Thrush and they are tiny compared with our own Song Thrush. We might have missed the King Eider but being on Yell meant we were in striking distance of the Swainson's; we just needed to traverse Yell and then take a ferry across the straits to get on to Unst. We had the time to get there and get it – with a bit of luck.

Swainson's was a big bird for both Tom and me. Any birder or twitcher will know what it is like to miss or dip out on a bird. Certain birds like to give you the run around and remain off your list for years. Fate, circumstances and the bird itself all seem to conspire against you. They are known in the trade as 'bogey birds'. Swainson's was currently top of our bogey bird list. My worst bogey bird as a kid was undoubtedly Nuthatch. I just could not see one for love nor money. It seems incredible now when I look back, but at the time I just could not put it to bed. The fact that I did not know their give-away call clearly didn't help matters. When I confessed this to my fellow birders on my YOC holidays at Gibraltar Point, the other kids were simply incredulous. I was desperate to get it on my list but the more I tried the more I seemed to fail. I can even remember being at a friend's house where Nuthatches regularly visited the feeders in their garden. I spent a desperate fifteen minutes peering out of their window that murky November morning. It was not happening. Dad arrived to pick me up and another opportunity slipped through my fingers. It took me until 1981 to finally catch up with one when I found my first in Padley Woods in Derbyshire. We were looking for Pied Flycatchers when at last one of those beautiful little blue and orange birds decided to shimmy down a moss-clad tree trunk in front of me. I was fifteen and it was well overdue. An embarrassing gap was removed.

In my adult years, I have had several bogey birds. I have already mentioned Sora Rail which I twitched unsuccessfully in Devon and Nottinghamshire. Both were long-staying birds that I managed to miss by leaving it too late and abject bad luck. I also had the phantom bird that 'never was' when a Spotted Crake was misidentified as a Sora on Scilly. We piled over on the boat from St. Mary's to Tresco to be hit with the bad news. I cracked it eventually on St. Mary's in 2005. The other bird that severely gave me the run-around was Penduline Tit. Tom and I possibly saw one back in 1982 at Blacktoft Sands RSPB Reserve, near Goole, Yorkshire, where an adult and a juvenile had been seen for a few days. Back then it was a very rare bird, whereas now it is an annual visitor, especially in Kent. Dad had taken us to Blacktoft on the off-chance something interesting might be present so we were delighted to hear that the Pendulines were around. There were loads of twitchers there; the weather was grim and everyone seemed to be dipping. For some reason, Mum and Dad stayed in the car. Tom and I were wandering around near a patch of reeds behind the hides when a small bird flew across the path. I glimpsed a rusty mantle and perhaps a greyish head in the most fleeting of views. At the time, we were convinced we had hit the jackpot. With hindsight, we were desperate to see it and there may have been an element of optimistic hallucination. Some years later, we both removed it from our lists. Mind you, if it was not a Penduline then I do not know what it was to this day!

In the meantime, I had managed to dip one at Hornsea Mere in 1987, literally missing it by seconds. I waited for hours but it never reappeared. I missed another 'one-day bird' in Nottinghamshire and had two further 'shots' at an erratic bird in Kent. Eventually, a male appeared in 2012 at Stodmarsh while I was working in Tonbridge. The weather turned out to be decent and the bird had been showing during the day, so I finished up at work and made a beeline for Stodmarsh. I was still in my suit when I got there. I became a car contortionist and somehow managed to change my suit trousers for jeans while sitting behind the wheel. It felt like a seedy thing to be doing – sitting in a car park with my trousers off! Surely fate was not going to conspire against me once again? It appeared so. I got there early evening and missed the bird by seconds. To make matters worse, there was a loud, garrulous birder present who was intent on telling all and sundry about his recent birding exploits. He had latched on to me when I was leaving the car and never shut up from minute one. He just banged on and on about how he had seen a Dark-breasted Barn Owl and a

Black-bellied Dipper the week before. He kept up his account all the way to the spot where the Penduline Tit had been seen. True to form, the Penduline literally did a runner the moment we arrived and all I saw was a little flying dot head into the bushes and that was it. It could have been anything. A non-tickable view was all I needed of such a sought-after bird. For the next twenty minutes, there was not a flicker of a bird. Not surprising really, because all that was going on was this bloke boring some other poor victim about the wretched barn owl and dipper. He was so loud, too. By this time, I was tense and the guy was getting on my nerves. Inevitably, my patience and temper snapped. I tried to be as tactful but my rising intolerance levels were hard to disguise.

'Look mate, you're going to have to shut up and be quiet as it's not going to come back, is it? I've come a long way and I want to see this bird, so can we have a bit of hush for five minutes?'

He looked rather hurt so I moved away further along the path as I was aware that everyone present probably thought that I was a bit of a maniac. They were right, too. I was feeling crazy! A bogey bird was giving me the run round AGAIN!! Anyhow, after a few minutes of relative peace, I caught a glimmer of movement on a reed mace. I raised my bins and there it was – a cracking male Penduline Tit feeding away in glorious sunlight. A little orange-coated highwayman, complete with a black robber's mask. A miniscule Dick Turpin in feathers. The elation and relief were for a few seconds indescribable. The lid of the Penduline pressure cooker had been removed and I once again became a reasonable human being. It mattered so much to me. I called the others over and made peace with the chatterbox man by painstakingly directing him and his video camera onto it. He was able to add it to his barn owl and dipper footage. I assume some poor birder got the Penduline Tit treatment a few days later at his next twitch. Generally, I am quite a calm person but do have my moments. That is what a bogey bird can do to you when the pressure is on. I would do the same again tomorrow. After all, I had come for Penduline Tit and not to listen to tedious anecdotes.

Swainson's held painful memories for us both. *Catharus* thrushes can be very skulking at times, so we knew that it might be a tough bird to see. My wounds concerning two different Swainson's Thrushes missed on Scilly were festering and open. I wanted to see this bird and badly. We managed to get straight on the ferry as I drove like a rally driver to get to the pier. Aboard, a man with a brown Sheffield United beanie on his head approached the car. It was another Birding Blade, a lad called Andy Mack. Again, the Blades air freshener hanging from my mirror had done the trick. This chance encounter was to have profound consequences for me a few days later, but at the time I was blissfully unaware of how fate was playing its poker hand. The whole Blades and Birding thing was getting a little bizarre. Every time I got on a ferry I was meeting Blades fans with binoculars, it seemed. We got chatting to him. He was with a crew of lads and was on tenterhooks about connecting with the Swainson's Thrush. He needed it, too. Apparently, a Leeds fan had found it, which slightly tainted the bird to my mind; even so I had to be grateful to him. You can't always pick and choose. Andy knew the gen on the thrush, so we said that we would just follow his car. They drove at breakneck speed, topping 90mph at times. I did not bother trying to compete as it was downright nuts on occasions. Don't get me wrong, I was hitting big speeds too, but I didn't want to widow my wife, leave my son fatherless or miss the Swainson's. Eventually, we pulled up at Norwick outside a small cottage garden where the bird had been found. One of the guys had already flushed it inadvertently, so there was a little bit of confusion as to where it was exactly. We crept round to the side of the garden where we could see a low breeze-block wall. The Swainson's instantly popped out and gave stonking views from about ten feet away. What a little gem! It had a corking eye ring and was in fantastic condition. I had seen quite a few earlier in the year in Costa Rica but this was very special indeed. Tom and I were elated. We touched fists and had a swig of fine Cognac from my hip flask. This is what we had come for. Our bogey bird was gone and I had moved a significant step closer to hitting 400. Just two more to go.

My next bird was a White's Thrush. This is a particular favourite of mine, having seen a few in Hong Kong. It was just one of those birds that I seemed to be able to turn up. My best sighting was of a bird sitting out on a lawn at my government quarters in Mid-Levels in Hong Kong. I watched it for so long that I got bored and went inside, which was a shame because I did not see it in flight. News broke of the White's Thrush on Shetland during the early evening. Unfortunately, we were a bit too far away to get there with the failing light. The weather was poor though, so I felt reasonably confident that it would not disappear overnight. It was a complete lottery whether it would stay or not. Anything can happen with these ultra-rare birds. They can clear off, move sites or simply die of exhaustion. My confidence was fortunately well-placed as I ended up getting amazing views of this eastern vagrant. Compared with the diminutive Swainson's Thrush, the White's was a veritable monster of a bird. I even managed to get a half-decent photograph. Most people's experiences of trying to see White's Thrush have been limited to poor flight views or obscured profiles of it skulking in the undergrowth. Not this bird – it performed like a dream. I did have my moments not seeing it. It was described as being near to 'the pampas grass' where it could be seen perched in the open. Everyone was cooing with delight. I kept looking at the pampas grass and not seeing the Thrush. After it had disappeared, I realised that I was looking at the wrong pampas grass! Fortunately, I saw it a few minutes later, feeding out in the open on the lawn. I was now one away from my goal. That same day, we observed a fantastic Myrtle Warbler. For me it was not even a year tick but it was a lifer for Tom. I had seen the wintering bird in Durham a few months before. Ironically, I had thought at the time that there was no chance that Tom would see one of these! Well, that was a short-lived view and served me right for being so smug.

On our penultimate day, we were back on Unst, clearing up on birds that we needed to see. The birding was extremely pleasant with a nice mix of migrants, including Eastern Subalpine Warbler, Barred Warbler, Siberian Chiffchaff, Red-breasted Flycatcher and two Yellow-browed Warblers. We had returned to an area called Baltasound where someone thought they had flushed an Olive-backed Pipit earlier in the day. It was worth a shot trying to re-find it and get our names up in lights. As we parked up, the pager beeped but the message was garbled due to poor reception.

'Shetland: Siberian Rubythroat.'

The pager message was scrambled with a few random letters instead of the location. It was an appalling moment. Siberian Rubythroat is one of the migrant birds that everyone wants to see in Britain. It is the ultimate rare migrant and epitomises what birding is all about. It is why we were on Shetland in the first place to see birds such as this. Here we were, actually on Shetland, reading a scrambled message on the pager about arguably the most sought-after bird on the British list. We compared notes with some other birders. We all had the feeling that it would be on Fair Isle but we had to know. It could even be on Unst. We just did not know. We did not dare even leave. Anxious minutes passed as we tried to get internet connection on our phones but were in a bit of a black spot. Everybody looked tense and a bit sick. It was a potential tick for everyone. Eventually, someone finally got a connection – it was at Levenwick on the mainland. My god, so close, yet so far. We might have been on Shetland but we were seventy miles away with two ferry rides to make.

I drove like a man possessed, white-knuckled and gripped, whilst Tom was nervously babbling throughout the journey. I just tried to shut him out as I had to concentrate on driving at speed on roads that I did not know that well. There were plenty of sheep about too, just to add a bit of spice. The journey was a blur of overtaking and going for it. We were on the cusp of allowable time before it got dark. I finally pulled into the lay-by above Levenwick and we jogged down to the garden where the bird had been found. The news was promising as we approached. It had been showing well, not a characteristic usually associated with rubythroats. We found an area with a reasonable view and waited. Not much happened. I could see some of the Birding Blades nearby. However, no one was on it where we were standing. Precious time was ticking by. Eventually, Andy Mack, the Sheffield United birder who we had seen at the Swainson's sighting told us the other side might be better. Minutes later he returned breathless:

'I've just seen it on the other side of the garden, I've come to get you both. You won't get it from here. It's doing circuits. Quick follow me.'

What a top lad to come and get us. We legged it round to the other side of the garden where there was quite a gathering of birders. Andy then told me exactly where it had been and where to look.

'It keeps running across that little patch of paving into the Fuchsia. It then comes out and stops and runs into the Hebe. It sometimes comes out on that little terrace above the bushes, too.'

'Okay, cheers.'

'Don't take your eyes off that spot.'

'I won't, mate. I won't.'

As birding and tension goes this was right up there. That clock was really ticking. I had to connect and do so right now.

It was approaching half past six in the evening and the light was on its last legs. There was still a bit of sun though. Maybe, just maybe. I nudged my way forward to the edge of the crowd of birders, who were lined up in a sloping field against the hedge of a well-maintained garden. I was trying to see a patch of gravel and a terraced crazy paving, neatly sandwiched between a Fuchsia and Hebe bush. I had been given precise instructions on where to look. The problem was going to be the vantage point. My view was obscured by strands of the garden's hedge and I was behind a couple of other birders. I was on my tiptoes trying to make the best of a bad elevation. I was desperate but this looked to be as good as it would get. The bloke next to me turned and said:

'Have you had it yet?'

'No.'

'Come in front of me then. It's in the Fuchsia now, so watch that patch of gravel right in front of it. Just concentrate on that. It's been doing circuits. It should show any time now.'

'Cheers mate – appreciate it.'

Jesus, he sounded confident. I could not dare to believe it though. I moved forward into pole position at the front of the hedge. I could have kissed the guy, but there wasn't time. I would kiss him later. I had to see this thing. I was ridiculously tense. I would never get another chance and most likely it would be gone tomorrow. The light was going and it could not be long before it would go to roost. It was now or almost certainly never. Within seconds, a small Robin-like bird hopped out onto the gravel. I raised my bins and got straight on it. It paused momentarily before scurrying off like a rocket into the Hebe bush. It had a bright ruby-red throat. BOOM. That fleeting pause enabled me to see every single feature of a first winter male Siberian Rubythroat, my 400th British bird, and one of the most sought-after iconic gems on the British list. I turned round in triumph and high-fived Andy who was behind me. He had got me that bird. What a sound lad. Bloody magic!

I had done it. A lifetime's achievement. I had made 400 and what is more it was with a Siberian Rubythroat. It is like scoring a double hundred at Lords and finishing it off with a six. It was like Geoff Hurst scoring a hat trick at Wembley to win the world cup for England (the day I was born!). It just does not come any better. Birding poetry. My birding poetry. The added beauty of it was that I would not have got that bird if it had not been for Sheffield United. We would never have chatted with Andy on the ferry and he would not have come to get us if we hadn't all been Blades and if it hadn't been for that Sheffield United air freshener that my lovely son, Jack, had bought me for my birthday. The two worlds of birds and football had never collided before in such a mad way and here a crazy cameo of Birding Blades and ferries had enabled me to get my goal. It was as bizarre as it was beautiful.

That bird epitomises my birding life. Non-birders generally don't get the birding thing. They may perhaps do so if they read this book. That is my hope. I hope birders enjoy it too and see something of themselves in me, hopefully the pleasanter side and not the rest! I guess this fanaticism is the culmination of a birding 'journey' over many years that started at Loch of the Lowes, took in Suffolk, the Scillies, north-east Scotland, the Far East and, latterly, virtually every overseas country that I happen to visit. I have birded on land and at sea. I have birded at work, on holiday, in the garden, on the train, in business meetings and from the car. I have neglected my family and friends. I have left my wife stranded in the street. I have tarnished our family holidays. I have been selfish. All has been due to birds. Put simply, I have birded wherever I have been and whatever I have been doing. Birding has been my crutch at times of strife. It has taken my mind to other places when the real world was too painful and been a constant companion over nearly forty years. It has given me joy and distraction, even when my father was dying of cancer. Birding has always been there for me. It has been part of my family, creating memories and moments. It has also held us together through life and death.

I have written down what I could not say – for example – at the photocopier. It has taken years of effort to get to this point and for me to rationalise a complexity of emotion, experiences, myself and my life. The answer is long and tortuous, yet in some ways it is simple. I have a passion. Perhaps the next time I am at the photocopier and I get asked the dreaded 'tweeter' question, then I can hand over a signed copy of this book and say, 'read this'. I am a birder and I am proud of it. A little bonkers, too, maybe!

Other Birding Books by Brambleby Books

Those with Webbed Feet – All about British ducks, geese and swans
Edward Giles
ISBN 9781908241573

Walking with Birds
Colin Whittle
ISBN 9781908241351

Arrivals and Rivals - A duel for the winning bird

Adrian Riley

ISBN: 9780954334796

A-Z of Birds – A birder's tales from around the world

Bo Beolens

ISBN 9781908241238

Birduder 344- A life list ordinary

Rob Sawyer

ISBN 9781908241092

Scilly Birding – Joining the madding crowd

Simon Davey

ISBN: 9781908241177

The Ruffled Edge – Notes from a Nature Warden

Pete Howard

ISBN 9781908241061

Winging it – Birding for Low-flyers
Andrew Fallan
ISBN 9780955392856

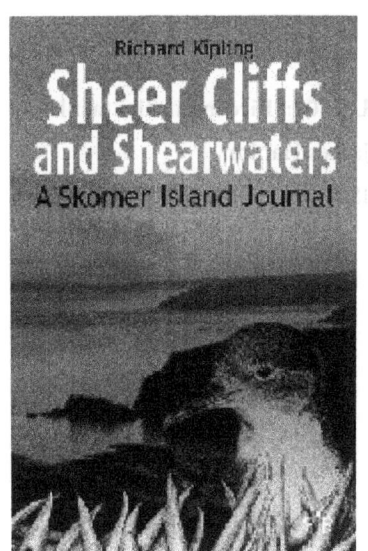

**Sheer Cliffs and Shearwaters –
A Skomer Island Journal**
Richard Kipling
ISBN 9781908241214

The World of Birds and Laughter
Richard Pople
ISBN 9781908241375

UK500: Birding in the fast lane
James Hanlon
ISBN 9780954334789

www.bramblebybooks.co.uk